THIS HEART SHAPED LAND

Finding the magic & leading a school in the Forest of Dean

Written by Robert Charles Ford

Mirabelle

Published by Mirabelle

Copyright

Praise for This Heart Shaped Land

"I am deeply indebted to John Rolfe, Bill Bixby, Maria Mendal and Carl MacCarthy for their support of this book" Rob Ford

"This timely collection of writings addresses the critical role of reflective teachers, students and parents not only in the life of school communities but also in society per se across different national contexts.

The author presents his thoughts - fears and hopes - immersed in the crisis reality of the end of the last decade, lived together with students, their families and local communities, with visible concern for all of them and - invariably - oriented towards the future, a better world to come.

The thematic scope of the volume is exceptionally rich – spanning educational policy, school cultures and specific practices of student, teacher and parental involvement in education, which - for the author - is a commitment to social and political issues (by the way, it must be strongly articulated here that politics is understood in this book in Aristotle's terms as a space of common goals, commonality).

The author addresses key issues by going through a variety of perspectives explaining why and how students, teachers and parents need to question and challenge educational structures and setups that reduce their opportunities for involvement. At the same time, the texts sensitively refer to the current predicament of schooling in late capitalist societies (such as the UK) or others, such as Moldova. In every case, this situation forces schools to undergo extraordinary pressure and the author clearly presents the resulting limitations and the possibilities of democratic cooperation.

The entire content of "This heart shaped land" expresses the author's thought that we all need "to get on with the things that really matter in life and what will last long after we are gone".

Looks like Robert Ford has found the way to this and guides the reader beautifully with his book."
Professor Maria Mendel
Professor of Education, University of Gdansk, Poland
Visiting Professor, John Hopkins University, USA

"I am very proud and honoured to work with the inspirational global educator Rob Ford. I have collaborated with Rob for many years and never cease to be hugely impressed and amazed by his great commitment to, and profound belief in, the key power, inclusive value and wide benefits of international teaching and learning. 'This Heart Shaped Land' is apt tribute to his incredible drive, sheer professionalism and energy; but Rob also possesses a huge and generous Heart; a Heart full of experience and a true authenticity and a Heart that shares, celebrates and collaborates in all aspects of excellence in education.

This is a truly delightful, hugely enjoyable and wonderful book; it celebrates both Rob's fantastic long term commitment to education but also all internationally minded educators; that incredible global community who bring the world into their schools every day; often amidst a range of many challenges.

Thank you Rob; thank you for all your brilliant work as a greatly valued British Council Schools Ambassador and for your innate humanity and huge skill, talent and constant belief in the importance of international education; you've always believed that this knowledge cannot just come to you but you must always reach out for it; I am always grateful to you for this reaching out and my very best wishes with your important work."
John Rolfe MBE
Schools Outreach Manager,
British Council, UK

"In a time when society and education often confuse schooling with education and prize quantitative outcomes over empowering students to become life-long learners, Rob Ford 's This Heart Shaped Land reminds us of the value and power of being human. His four-year story is one of a leader striving to be engaged with his students, staff, community, the outdoors, and the world. Rob reminds us that most of all leading students and staff is about being thoughtful, reflective, empathetic, and most of all human. This Heart Shaped Land reminds all of us about why we are engaged in the work of empowering young people."

William G. Bixby
Associate Superintendent of Schools
Prince William County Public Schools
Manassas, Virginia, USA

Dedication

To Les Jones, a true teacher and I hope
I always carried the flame and defended
the weak.

Table of Contents

Preface

The Forest of Dean, that far west part of the English county of Gloucestershire bordered by Wales and shaped by the rivers Wye and Severn right down to Beachely, where they flow into the sea, is one of the least known parts of the UK. It is also a rather beautiful and magical place, so it is not surprising to see the number of writers and poets it has inspired from William Wordsworth at Tintern to JK Rowling and the Harry Potter series of children's books. It is to another writer I took my inspiration from, Dennis Potter, whose famous description of the Forest of Dean as a "Heart shaped land" gave me the idea of the title of the simple blog I would keep to communicate my thoughts and routines as the new Headteacher in 2015 of the secondary school, Wyedean, that sits at the very southern tip of the Forest overlooking the Wye, at the ancient Norman town of Chepstow over the A48 bridge and into Wales.

I wrote the blog not with the intention of collating a possible book and certainly wasn't inspired by Wyedean's most famous literary daughter, one Joanna Rowling, even if occupying "Dumbledore's study" for four years and the office of the first Head and possible role model in my predecessor, Ken Smith in the 1970s, may have had some small part.

Whenever I video conferenced from my room to schools from Canada to Kosovo to Indonesia, students loved to hear the stories older colleagues could still remember. Not exactly Hogwarts towers and turrets though, in its seventies municipal drabness with the functional rectangle school blocks of a buildings, but it is what went on in those buildings daily that was the real inspirational educational magic. When I was appointed, having spent time already as a senior leader in wonderfully strong school communities in Royal Wootton Bassett in Wiltshire and Crickhowell in Powys, I wanted to be able to show my thoughts, my hopes and at times my fears, especially in the tumultuous World of the last half of an extraordinary previous decade of Trump, Brexit, severe public funding cuts, and the dominance of neo-liberal capitalist theory in English education gone crazy. Who would have guessed the global pandemic of Covid19 at the start of the 2020s would have made the previous decade look almost like a Nirvana as we still grapple with the possible longer term consequences of the virus inflicting damage deep into our societies' core and having a lasting impact on our young people.

The story that has emerged over 4 years in "This Heart Shaped Land" is a valuable one, especially for those in education looking for hope and how the answers are there in our local communities and in our young people. This is what I found at Wyedean and it was a deep honour to serve as the principal of this remarkable community on the Welsh/English borders. I arrived knowing that the strategy and mindset of an outward facing school and a positive school culture would build a shared collective ethos and repair a damaged school community, giving leadership, ownership, and hope back to the wonderful team of colleagues, families and students, there. We brought the World into classrooms daily, living Dr Arnold's maxim for education as *"an introduction to the best that has been thought and said"*. We empowered and challenged throughout the vicious cycles that had ground people down previously, to virtuous ones. We widened the curriculum for all and put key accepted educational concepts in other parts of the global educational World such as deeper learning, creativity, critical thinking, digital & cyber learning, coding & languages, and international mindedness, at the heart of our school vision and values. The story here shows this narrative and hopefully will serve as a model of leadership for others in education who need to know they are not alone; and the false binary shrill debates in education are just that.

After four years, and a superb leadership team in place, supported by leaders across the school and a sustainable model of school improvement ready for someone else to take it on further, the pull and call of my first love in education, global learning, took me to Moldova and the challenge there in establishing the first truly international school in that part of Eastern Europe. Having been a British Council school's ambassador for nearly two decades and worked as a speaker and advisor on leadership, school improvement, curriculum, the pull and call took me to the other side of Europe to another land and people I love, placed at the crossroads of Europe, and my new blog, *"Mail from Moldova"*, has already had over a year in writing.

https://mailfrommoldova.home.blog/author/robford73/

It is a rare privilege to know the Forest of Dean and Welsh borders and in my very last piece in May 2019, I signed off, fittingly, quoting famous Forest son, Dennis Potter and his description of the land and people of his home. ***"A strange and beautiful place, with a people as warm as anywhere else, but they seemed warmer to me"***

I hope you enjoy the book and the journey a wonderful school community took to continue placing value in the daily education of its young people and the communities it served. We all need to find the magic to create, value our precious time, and get on with the things that really matter in life and what will last long after we are gone.

"What you do for yourself dies with you when you leave this world, what you do for others lives on forever."
Sir Ken Robinson

Rob Ford, Chisinau, Moldova, August 2020

PART 1: SEPTEMBER 2015- JULY 2016

4th September 2015

"Life starts all over again when it gets crisp in the Fall."
F. Scott Fitzgerald

Summer is over, autumn is here, and a new academic year has started. It also happens to be my first week as the new Headteacher of Wyedean School following the retirement of my predecessor, Clive Pemberton. Clive's predecessor, John Claydon (Head, 1990-2005) wrote a welcome card for me to read on my first day in the job. *"You'll find a tremendous well of goodwill in the local community and amongst the staff".* One of the reasons I wanted to be the next Head of Wyedean School was due to its close relationship with the community. Having worked in schools in England and Wales where the community has a good and close relationship with the school, I know how valuable this is for the success of the students. I am impressed with the dedication, professionalism, and hard work of the staff at Wyedean and I am very proud and privileged to be the next Headteacher of the school.

All sorts of studies show how important these weeks and months are in autumn for successful learning, and watching the new Year 7s arriving on Thursday eager to get started in secondary school made me think how quick the time also flies by in a 39 week academic year. The Sixth Form have just had their best A Level results ever, and by the time we have reached Friday with the rest of the school returning, we are already back into the swing of school life. The staff worked hard on the inset days on excellent teaching and learning with a real tangible buzz and excitement about the year ahead. I want to build on the strengths of the school identified rightly by last year's Ofsted and the summer result. In our priorities for the year as staff we discussed developing further outstanding learning, Digital Learning, International Education, Creativity, and Learning skills that a changing and fast paced C21st society requires. There are some great learning opportunities planned for the year ahead for our students.

This week has seen the worsening of the heart-breaking humanitarian crisis on the shores and borders of Europe. As we start this academic year with this backdrop in the news, the reasons why we value education and the nurturing and development of our young people in the ethos and values of our community and society have never been more important.

11th September 2015

"Three things students want to hear - I believe in you; You have a purpose; How are you?" Edutopia

It is interesting how staffrooms used to echo with the infamous piece of advice to younger teachers "don't smile until Christmas". It is not something I have ever been able to manage to see the point of, and walking around the school this week in our first "normal" week back, the amount of smiles and greetings from the students makes it impossible but to break into a broad grin. There is a lot of academic work around the idea of "positive school culture" and how schools need to be learning laboratories where students and their development are at the centre of all that we do. I have been impressed in my first 2 weeks at Wyedean at the level of commitment and hard work from the staff going into making sure this academic year starts as well as possible, building on from last year's success with Ofsted and the summer results. The conversations I have enjoyed this week include discussing what sort of things we should be focussing on in schools in terms of new technologies supporting learning, the powerful impact of creativity, the need for global learning as well as ensuring our curriculum offers as many opportunities as possible. I had a wonderful moment when I went into the JK Rowling library in the school and heard our Carnegie Shadow reading group discuss their next book; *"1984"* or *"A Clockwork Orange"*. My educator's heart beat a little faster to hear such a discussion.

2

One of the more interesting discussions I had this week with students is a question about uniform. I did point out to a group of Year 9s that as a new Head, I would prefer for them to ask me about what will I do to develop new opportunities or new ways of making learning exciting. One of the highlights of the week was the agreement with the Confucius Institute to bring Mandarin teaching to Wyedean School for the next few years, and to share with our local primary schools as the new hub for Mandarin teaching in the Forest of Dean/Monmouthshire area. Wyedean School believes passionately in international education and the school is supporting the local charity "Help Calais Chepstow" in collecting food and clothes as well as raising awareness about the refugee situation in Europe. All week the pastoral teams have been focussing on the issues behind the refugee crisis. From the global to the national this was the week where Queen Elizabeth II became the longest reigning British monarch in over a 1000 years whilst this Saturday it will be the flag waving of "Last Night of the Proms" signalling for many the end of summer. I know I will be going into my weekend smiling as another good week ends at Wyedean School, ready to smile on Monday morning as the kids come back in for another week of learning. I won't even be thinking of how many weeks it is until Christmas – despite my local supermarket's best efforts with the Christmas decorations out already! Now there is a reason not to smile.

18th September 2015

"Education is not the filing of a pail, but the lighting of a fire." W.B. Yeats

We have come to the end of week three and thirty six more learning weeks to go; without the holidays. Autumn is definitely here, not just from the lovely iconic scene out at the front of school on Thursday with some of the primary school students knocking conkers from the trees, but also from the torrential rain, mists, and cooler air this week's weather has brought around the school campus. Saturday evening at Wyedean School saw the incredible school's gospel choir perform for their 10th anniversary concert with a lovely mixture of past and present students singing their hearts out.

What struck me most sitting in the audience listening to students talk about their love of the songs was the incredible confidence these students had speaking to parents and their community. In the week that Jeremy Corbyn tried a different style of engagement at Prime Minister's Questions and the rugby World Cup is about to get underway engaging the rugby world, the week at Wyedean saw engagement of a different kind with the huge turnout on Thursday at the 6th Form Information Evening. I spoke to the 6th Form about something that had inspired and engaged me in my life and it was interesting to listen to the experiences of our Year 12s and 13s and what had influenced them to do the subjects they wanted to do, and the university and career paths they are looking at following now. I did respect the one student who paused for a moment and said "*sir, I am 17 and to be honest I haven't a clue but then I am hoping school gives me something to think about*". Well, he is right. School will be giving him plenty to think about as he goes through his A Levels.

I spent some time with Year 11 and the English Learning Area this week and was impressed at how all the students could tell me where they were in their progress, what they were studying, and more importantly who they were currently reading! A visitor walked with me around the school on Thursday and was struck by the innovation and engagement of the students in the school's motorbike club, aka "Barry's Bikes" after our long serving caretaker who gives his time to spend with these students each week. The Leadership Team has been working through the wonderful educational acronyms of SIP, SEF, QA & PM as well as looking at the Aspirational 8 and Progress 8 targets – the latter where the awful "bucket" system of rating subjects (Yeats would be spinning) is now how we describe the curriculum. What has sustained me and my colleagues through the week though isn't the thought of "filling buckets", but how the sparks of learning and opportunities are setting alight the individual imaginations of our kids be it the gospel choir, the inspirational literature, the new Mandarin lessons, or the motorbike club. I have made a mental note to ask the 17 year old A Level student in a few months if the school has indeed lit a few sparks of inspiration in his mind. I hope it will. One final thing on a Friday, is it England or Wales in the World

Cup in this corner of the UK? A colleague has Fiji in the sweepstake so that answers that one for him at least.

25th September 2015

"The best way to predict the future is to create it." Peter Drucker

When I worked in Wiltshire I used to love the drive down to Avebury at this time of year, in particular to see the modern day druids on the stones for the Autumn equinox there emulating their Celtic ancestors from 2000 years ago. The idea of "equal-night" in Latin is the idea of balance for the Earth in terms of equal hours of daylight and night. My other favourite drive this time of year is through the Wye Valley to see the forest in all its autumnal glory. The academic year is already coming to the end of September and it is hard to think that it is October next week. This week in school has seen a lot of innovative foundations for the academic year ahead. The school's commitment to global learning and technology leapt forward with the beginning of Mandarin lessons and the visit of our new teacher from the Confucius Institute. I was lucky enough to spend time with the respective Heads of Offa's Mead and Tutshill primary schools in the last week and we will be able to develop Mandarin with these schools.

Today I had a group of students taking part in a video conference with schools in Moldova (where? Yes, the first question – which the Year 8s took straight to their geography teacher) and with France as part of our celebration of European Languages Day. Two Polish Year 8 girls here at Wyedean spoke eloquently about their ability to use English having lived here for a number of years, still feeling Polish, yet wanting to support either Wales or England in the World Cup this weekend (both are either side of the Wye). The technology is fantastic to aid this learning but not as tasty as the MFL café at lunchtime with huge queues out of the door with students tasting French, Spanish, and German foods. All were using their foreign languages as they were served.

I walked around the Science Learning Area this week and was pleased to see the engagement, independent learning, and the enquiring minds being challenged in the lessons. I joined Science Club on Tuesday where we made planispheres, only to be told by a very confident Year 9 there was a brilliant app called StarApp which allows you to simply point your phone to the night sky to get the names of the constellations. His confidence fell when he didn't know who Magnus Pike was though! His pitying look towards me as Headteacher said it all, so I went with Brian Cox instead.

The creativity today in Year 9 DT was incredible and it was nice to see students using their technology to enhance their learning as they actually made something physical. I still have the footstool I made in DT lessons myself, all these years later.

It has been hard to ignore the rugby this week and a colleague said the fan zone in Gloucester had been a very memorable experience. The year 10s on Wednesday soundly beat Dean Academy and drew with King's College Gloucester in their midweek rugby game. Friday finished off well for me with the Year 7s performing a very scary Haka. I think even Sam Warburton would think twice about walking up close to face off these guys.

My educator's heart beat a little faster a few times this week as I walked around the campus seeing the school working as it does. I am still astonished at the hard work the teachers and support staff put in every day to make the school the success it is. The "World's Largest Coffee Morning" for MacMillan on Friday in the staffroom saw a side to the school we sometimes lose in the grade-grind Govian/Post-Govian era; colleagues talking, relaxing, and being ready as professionals to make their lessons the best they can be for the students. My colleagues have led the implementation of GCSEPod to improve learning and revision for KS4 to use digital learning in a very positive way. The Positive School Culture here at Wyedean is helping us become the high performing World Class School we all aspire to be for our C21st learners.

It is Wyedean's Open Evening next Thursday 1st October. The staff cannot wait to show our community the experience and education that goes on in Wyedean every day, as we work hard to balance all that we do so that as educators we are creating the opportunities for students through compelling learning linked to student success. I once worked far from Wiltshire for a while, in Bandung in Java. One of the principals

I worked with repeated daily that we had to turn the dreams of kids into their futures. I have thought about that frequently as an educator as I reflect on the way we prepare our kids for their future. A week like this week and a month like this month tells me as a parent and an educator at Wyedean we are in the right direction and doing just that.

2nd October 2015

"The most influential of all educational factors is the conversation in a child's home." William Temple

I drove back through the Forest of Dean today from a meeting of Gloucestershire Secondary Heads. The sun was shining and it was just glorious. One moment in a room full of serious conversation regarding the new Ofsted framework and potential further funding cuts, the next driving through the glorious sunshine of the Forest with the colours of autumn everywhere. The backdrop from crossing the old bridge at Brockweir and through the Wye Valley and Tintern lifted my soul. You can see why Dennis Potter called it a heart shaped land on a day like this. On Monday, I looked across the Severn when I visited Woolaston Primary School – what views. Actually what kids and staff at that school! Chepstow was bustling on a Friday as I passed Wyedean students on a field trip with Geography walking through the town.

On Thursday Wyedean School opened its doors and saw its community come through in their hundreds, from both sides of the border. Staff, students, and governors showed off our school as parents and carers of years 5 and 6 came to look at their next destination in their educational journey. And a rugby match for Wales on as well! And we won! Cymru am Byth! Now England needs to beat the Aussies. I asked my wife what I should be saying in my first Open Evening speech as the new Head after 5 weeks. It was easy; this school cares for all of its students and wants the best for every individual. If parents and carers want a school that takes their children and gives them support, and stimulating, compelling learning, and opportunities – come to Wyedean. And Open Day is every day for anyone at this school. We have so much to see here. I walked around the Creative Learning Arts area this week and was amazed at the creativity and original ideas from students in music, drama, and art. I wrote to staff after Open Evening saying I was bursting with pride at the leadership and confidence of our students supported by the dedication and hard work of our professional staff.

The faith in the school and the strong foundations here have been rewarded with Wyedean School being chosen as only one of a handful of schools in the South West to work this year directly with the South West Regional Education Commissioner, Sir David Carter, on his group of schools working to become outstanding. This is an incredible accolade for the school and the staff as we continue to strive to deliver and develop World Class C21st learning here. The Ofsted meeting on Monday in Cheltenham was to look at how we should be working on progress for students as we shape as a school our curriculum and qualifications without capricious fads.

My Year 10 Critical Thinking group met with me on Thursday for our lesson and we looked at what we would need for an isolated existence other than food, shelter and water. The students all talked about stimulus for their minds. It was an enlightening discussion and refreshing to hear them say they would need to keep their minds active and to be engaged with the natural World. I mentioned Henry Thoreau living isolated in the woods in a cabin in Massachusetts to stimulate his senses for his writing. Not many of them fancied this for 2 years but wanted to get into the Forest of Dean this weekend, especially for the Forest Food and Drink festival this Sunday. I am going to take my wife and daughters. The festival of autumnal abundance and harvest bounty made me give another push to the school's Harvest Festival support of Chepstow Food Bank appeal (see our school Twitter) this week. So with the sun shining and our heart shaped land looking at its best in autumn, I finished the week looking at the plans for the school's International Christmas Market on the 9th December. How long until Christmas? Staff are definitely smiling after this week in school.

9th October 2015

"We know what we are, but know what me may be."

I was able to take my family to the Forest Festival on Sunday near Coleford at the kind invite of a parent of students at Wyedean. The sun was shining and the colours of the Forest around the festival ground gave the day a lovely sepia feeling. My daughters didn't do too well at the turnip throwing competition but last year's champion, "Bread", sent a nice message over the school's Twitter afterwards. It was good to see so many students from the school helping at the Festival and with their local community. I even managed to take in the steam railway at Parkend on the way back.

It was a delight to welcome the former Headteacher, John Claydon, into Wyedean School on Monday. John was Head from 1990 until 2005 and there were plenty of colleagues who remembered him and loved seeing him back. I visited St Briavels primary school on Monday afternoon and was just bowled over with the views from the playground looking down on the Wye Valley. The learning and atmosphere there was pretty impressive too. The week has seen a constant flow of parents and year 6s walking around and seeing the school working following the open evening. It has been interesting to take questions about education from a national policy point of view from a lot of parents. We have the Rt Hon Mark Harper MP in next week so maybe I will raise a couple of things with him as he sits in Cabinet.

The school's cycle of looking at learning and progress is well under way; colleagues have been looking at lessons, learning and the work students produce as a focus. I walked around the Applied Learning Area this week, and it was a great experience to see a range of subjects from Computer Science, Design Technology, Food Technology, and Business producing some really compelling learning. The sophisticated use of digital learning was particularly impressive. School leaders looked at a really clever App in the Leadership Meeting on Thursday as a way of having a "Wyedean School" App that can help with better home communication with the school. The Year 11s had their information evening on Thursday and colleagues worked with parents and students in ensuring the students have a plan of action and support for the year. We are talking about "war boards" in leadership at the moment as we get to grips with the new Progress 8 measurement (another question perhaps for Mark Harper) and sometimes in education it does seem like you are preparing a military strategy. It's why the talk of Christmas trees and the International Christmas market on the 9th Dec took my mind off Ofsted and government educational policy and back to the wonderful enrichment of whole school life. It was interesting to see how many students and staff could quote their favourite poets on National Poetry Day. We tweeted a particular nice take on Philip Larkin's poem, *"This be the verse"*. Yes, THAT one.

So, week 6 ends and half term is a little over 2 weeks away. Halloween and Bonfire Night still to come. The school's Harvest Festival appeal for Chepstow Food Bank is in full swing and many thanks to all who have donated already. There is still time to donate. No mention of the rugby only to say if Wales need Mr Jenkins and Mr Thomas to plug the injury gaps against the Aussies we can let them go for a fee, a large fee.

16th October 2015

"Education, therefore, is a process of living and not a preparation for future living." John Dewey

I have to start my weekly blog by praising my colleague and the students of Applied Media. I missed them out last week when I mentioned how impressed I was walking around the Applied Learning Area. The week has been filled with colleagues working hard on looking at how they mark work, the dialogue that follows and how students improve their learning as a follow up. Senior and middle leaders looked at work this week as part of how we all work together to ensure there is consistency in marking and feedback. Hattie stressed the importance of this in the way a student learns and progresses. As part of looking at the quality of learning around the school the first round of lesson observations are well underway. As a new Head to Wyedean I am really keen to see students learning in their lessons across the curriculum. I have been lucky enough to see many lessons in schools around the UK and abroad in my career. I was once doing a joint observation in a US High School where half a dozen students were asleep. I was writing my notes about the lesson reflecting the sleeping students when the superintendent for that county's schools told me I had to ignore the factor of the kids asleep and look at the others. The lessons I have seen this week were anything but about putting kids to sleep. The buzz for learning, energy, and the engagement was something I would like to show the US high school I was reviewing back then as an example of real LEARNING.

I went to the first meeting on Thursday in Nova Hreod School Swindon for Wyedean School as we are one of the handfuls of schools Sir David Carter has invited to work with him on his high performing schools programme as the regional commissioner for the South West. Lord Nash, the Minister for Academies, spoke at length there at how he had seen some of the most under performing schools in London improve because of purpose and leadership in a school. Sir David talked about "not a minute lost in lessons for learning" which resonated in my head as I watched a colleague deliver the most elegiac lesson to her students in year 11. It was like watching educational poetry in action. The work of Sir David's group is about "Good" schools like Wyedean moving to "outstanding" as high performing schools in the South West. I am looking forward to the next 12 months working with my leadership teams collaborating with schools across the South West in this group.

This week the three World Class learning strands of digital learning, creativity, and global learning that we believe at Wyedean are our fundamental to C21st learning took a huge step forward with the various developments in learning across the curriculum and especially with our primary schools supporting all through education. The school hosted the Rt Hon Mark Harper MP on Friday morning where we spoke to Mark about the developments in English education. Mark saw our impressive gospel choir sing to him in the JK Rowling library which was light relief after 6th Form students scrutinised him over a range of topics from the EU referendum to Corbymania. Mark spent time with staff, students and governors as the GCSE Catering group hosted the event with cakes that would put a Parisian patisserie to shame.

We have had lots of community events this week including meeting with Chepstow Rotary Club, seeing our parents at Beachley Barracks, and the Year 10 information Evening. A busy end of week 7 finished off with the agreement of Latin being funded and introduced in the school in November and our partner school in Montreal holding a video conference with our Year 9 students who are working on a range of projects for their joint Quebec exchange programme in 2016. The Science learning area had the most incredible learning day with "Tomorrow's Engineers" – if you have a look at the school's Twitter there are great photos of the event.

Definitely nothing to fall asleep in class here at Wyedean. Half term starts after Wednesday next week and I think I am more than ready to see my beloved Brittany again at my wife's family's place on the coast to recharge my batteries.

6th November 2015

"A good decision is based on knowledge and not on numbers." Plato

I have struggled all week to comprehend how miserable, grey, and wet this first week back after half term has been, in contrast to the sunshine during the break. It's hard to believe my 3 kids were playing in the sand and running into the sea at Brehac beach, northern Brittany this time last week. I drove up to visit Forest High School on Tuesday at the invite of the Head to see the hard work this school is achieving. The drive through the Forest in the autumnal fog was very atmospheric and I more or less stumbled upon the school as I arrived in Cinderford; the fog was that thick.

Wyedean School is very much about working in partnership and collaboration with all sorts of partners and networks, and on Wednesday our Mandarin teachers arrived from the Confucius Institute to begin teaching Mandarin to our primary partner schools at Offa's Mead, Tutshill, Bream, and The Dell. We have a couple of global partnerships we are hosting exchange programmes with, and our students who are hosting our Spanish partners were very excited to receive their letters and partner information. We are also working with a school in Montreal, and this week Ecole Beloil held their information evening for parents and students as Wyedean students will be staying in Montreal next year with their exchange partners. As part of my work for the British Council, I have been speaking over Skype to a number of schools looking at British political, cultural, and historical issues. On Monday, I spoke to our partner Lycée Rabelais in Paris about the importance of Remembrance and the Poppy in the UK at this time of year. Wyedean School will be taking part in the national remembrance observance next week and a representative group of staff and students will take part in local community remembrance. At half term, a large group of History students from Wyedean School visited the WWI battlefield and commemoration sites in Belgium. Even 100 years on the sheer number of names representing lives lost in this war and subsequent wars is hard to comprehend.

This week the success of the school was further recognised when the Rt Hon David Curry wrote to me inviting the school to contribute a case study to The Parliamentary Review annual publication. He cited in particular the 6th Form results and success as well as the recent invite by Sir David Carter to the school, recognising it is moving to "Outstanding" as a high performing school and a beacon of success in the area. I am very proud of the school always and the hard work staff do here day in/day out, but this is wonderful recognition of what we are achieving here at Wyedean School.

Education is never far away in the national news and staff and parents were interested in the Secretary of State's announcement of the possible return to testing for 7 year olds just as we are all getting used to "life without levels" at KS3. For Wyedean, as an academy with the relative freedom over its curriculum and qualifications, the relaxation on the EBacc was welcome news but the debate still continues. It has also been a week of year 11s here and from outside requesting information about the 6th Form Open Evening on the 3rd Dec.

I was lucky enough to visit the site of the proposed UTC today at the site of the decommissioned power station at Berkeley and was given a tour by the executive principal of South Glos' & Stroud College group. It was very strange to be staring across at the Forest and Lydney from this side of the Severn.

My critical thinking group had a very lively debate in my room on Thursday as we discussed the meaning of "happiness". With Halloween gone and Bonfire Night upon us my definition of happiness right now is watching a roaring fire and lots of noisy fireworks as we enter November and darker nights and mornings. And I would also be happier if some of my Year 7 boys didn't get so muddy at lunchtime!

13th November 2015

"Look deep into nature, and then you will understand everything better." Albert Einstein

A school I work with in Delhi, Bal Bharati School, sent me greetings for Diwali, the Hindu festival of light. I gave a talk over video conference this week explaining Bonfire Night and the importance of light also in the increasing darkness of late November with winter around the corner, a long way to go before the end of term at the end of week 10 and the shortest day still far off in December. Like any good educator, I felt I had got this across well. First question: "So Guy Fawkes. You light bonfires and have fireworks to celebrate the fact he tried to blow up Parliament?" My silent response was a little longer than I wanted it to be before I said no.

Another annual November commemoration was marked this week with the community act of Remembrance held in Tutshill to mark the 11th November Armistice with a very fitting service and the two-minute silence. As I stood with my students from Wyedean School I could see other local schools represented, representatives from The Rifles battalion were there, local scouts and guides organisations, Rotary Club, The British Legion as well as other members of our Forest community. All to remember the significance of the names of local people read out who made the ultimate sacrifice and truly did give their today for our tomorrow. The strength of our community at that moment was very powerful. It is incredible what can be achieved when we come together for a common purpose.

The thought of community wasn't lost on me as we held our autumn "Academic Mentoring Days" on Thursday and Friday at Wyedean. I have never known a successful school that doesn't have a good working partnership with its parents and carers. These opportunities are vitally important so parents & carers get the chance to raise issues with their child's teachers, sometimes difficult ones, but often to reassure and all in the shared spirit of wanting the absolute best for our young people. It was so good to see so many parents & carers over the 2 days in Wyedean School. Our staff here never cease to amaze me with the time they will spend making sure the constant dialogue with home gets the best and gives the very best for our learners. I'll say it again; I am privileged to be the Head of this school.

I am conscious of how we are a quarter of the way through the 39-week academic year already – minus the holidays. I gave two assemblies this week to Years 8 and 11 on the theme of "Time". As a History teacher, time for me is often a timeline with a start and finish with events in-between. For Dr Who it definitely isn't. With the risk of being controversial, I used the lovely clip from the best Dr Who ever, David Tennent, where he explains time as more like a "wibbly wobbly ball". I know, possibly Christopher Eccleston. Sometimes we are not conscious of the amount of time we have and how precious this time is to make something good from it – hours on Candy Crush or Minecraft doesn't count in case my family are reading this. My Year 10 Critical Thinking group on Thursday got so engrossed in their discussion on the refugee crisis they overran into their PE time – apologies for that.

Next week is the annual British Council's "International Education Week". Wyedean School will be using the week to focus on raising global awareness with our students so that they are increasingly connected to the World in which they live and understand that technology and media are a key part of this when used in a positive way. That awareness of ourselves as an individual, in our local community, in our national community, and in our global society isn't something unique to the C21st. It was there long ago in the minds of those people whose names were read out across our corner of the Forest on Wednesday morning as they were remembered in time.

20th November 2015

"Human history becomes more and more a race between education and catastrophe." H. G. Wells

Like many people I woke up on Saturday morning to be confronted with the shocking and appalling events that were still unfolding in Paris following the IS terrorist attacks on innocent people doing nothing more than enjoying their Friday evening in Paris, at a football match, in restaurants, cafés, and a concert. My friend who teaches and lives in Paris spoke about the absolute numbness she felt and had spent this week calling friends and parents to see if they were ok. This week in school students and teachers have been discussing why this senseless violence has been perpetrated. I have been proud of my students when I have heard their discussions, who see these people from IS not as a representation of Islam but of something more akin to nihilism and senseless destruction of innocent lives. A Muslim teacher colleague and friend from Indonesia who I worked with in Bandung on Java, Ibu Eha, spoke to me and said "Tell your students & community IS doesn't speak for Islam. As Muslims our teachers, parents and students believe only in peace and tolerance".

In school we had to decide whether our visit to France for Year 7 should still go ahead, scheduled for this week. The decision to postpone until after new year was the right one, later confirmed by the FCO website advising no school travel to France this weekend. Our parents were brilliantly supportive and we cannot thank them enough for the way they have worked with the school on this. I was interviewed by BBC Radio Gloucestershire on Monday about the decision we had taken as a school to postpone the visit. I also spoke on the programme about what we do as a school to ensure our students are educated about World events such as the Paris Attacks and how we develop their ability to understand these events. The HG Wells quote in this blog has never been more apt for me as an educator. This coincided with the school marking the British Council's "International Education Week" with a series of events as Wyedean School believes so strongly in the high importance global education plays in C21st learning. We have been working with our Quebec and Spanish partner schools this week and it is so good to hear parents and students in our partner primary schools praising the joint transition work through the innovative Mandarin learning we have provided.

The Creativity Learning Area held their annual Year 7 music concert on Tuesday night. My surprise swung between the sheer talents this year group has in those amazing singing voices to how so many parents had made it into school beating Storm Barney. It was also good to see the entire year group performing confidently together and how proud parents and teachers were of the performances. On Thursday KS3 were treated to a workshop provided by G Dance and the disabled actor Nicola Miles-Wildin. Wyedean School sees creativity as another key element in C21st learning and this was a great opportunity for the students to create great dance set pieces. Nickie is coming back in January.

11th December 2015

"Leadership and Learning are indispensable to each other." John F. Kennedy

The end of the penultimate week... almost. It feels a long term and I know educators, support staff, and students are gearing themselves up for that final week, week 15, of this long term. I am talking about my Headship experience in Bristol on Monday and I have been doing a lot of reflecting over these last 3 months as the new (newish now) Head of Wyedean School. I had an opportunity to have such a conversation with the director of education for Gloucestershire, Jo Grills, who very kindly came to visit the school on Wednesday. Jo made a very astute comment as she left about the school reception and how important this first impression of the school is for visitors, staff, and students. Jo was very complimentary as were the parents who came in for the Year 13 evening last night. I had a similar experience in Severnbanks School Lydney on Monday when I went to visit the Head there, Pam Howells. It was lovely to hear the singing of the students rehearsing the Nativity play as well as talk to Pam about how the schools in the Forest of Dean need to work more closely, and how we should continue to lift the aspirations of our students. Pam is a very inspirational and dedicated Head and she referred to herself several times as a "proud Forester". Those students and the community know how fortunate they are to have an educator like Pam as Head.

I have been really keen as a Head to keep building the links we have with our own Forest and Wye Valley communities here. I have only ever known strong community-school partnerships and how we work together to raise the aspirations of our young people. I have seen so much of this partnership over the last 3 months and it was very evident this week. The new food hall for Marks & Spencer recently opened up in Chepstow and on Tuesday the Gospel Choir were invited to sing at the opening. The manager was thrilled as were the many shoppers who were not necessarily walking into the store but stayed listening to the singing. On Wednesday evening, the school held the first ever International Christmas Market for Wyedean. It was a lovely event as many parents and students turned out to support the evening. This will be an annual event for the school and community, and plans are already underway for next year. This may read strange for a Head to write but I really enjoyed the Full Governing Body meeting on Tuesday. We welcomed many new parents and academy governors and although items such as the cuts in education across the country are sobering topics, the support and ideas from the governors supporting the school was a perfect example of leadership for me. Every stakeholder at Wyedean wants this school to be even more of a high performing school and even more aspirational than it has already reached.

I met with PGCE teachers this morning ahead of their second placements. It is heartening to know the quality of new teachers and their passion for learning means a torch of education is continually being passed on. I was reminded of the moment in "The West Wing" quite a few years ago where the character Sam Seeborn gives a speech where he declares "Education is the silver bullet, education is everything". Never a truer word said.

One of the best parts of the job is like this morning when my head of MFL came into my room at 7:45am and told me the plans she has for Mandarin and Chinese as Wyedean as a Confucius Hub. It is poetry to hear of the opportunities for students and staff such as Chinese New Year on the 8th Feb, a Chinese Business Etiquette course for Sixth Formers, Shanghai Maths teaching model and more Mandarin for our primaries. And on Tuesday we Skype with the University of Bristol Classics School to discuss the Latin programme we are starting here at Wyedean. I know we live in austere times but we have reservoirs of hope in how we look at learning and life opportunities for our students.

A couple of years ago Wyedean School students campaigned in the Welsh Assembly about the lack of safety on the Chepstow-A48 bridge. This week we cannot say thank you enough for the completed safety barrier that allows our students crossing from Chepstow to get to school safely. I am about to drive back across that bridge and see my middle eldest daughter in her first primary school nativity play this afternoon. I will be thinking of those kids in Lydney performing to their proud families as I watch my Annie as a proud dad this afternoon. Education is about these moments! More of them please.

19th December 2015

"Christmas isn't a season, it is a feeling." Edna Forbes

The buses have all left with our students heading off for a much needed break, staff have gone home to their families, and the school is about to close for the holiday season after a long 15 weeks of a 39 week academic year. Term 1 is finally over and it is 2016 when we come back. And I need to see the new Star Wars film before the spoilers really take hold of cyber-space.

I spoke on Monday in Bristol about Headship and some of the challenges and rewards that go with the role. I have continued to be impressed every week with the talents and abilities at the school and Wednesday night in St Mary's Church, Chepstow was no exception for the school's carol concert. This was a great event where the community had celebrated, commemorated, mourned, and come together in this ancient building for hundreds of years. Hearing the various bands play and choirs sing their hearts out to the rafters made me think about the importance of marking moments of life and the cycle of a year in a community.

I had a meeting in Shire Hall, Gloucester, mid-week to look at ways schools can manage shrinking budgets with the expectations of "doing more for less" – I drove back through the Forest of Dean knowing the new year will mean more creativity in how we look at getting additional funding and how the skills of leadership in planning this strategically are going to be needed even more. This will be the challenge for every school now and for the foreseeable future. I am very lucky at Wyedean to have incredibly professional and dedicated leaders at all levels and throughout the school. I was looking at the December newsletter (available now on the website) and the CPD review for this term, amazed at how much my colleagues do to make sure kids get the best learning and the school goes forward. My optimism for the New Year ahead is already brimming over as we planned this week the applications for a regional arts centre to be here at Wyedean as well as for the Chinese New Year on the 8th February, The Year of the Monkey. Colleagues from English and MFL Skyped with the Classics department of the University of Bristol and the development of Latin to support English and language learning is one of the most exciting foundations we are putting down here to benefit all learners.

Year 11 mocks have just been completed and students are looking at their results planning what they have to do for the time they have left between now and exams. I had a few Year 11s in with me today going over revision tips and again telling me how supportive GCSEPod has been already. I want all students and staff to get a good break over Christmas ready for the new year ahead and have emphasised this point strongly whenever it has come up. Staff who are retiring or going on maternity said their goodbyes this week. To Jenny Rickards, learning mentor for 13 years and supporting countless students we send our very best wishes as a school for your service and dedication. Enjoy the next chapter.

I have a couple of key appointments in January to my leadership team including a new finance director and a deputy head so I am definitely getting some rest with my family over the break. I am itching to see the new Star Wars film and will hopefully see it sometime next week. So it is time to face the "Black Friday" traffic and the queues of traffic trying to get to

Cribbs Causeway. It is meant to be the warmest Christmas Day on record this year and I have wondered whether the "Christmas jumper" day that has now become a regular event shouldn't be a "Xmas t-shirt" as I sit here in mine way too hot.

I wish all our Forest & Wye Valley communities at Wyedean School a Merry Christmas and best wishes for the New Year. PS: Don't forget to download free from the App store – WS - "MySchoolApp".

8th January 2016

"In the depth of winter, I finally learned that within me there lay an invincible summer." Albert Camus

Happy New Year. Like many people this morning I found myself scraping ice off the car at 6am ahead of driving to work. It seems the deluge of rain we have experienced throughout the winter so far is about to be replaced by a cold spell next week. I had a Year 9 boy ask me in the corridor at break yesterday about "snow days". He did grin as he finished his question.

We started Monday back after the break straight into a school day and straight on with lessons and learning. I think this is the first time for many years as an educator I have started back in January without an INSET day. I know my daughter's school had an INSET delaying the inevitable return to a Tuesday and she also has a very short half term to February of only 4 weeks. Not a lot of time compared to the 15 weeks between 1st September and Christmas. This stretch of the academic year is always about consolidating the foundations of the autumn and quietly concentrating on and building 'learning-knowledge-understanding' for all classes but especially the exam groups ahead of the summer. We have the Year 9 option process ahead this term and the timetable for 2016-17 is more or less underway following the first release of numbers for projected Year 7s and 12s potentially starting in September 2016.

The Year 11s had their subject consultation evening last night and I continue to be impressed with this year group especially the way they approach their learning, their post 16 options and the general way they have developed as independent learners. Parents were full of praise for the support the school is giving and there is a lot of appreciation for how useful GCSEPod has been in learning as well as the improvement in communication through the Wyedean "MySchoolapp".

I was thrilled this week ahead of the UCAS 15th January deadline to see the range and number of offers Year 13s have been getting from universities, including a number of students getting into Oxford following December interviews. The record surge in applications to Year 12 is encouraging and we are still accepting applications for Sixth Form. In Year 7 we have had to create another teaching group mid-way through the academic year to accommodate the request for places and I am pleased to say we have created those places for parents who have contacted us to bring their child here to be educated.

One of the initiatives at Wyedean School now underway in 2016 is the school's development of Latin in the curriculum. I once attended an international conference where one talk was entitled "Where once we taught Latin we will now teach Coding" – my first question was simple: "why not both?" We are working in partnership with the University of Bristol and the educational charity "Classics for All" to develop Latin as a cross-curricula project between the English and MFL learning areas. Colleagues from both Learning Areas are at Bristol University working later this month. Studies show how Latin can significantly improve literacy and confidence in students and it is an example of the innovative way we approach learning at Wyedean School. This year, the severe national funding situation restricting schools in the way they develop the curriculum means educators have to be more innovative in ensuring all of our students continue to get a wide range of opportunities that challenge and stretch them as learners. I am extending this as a 2016 learning challenge to parents and the community with the start of free adult Mandarin courses here at Wyedean as part of our very successful adult learning programme and as a centre for the Confucius Institute. We are always learning and all of us are learners.

This week the SW Regional Schools Commissioner, Sir David Carter, has been named as the next National Schools Commissioner. Sir David is a very inspirational educational leader with a total commitment to every individual student getting the best education possible. Although a loss for the SW, nationally this is a very positive start to 2016 for schools and academies in England. I have been thinking of leadership all week especially looking at the news from Westminster regarding the forth-coming EU referendum and the Labour re-shuffle. One of the most striking images of the week was President Obama announcing his decision to introduce gun controls with tears streaming down his face. It is hard to believe this is his last year as president and I know friends in the States are anticipating a potential Trump v Clinton vote come November. I read a little over Christmas and can heartily recommend the travel writer Paul Theroux's book "Deep South" to try and understand modern America. As my American friend once said: *"we are you, we just took a different route after 1776"*.

If Monday was supposed to be the "worst" day of the year as people returned back to work and school, today is supposed to be the day when all the resolutions on getting in shape are thrown out of the window at the end of a busy first week of 2016. I know some will be thinking of "snow days" next week but personally there is too much to do and February half term is only 4 weeks away.

15th January 2016

"Life's most persistent and urgent question is, what are you doing for others?" Martin Luther King Jr.

The sunshine on Friday was just so bright. I had a meeting for Headteachers in Shire Hall in Gloucester to look at ways we can collaborate more to get even more for the students in our county and in the Forest of Dean in particular. Despite the Thursday night forecast there was no Arctic blizzard hitting Bristol anytime soon as I drove up the M5. The cathedral looked magnificent in the morning winter sun and I prepared for a couple of hours in a room potentially feeling the opposite of what I was feeling walking through the medieval streets, due to the severe financial situations all schools are now facing. I have a wry smile whenever I hear anyone official say "we have to learn to do less for more". I am still waiting for guidance on how I tell that to my support staff doing everything and more for the school or my teachers who are ensuring every lesson is a compelling learning experience by working long into their evenings.

Thursday had been a long, intense but necessary day as the school held interviews to appoint the next Deputy Head. We were very fortunate to have such a strong field of candidates apply and at the end of the process the acting Deputy Head, Rob Wagland was appointed permanently to the post. This week we have the same process for the Finance Director role. As a new Head, relatively speaking now, both posts are crucial in helping me to take the school forward and develop an outstanding educational experience for the students of Wyedean. I took my assembly with Year 11 on Monday with this in my head as I talked to them around the theme of motivation. Year 11s are now more than half way through their academic year and we have had the mocks and latest round of progress updates to make sure everyone is on track. I am always a bit wary of using my own experience to "motivate" anyone because an individual's experience doesn't speak to everyone and can backfire. My experience is fairly straightforward. My father worked underground digging coal for nearly 40 years and I was very lucky to be in a school where teachers saw education as the ladder of opportunities and literally would push books at you whether you liked it or not. There was a real passion for developing a love of learning and to be curious about the World. Teachers did really talk about "lighting a flame" and passing it on. I think of this often when I talk to any students.

The Historian (and famous descendent of possibly my favourite president, John Adams) Henry Adams once famously said "*A teacher affects eternity; he can never tell where his influence stops*". I think it is still true, even more so. One of the joys of watching my colleagues when they teach is that passion and enthusiasm for the very thing that once lit a light in their head. The area I came from is full of history. Any visitor to my beautiful heimat of Shropshire gets the "15 minutes of 3000 years of British history" just by driving from the Iron Age hill fort on the Wrekin, past Roman Wroxeter, by the medieval Abbey at Buildwas and through the Coalbrookdale valley to Ironbridge where the modern age began in the early C18th and the birth of the Industrial Revolution. It lit my spark for history a long time ago!

The UCAS deadline for applications on Friday made me think back to how lucky I was that teachers I knew pushed me to get GCSEs, A Levels, and then to look at university as the first person in my family to do so. I thank all those wonderful educators daily in my mind. So back to how we do less for more. I think in the current climate all educators, support staff in schools, community, and parents need to collaborate and do more together. I have also seen the power of better meaningful conversations about better education and how we all achieve this goal. Over the last couple of weeks, governors, parents, staff, and students have been working out how we can develop a "learning garden" at the school. I saw how powerful these were in places like northern Thailand for the students as areas to learn and especially for independent learning. We could give up and say there is no government money and budget cuts or we can look at how we look at other ways funding this and make it happen.

I left the meeting on Friday very optimistic about what could be done for our schools and communities in the Forest of Dean and Wye Valley. It takes leadership and persistence. And maybe the odd prayer in Gloucester Cathedral. In the week of Martin Luther King Day, a day marked as a Federal holiday in the US, I caught the film "Selma" over Christmas about the Civil Rights movement in Alabama and the freedom marches of the mid-60s. When LBJ stands in front of Congress and utters "We shall overcome" you know we can. "Yes we can" as the man said running for president all those years later.

22nd January 2016

"The terminology of 'a culture of high expectations' is in itself complex and problematic, but any opportunity to explicitly raise expectations should be seen as a moral imperative." Julie Smith

I spent most of Friday at the Gloucestershire secondary Heads conference listening to a variety of speakers talk and debate some of the most pressing and pertinent issues surrounding education today. Sir John Dunford, the "Pupil Premium Champion" gave a very forthright account of what the best schools are doing to ensure a big chunk of learners are not written off and actually have measures put in place to allow them educational opportunities that raise their expectations as well. Bradley Simmons, head of Ofsted in the SW, talked through the new Sept 2015 framework and what this means for schools especially in terms of the deeper expectations of the role of governance, safeguarding, pupil premium, and more able students. Wyedean School wants to move from "Good" to "Outstanding" and to be considered "high performing" in everything we do so it was with interest I read the final DfE League Tables published last week comparing the GCSE 5x A*-C with English and Maths.

Educational funding policy concerns all schools and there was nothing reassuring at the conference from the chair of the Commons select Committee, Neil Carmichael MP, for any school leader in the room. Telling schools to "do more for less" and expecting them to aspire to "World Class" education on funding levels last seen in the mid-1990s challenges even the most optimistic of school leader. One of the other areas of contention is the government's wish for "90% of children" to be studying EBacc subjects. The Chief Inspector of Ofsted, Sir Michael Wilshaw, has publicly challenged the thinking for this proposal and consultation with the DfE ends on the 29th Jan (English.BACCALAUREATE@education.gsi.gov.uk)

My background is strongly with the International Baccalaureate (the IB) and I have looked on in bemusement over the years as several different governments, both sides of the border, have attempted to take the word "baccalaureate" and apply it to suggest they are actually joining a curriculum together with cross curricula subjects and strands that enhance learning. I do believe the days of viewing education as dry, stand alone, disjointed, and disconnected subjects forming a student's curriculum are long gone, but educational debate still needs to go some way to look to the sort of education the IB provides, and make sure all students have the opportunity to develop knowledge and skills to equip them for life-long learning and high aspirations. Last week we held our Year 9 "Options Evening" and we have worked hard to provide different curriculum pathways and individual learning for our students. What all staff here want for Wyedean is a curriculum, both formal and informal, that raises expectations, challenges all learners and equips students for the C21st globalised World.

A clear example of this comes from the Science Learning Area on a daily basis. Students were fortunate enough to go to the GCSE Science Live event at Oxford last week and we are delighted that our students are through to the Science Fame Lab final at the Cheltenham Festival in February. I have also been following the recent sporting success of our very own "Wyedean Warriors" on Twitter. The student council executives have moved our proposal for the school's "learning garden" forward and we were really pleased to be awarded 420 saplings by the Woodland Trust as part of this commitment to the learning environment of the school. We are in the Forest of Dean after all. The respective coordinators of digital, creative, and global learning all presented to the Full Governors on Tuesday and it felt reassuring to see how expectations for all learners are being raised. I agree totally with my colleague in English, it is our moral imperative as educators to have a culture of high expectations for all of our students from all of our staff.

29th January 2016

"Learning is not attained by chance, it must be sought for with ardour and attended to with diligence." Abigail Adams

It's hard to believe we are at the end of January already and we are talking in school about February half term. This Friday lunchtime I was asked several times by students "when do we have the next break?" The weather doesn't feel very wintery right now especially in contrast to the snow scenes from North America last weekend. Life in school very much feels business-like as progress is made through courses, especially those with summer examinations looming. Year 11s have started their individual formal guidance meetings in school and I was struck this week how focused various students I met with were fixed on their hoped-for pathways at Wyedean Sixth Form after GCSEs.

I think I have mentioned before how I was surprised by the large number of questions from students in September about my plans for uniform. As opposed to questions on learning or opportunities in school I had in mind as a new Head. I do believe strongly in school identity and students and staff feeling pride in their school. Well this week we had the Year 10 Careers interviews. These are supported by local organisations, employers, governors, and local business people. It gives students the opportunities to meet with them and be interviewed and go through where they are right now. It is very powerful and necessary as we prepare students for the World outside of school. The Year 10s came dressed in "business wear" and looked very impressive in how professional they looked. I joked with a lot of them that this could be the new uniform. Have a look at the school's Twitter for an example.

In Wednesday's Teaching and Learning briefing the Creativity Coordinator gave a rich talk on what she has done with the brief of Creativity and staff have lots of ideas already concerning the school's "Creativity Festival" scheduled for early July. We are looking forward to our primary partners, local communities, and even some of our international partner schools joining us in this celebration of creativity. Just after the briefing I caught up with my colleagues from English and MFL who had spent the previous day with the Classics Dept of the University of Bristol preparing for the Latin courses we are introducing. It is fair to say they were definitely buzzing from the day and ready to get going.

I was lucky to speak to a number of parents on Thursday at the Year 8 consultation evening and this is always a great way of being able to catch up – much more preferable to email. I sat with a number of individual parents who wanted to talk about how Wyedean can support the number of students from Welsh medium primaries who choose the school but would like to continue with their Welsh. Well, in what we think is a first for an English school, we are introducing the opportunity for these students to continue with their Welsh at Wyedean. I need to add here, and apologies for the boast, but last year from my school in Powys I did get Welsh onto Skype Classroom as one of their languages. The Music department are also working on the programme for the school's Eisteddfod in March.

I get a number of emails from parents regarding homework/home learning and this week as part of our commitment to better digital learning, our digital learning coordinator came back from BETT 2016 with a great tool and app (Show My Homework) that will really ensure home learning supports and complements school learning. This will also support further independent learning for students.

I have witnessed a battle royal of student leadership this week as the two respective Prom Committees for Years 11 and 13 have fought it out for the coveted "Valentine's Disco" slot for lower school. Even dividing a brother and sister in those year groups though to see their student leadership in action is just a delight. It's a big part of what makes this job so rewarding. Finally best of luck to Jessica Fudge this weekend in the area final of the Rotary Club "Young Chef" competition and I hope the weather is good for Year 7 on the French trip going out tomorrow. My thanks to Beky, Dai, Martyn and Gwenda for all of their hard work on this early start tomorrow at 5am!

5th February 2016

"Becoming is better than being." Carol Dweck

I have been fascinated by the Iowa caucus vote this week and if you are interested in US politics and history there is a podcast every Sunday until the November election from the Washington Post taking each of the 44 presidents and examining their lives and legacy. The becoming in this case is very often more fascinating that the being. Interestingly Jefferson doesn't have being president on his gravestone as a legacy. And it is astonishing to think that he and Adams both died within hours of each other on the 4th July fifty years after the Declaration of Independence.

In a week where a group of Sixth Formers gave me a divided analysis on Britain's future in the EU we welcomed staff and students from a French partner school in St Tropez to spend the day in Wyedean on Tuesday. And as if by magic the sun shone like a warm spring day, not quite the French Riviera but almost the Côtes de Wye. Our year 7 left in the early hours of

Saturday morning for their long awaited visit to France and if you have a look at the school's Twitter they had a superb time this week and my thanks to staff, parents, and students.

The Science Learning Area here at Wyedean continues to take curriculum enrichment to another level and I am pleased to see Year 8 have been chosen to represent the school at the Salters Festival of Chemistry at the University of Bristol. On Wednesday, the year 9 finalists went before an audience and an outside panel of experts for the final of Fame Lab UK and a place at the Cheltenham Festival. A huge thanks to all staff and Fame Lab for their support of this very powerful competition. Just have a look on the school's Twitter. I am very proud of our students, none more so than in those moments listening to individual students talking knowledgeably and confidently about their chosen topic. Well done to all the student finalists! I met with Gwent Wildlife Trust on Thursday and incredibly Year 8 Sean Crabbe has won the John Muir photography award. Well done Sean!

The Gospel Choir took part in the Music for Youth Primary Promenade concert in Cheltenham on Thursday and the Wyedean Warriors continue with their sporting success this season. The Year 9s won 2:1 against Dean Academy this week and the Year 7s beat them 10-5 at rugby. With the 6 Nations starting this weekend there will be a lot of friendly rivalry over the next few weeks between our English and Welsh school components, with the odd dash of loyalty to Scotland, Ireland, France and even Italy. The Sixth Form football team beat Newent 2:1 in the County Cup and are through to the next round.

I met with the new intake of PGCE teachers from UWE this week and the school's partnership with universities like UWE and Bristol is having a very positive impact on our priority to ensure that the Wyedean approach is about compelling learning experiences challenging all of our students. One of the English teachers, Lucy McManus, has just received an outstanding commendation from UWE for the work she has done with them on training PGCE teachers in effective A Level teaching. Lucy was commended by visiting Danish colleagues in partnership with UWE in October for her work.

We are now more than half way through the academic year at the end of week 20, and as I hear Year 11 go off down the corridor for their 2-hour walk and talk Maths mock, their approach towards this final stretch of learning and revision before the exam season is impressive. Next week we break for half term and the staff have a two-day inset on Thursday and Friday aimed at improving even further teaching and learning. It is our core business and the reason we are here. Next week we say goodbye to our friend and colleague, Finance Director Jeanine Allen, who is moving to a school in the North West. Jeanine has given the school 10 years of dedicated service and she leaves with our warmest wishes.

26th February 2016

"Education is the silver bullet. Education is everything."
Sam Seaborn, *"The West Wing"*

My apologies for being slightly political here, but in line with the national focus in schools on "British Values" and this week the topic being democracy, I have been exchanging a few emails and Skype sessions with friends in the States about the consequence of a possible President Trump come November's presidential election in the US. They, in return, have asked what happens with a possible "Brexit" here in the UK if the referendum vote chooses to support Britain leaving the EU. I don't know what will happen but it was the two main topics of conversations with Quebec partner school, Ecole Ploybel Montreal, we spoke with over Skype this week. We did intend to talk about the planning of our partner exchange visit for 2017. I have been indulging a more idealistic, albeit fictional time, in American politics by catching a few re-runs of 'The West Wing' recently. Sam Seaborn, played by the actor Rob Lowe, not only quotes education is the silver bullet but his character goes on to declare that *"...schools should be palaces"*.

I saw a school that did look like a palace this week in the shape and form of Torquay Academy as they hosted the latest conference of the National Schools Commissioner, Sir David Carter's "Race to Outstanding" group. Principal Steve Margetts, together with the staff and students of Torquay Academy, has a school that has not only significantly improved standards and attainments, but considerably raised expectations and the aspirations of the kids and community it serves as a school. The members of my leadership team who participated in the conference took back a lot of ideas from the day that we could look at incorporating at Wyedean as we continue to strive to be a high performing school in all that we do. Talking with Sir David at the conference, it is clear there is a real momentum to continue to build networks and partnerships between academies that raise outcomes for students and the communities the schools serve. It is a real privilege to be in this small group of schools and work with school leaders dedicated to sustainable and meaningful school improvement. One of the lasting impressions I have taken away is Steve Margetts' firm belief in high aspirations and expectations of his staff and students. This was clear in the powerful learning environment created in the academy.

I came back late from Torquay but in time to catch the last hour of the Year 7 consultation evening. It is hard to believe Year 7s are over halfway through their first year. It is always one of the best parts of being a Head to be able to talk to parents directly and openly at such events. We have also been running a wide consultation with parents about the school as a fact-finding forum and if more parents want to be involved in this forum then contact me directly at the school. A huge number of parents have taken advantage of the free Mandarin being offered by the Confucius Institute as part of the Adult Education programme we have at Wyedean that was launched this week. This coming Monday at 6pm we have a huge Chinese Festival on at the school to celebrate Chinese New Year. Next week the preparations are under way led by our JK Rowling library for "World Book Day".

Today Wyedean has organised a "Wear it Purple" day to commemorate what would have been Natasha Scott-Falber's 18th birthday. She died of Toxic Shock Syndrome in February 2013. Purple was her favourite colour. The students will pay £1 to wear something purple for the non-uniform event. All money raised will go to FISCH, a charity that is building a drop-in centre for street children in Tanzania. Working in Africa was close to Natasha's heart after she visited Tanzania with her church while in Year 8. The event on Friday also serves to raise awareness of TSS. In addition to Wear it Purple, three Wyedean students are taking part in a sky dive to raise money for FISCH this weekend.

It is my eldest daughter's 7th birthday today and I am torn between this and the 6 Nations with Wales v France tonight - a fixture that is important in my family because of ties to both nations. Certainly the two most stirring anthems of the nations involved. Hopefully I may get back to watching a bit more of "*The West Wing*" over the weekend as well as my daughter's "cinema party" for 40 of her "closest" school friends. To finish another long week and in light of Sir Michael Wilshaw's comments today about the teaching recruitment crisis and teachers choosing to go overseas the full Sam Seaborn quote I started this week's blog with is worth a re-visit for inspiration.

Sam Seaborn: "*...education is the silver bullet. Education is everything. We don't need little changes, we need gigantic, monumental changes. Schools should be palaces. The competition for the best teachers should be fierce. They should be making six-figure salaries. Schools should be incredibly expensive for government and absolutely free of charge to its citizens, just like national defense. That's my position. I just haven't figured out how to do it yet*".

4th March 2016

"*Tell me and I forget. Teach me and I remember. Involve me and I learn.*" Benjamin Franklin

The partner school in Chisinau, Moldova, who we work with as a school, Lycee Gheorghe Asachi, celebrated the start of spring this week, with a festival and the giving of red and white ribbons, known as "martisors". They bring luck for the rest of the year if worn. Our Eisteddfod for St David's Day hasn't quite fallen on the 1st March for Dewi Sant but it is a similar principle over on this side of Europe to Moldova (there is a board game called "Where is Moldova?" – great Cricova red wine, a favourite of the Royal Family going back to Queen Victoria). I sat with a group of Year 11s earlier on in the week as we went through the Year book and Prom arrangements. I wasn't sure if their being relaxed and confident as we sat in my study was a good sign or not as their exams approach even faster, or so it seems now we are in March.

I think the two things I have enjoyed most this week are the assemblies I have taken and the Head's drop in as I have been walking around various learning areas with colleagues looking at the work we do especially on supporting PP students and delivering stretch & challenge in learning. The theme for the assembly has been based on British Values and The Rule of Law. My stretch and challenge as an educator was to spend 15 minutes from Monday to Thursday at 8:45 ensuring I made this appealing as a topic to the various year groups. I did manage to get in The Simpsons, John Locke, Magna Carta, Charles I, the Founding Fathers, Hitler, Jim Crow Laws, Brexit, and finally Donald Trump. In my walk around three learning areas I saw very effective feedback and review in Social Studies/MFL, tracking and independent learning in the applied learning area, and in Maths today not only sublime learning from the PGCE teacher but rich and stunning curriculum enrichment supporting extended learning for all maths students. These moments really are the best times of being a Head.

The school has been looking recently at exactly what sort of network and partnership with other schools and organisations we should collaborate with to ensure Wyedean School is a high performing & innovative school. We took a huge step closer this week as we looked in leadership and in governor meetings at a partnership with some of the very best and outstanding schools in England. Wyedean School believes in all sorts of networks and partnerships and one of the most successful ones we have been involved in over the last 6 months is the one with the University of Cardiff and the Confucius Institute. On Monday evening the school held its first ever Mandarin Festival and my thanks to local primary schools, parents, and the Confucius Institute for supporting the event. The Chinese Lion from the group at Bristol University was wonderful to see and certainly entertained the students from Bream and Offa's Mead in the front row. Some great photos on the school's Twitter also on Wyedean Sports Twitter showing the success of the Wyedean Warriors and well done to Year 8 and 10 girls football teams this week in particular. County finals at Rednock School coming up on the 15th March.

As the region Mandarin hub/hwb it is astonishing how we have been able to get Mandarin delivered to students from The Dell to St Briavels primary schools and many more in between in the Wye Valley and Forest of Dean areas. This week across England Year 6 students and their parents found out their 1st choice secondary school for September. In response to the many phone calls we have had here since Tuesday from both sides of the border, we will have places available and we have already created additional teaching groups. The same goes for Sixth Form places as we have had a record intake. We have been working with the Welsh Assembly to provide the opportunity for students from Welsh medium primary schools to continue their Welsh in what is believed to be a first for an English school. So from September, students will have the opportunity to study French, Spanish, Mandarin, German, Welsh and with our funding and partnership with the Classics dept. of Bristol University, Latin.

I am attending the annual educational leadership conference for ASCL this weekend in Birmingham where, amongst others, Nicky Morgan is giving the key note as well as Sir Michael Wilshaw and Sir David Carter speaking respectively. I am not convinced that despite the opportunity to see and listen to these heavyweights of education I wouldn't prefer to see the class of top set Year 9s that I saw working in Maths this morning so well with their teacher.

18th March 2016

"Our task is to educate their (our students) whole being so they face the future. We may not see the future, but they will and our job is to help them make something out of it." Sir Ken Robinson

It appears that the English educational system is about to enter another tumultuous period of change following the Chancellor's budget statement this week and the subsequent White Paper launched by Nicky Morgan. On one level it is actually a relief to finally see the educational strategy the government is outlining for the next few years so at least as educators we can plan accordingly. Over the last couple of weeks I have attended the ASCL conference, SW Education conference, and Gloucestershire Heads and listened with intent to the debates generated by the likes of Michael Wilshaw, Nicky Morgan, John Dunford, and David Carter as well as my colleagues leading their own schools. It is amazing how much thinking can be done up and down the length of the M5 motorway.

Everyone involved in education wants to raise standards and opportunities for our young people in an ever changing globalised and technology influenced society but how we do this is where people are going to obviously differ. The debates and dialogues are healthy though and what has worked previously isn't necessarily what is needed now to address the issues we are facing in education in 2016. I look at my own kids and the students entrusted to me as the Headteacher of Wyedean and want to make sure that the nurture and the learning we are providing for them gives the right skills, life choices, and well-being to allow them to grow and soar in this World. I don't know if making every school an academy or pursuing the EBacc curriculum or even every school joining a MAT necessarily achieves this ambition. I do know having dedicated professional teachers working hard offering challenges and stimulus supported and trusted by school leaders, administrators, and pastoral care is part of how we achieve this aim. I know the work of the school's governors & parents supporting and challenging the staff and students is a key part of achieving success for our young people. I am not sure if it was Steve Jobs or Abraham Lincoln (or neither) who said: *"the best way to predict the future is to create it"*, but Wyedean School has joined the highly successful Challenge Partnership network of schools this term, as a way of creating unique opportunities and raising standards further as we plan for our future here and avoid capricious educational fads. And more investment in schools is needed Secretary of State, not less as funding is now being reduced to a crisis level that will impact negatively on standards & what we are trying to commonly achieve in education.

There are two examples of what we can achieve in partnership from the last couple of days alone. On Thursday, one of our parent governors, her partner, our creative learning coordinator, and director of Sixth Form worked with our students planting over 400 trees kindly donated by the

Woodlands Trust to plant at the front of the school. The spring weather was glorious and it ranks as one of the best days I have experienced at Wyedean to date even with the various expected curve balls thrown my way during the same day. On the same evening, staff and parents worked in partnership having the often tough and difficult conversations with students facing exams in Year 11 and Sixth Form in just a few weeks but all in the spirit of support and partnership. I know from the conversations I have had this lunchtime with three of the Year 11 lads I am mentoring how important this support is from school and home. The latest round of lesson observations we are undertaking also reveals the compelling learning going on in the school and the impact this is having on the individual student's progress. We can't afford to waste any learning time.

It was Sport Relief today and I did let the younger more energetic colleagues take part in the staff netball match at lunch and opted instead for the judging role of the Easter Cake competition. My thanks to Year 10 Food Tech students and Year 9 entrants for the invite. The Student Leadership Exec' are currently looking at the Wyedean school uniform and dress code and in our meeting this week there certainly was a lot of "healthy dialogue" generated on the issue. As I looked at the whole of Year 9 in my assembly this morning, it reminded me of my time in US high schools as we held a non-uniform day in aid of Sport Relief and students wore their own clothes. I think it is fair to say Hogwarts style academic gowns are definitely a non-starter for now and the future.

24th March 2016

"A fo ben bid bont." ("If you want to be a leader, be a bridge.") Welsh proverb

The anticipation of the Easter break is palpable around school right now and not just because chips have been moved to Thursday from Friday on the canteen lunch menu. The A Level Geography students and staff are currently in Iceland (the country not the shop) on a field visit and a group of students and staff are anticipating decent snow on the French Alps as the ski trip gets off today. Year 11s have a shorter break as they are accessing the school's Easter revision sessions. I know it has been a shorter term but the Wyedean School Spring newsletter highlights a fair few enrichment and extra curricula opportunities that have taken place this term. There is a link on the school's website and social media sites:

http://www.wyedean.gloucs.sch.uk/downloads/Spring newsletter.pdf

One of the highlights of the term for me was to see the school's Eisteddfod concert last night. I know I am the Head of Wyedean so you would expect me to write this, but we don't half have some talented students at this school. The gospel choir recently won 1st Place at the Mid Somerset concert for schools across the South West. It was a great evening and my thanks to the staff and students in the Music department for putting on such a lovely night of music and song across the border in our corner of the UK. My thanks also to the Chepstow community groups who also performed in the Eisteddfod.

I spent a long morning in Shire Hall Gloucester on Tuesday and was able to attend a British Council/Global Learning Partners at Abbeyfield School in the evening. The current debate in education especially since the launch of the White Paper last week swims around my 3am thoughts, jostling with the budget, so it was nice to see some inspirational international curriculum stories from across Wiltshire. Also good to catch up with friends and colleagues from my Wiltshire and British Council days. Throughout my career as an educator I have been privileged to be involved and to witness some of the most powerful learning experiences in different parts of the World. I have more hope since Tuesday that there are classroom teachers who will still find the energy in an exhausting and time demanding day to give students additional opportunities to engage with the wider World. It is a key part of our vision for Wyedean School that we involve more our students and community in the globalized society. My Year 10 Critical Thinking group had an interesting discussion on symbolism linked to globalism this morning following the vote against changing the New Zealand flag. Year 13 A Level Politics had a couple of lessons looking at the US presidency with me today. I even managed to get through Bill Clinton's 8 years without too many meanders off executive power.

38

I spoke to Years 12 and 13 in the Sixth Form assembly on Tuesday morning ahead of my meeting to County. It was a talk based on motivation with exams so close but I based it around a quote asking what would you do with your "one precious life"? Unbeknown the tragic and terrifying events of Tuesday were unfolding in the terrorist attacks on commuters in Brussels at the very same time. Life is extremely precious and as I drove along the M4 in the afternoon to Chippenham, I heard the very dignified voice of the widow of the police officer murdered in Liverpool, leaving two young kids without a father and a wife without a husband. As she spoke, she talked about telling her daughters about their dad and then she said:*"I will always tell them there is much more good than bad in this World"*. Incredible wisdom and courage!

I met with Learning Area Leaders on Wednesday and was reminded it has been a whole year since my interview for the Headship at Wyedean School. I have been invited to speak to NPQH candidates at Cabot Learning Federation in April about being a Head. What to say? Despite the term having a fair few curve balls it is still the best job in the World by a mile. I wish all of our school community a restful and enjoyable break ready to come back refreshed for the long (warm and sunny?) summer term ahead.

15th April 2016

"Please can you pass on our sincere thanks to the terrific team for giving up their holiday time to take the students away skiing. Our son had a brilliant time and we are always amazed at your staff's patience, energy, enthusiasm and flexibility. As always the Wyedean Community enables students to be themselves whilst understanding their roles of independence, responsibility and enjoyment. Thank you too for your on-going support of all that makes Wyedean a wonderful learning and developing environment." Year 10 parents' email, 11th April 2016

There are some great photos and comments on the two visits that went out from Wyedean over the Easter break posted on the school's website, Facebook, and Twitter. I have no problem starting a new term back after Easter reading the very kind words from parents in the quote starting this blog piece. It's less than a month until the Queen's Speech and along with lots of educators I am waiting to see what form the education bill will take based on the March 2016 White Paper. The highly respected Institute of Fiscal Studies announced real term funding being cut by another 7% taking spending levels back down to those last seen in the 1970s. These are unprecedented times in the public services and in education in particular. Some of my A Level Politics class discussed the Brexit referendum and the possible consequences of either result being announced. For them this will be the first time they will also be eligible to vote.

The new day of the summer term kicked off with a huge burst of optimism when I went to see the Year 11 Motivation day with a very talented speaker from The Fix Up Team (@thefixupteam). I am resisting the temptation to constantly remind Year 11 how little time they have left before Study Leave but as expected, along with Sixth Form and A Levels, this dominates these few precious weeks before Whitsun break. The leadership team are in throes of planning the new timetable and I met some Year 9s to speak about how they chose their options especially in the context of EBacc.

The school has been working this year with groups within pastoral like EACH (Educational Action Challenging Homophobia) through assemblies and working with groups of students. I was impressed with a group of students who have recently set up a LGBT group in school to support their peers. It makes me very proud to see such leadership from Wyedean students. Another proud moment was seeing the outstanding creativity and innovation in the DT exhibition on Friday lunchtime for GCSE and A Level. Even the Dyson Foundation thought so on Twitter.

It was a strange moment to speak to staff last Tuesday at the School Priority Meeting as a sort of part "state of the union" address and part "try not to make them fall asleep". I think I got the balance right as a Head. I did work at a school once where the Head had about 72 "urgent" priorities for the school to focus on. The positive school culture along with the hard work and professionalism I see daily as I walk around convinces me that Wyedean School's priority to be a high performing school in all that it does is being achieved.

I was fortunate enough at Easter to spend a few days taking an elderly relative of mine to Arnhem to see where his cousin had died at the bridge as a paratrooper fighting there in September 1944. It was a very poignant visit especially when we went to the Commonwealth cemetery at Oosterbeek. Every September all the local schools go to Oosterbeek and lay flowers on every grave to remember and to also look forward. I spoke to a Dutch teacher who said how important it was in local schools to remember these moments in Europe, and the importance for younger generations to be aware of what it has taken to get the peace and prosperity we enjoy and perhaps take for granted in our continent today.

22nd April 2016

"A leader is best when people barely know he exists." Lao Tsu

I had the privilege to be invited over to the Cabot Learning Federation (CLF) in Bristol on Wednesday to talk to NPQH candidates about headship and school leadership. I undertook my own NPQH as an aspiring Head/Principal through the CLF Institute, and it is a model of leadership development and succession planning that allows schools and academies to continue to get good school leaders coming through. When David Carter set up the CLF he knew good succession planning was crucial to its success and the belief that everyone is a leader in school. This has never been more important than right now in this time of unprecedented educational uncertainties. I thoroughly enjoyed my NPQH with Cabot & the National College especially as it has giving me the leadership nourishment and challenge at the time I needed to prepare for leading a school like Wyedean.

Every day as a Head feels like it is an NPQH challenge and no two days are the same. Monday started off with the A48 closing at 7am for the roadworks not 9:30am as stated. The chaos this caused with students and staff trying to get to school was appalling. It's a good job I had planned my Year 11 assembly on the theme of humour and laughter after that start to a week. The power of social media, for good and for bad, never ceases to amaze. Parents, governors, local counsellors, and students were quick to take to Twitter and Facebook to put across the concerns regarding the two weeks of disruption this would cause to students being in school and for exam classes about to go on study leave. My sincere appreciation to Gloucester County Council and the Highways Agency SW for listening and acting.

As the week went on the Year 8 assembly theme changed to Friendship so things were definitely improving by Thursday and even the sun began to shine which finally justified my decision to turn the school heating off on a freezing cold Monday. My Year 7 History class went outside to work in the sun as we were looking at the topic of bad rulers in history, even picked up on Twitter by Horrible Histories. How will Elizabeth II be seen by history? Not quite the same as King John or Mary I. An interesting debate in class as the Queen marked her 90th birthday this week. My Year 13 Politics class grappled with the powers and role of the Vice Presidency. Who would Trump choose as a running mate if he is still there in the autumn? The Science learning area are involved in a fascinating project at the moment with planting "rocket seeds" that have been in space and I saw some great learning in Maths as I walked around the area. Year 11s are just off to the Maths mock now as I type this blog. Study leave beckons ever closer. We have a vacancy in Maths at the moment for September, so if you know of anyone interested the details are on the website. The Sixth Form football team sadly lost narrowly in the county semi-final to Tewkesbury but were a credit to the school.

The leadership team worked with Jackie Beard of the National Governors Association on Thursday as we continue to develop as a high performing school and my thanks to parents who came in this week after school to work with Jo Davies of the Ceridwen group for parent voice on improving the school. The teaching and learning briefing focused on the recent round of lesson observations and I saw a great example of stretch and challenge in a Year 9 DT lesson linked to global designs. I met with Caroline Harmer of the Global Learning Partnership to plan the autumn global conference being hosted here at Wyedean as well as our development of the global leaders' scheme.

To finish this week's blog, the hoax curriculum letter this week doing the rounds was spotted immediately by sharp eyed students - not the boxing lessons being an odd inclusion but the spelling being way too good in the letter to have come from me as Head. Exam students have far too much time on their hands it seems. At least they are motivated by what is happening politically to education right now in England. As for uniform rumours no striped blazers and boaters just yet but the student council are running a consultation on how we can improve the current uniform without major changes. The final decision on this will be communicated in June.

My thanks to Forest Activities Festival for the invite to attend on Sunday at the Speech House grounds Coleford and I know my three daughters are looking forward to it. I haven't checked with Mrs Ford yet but then this is where I hand over my leadership for the weekend when I get home.

6th May 2016

"March winds and April showers bring forth May flowers." English proverb

"Where flowers bloom, so does hope." Lady Bird Johnson

I am not sure about the May flowers right now in week 30 of the academic year but I know I am still scraping ice off the car first thing in the morning. Being able to sit outside this week to eat dinner in the evening sunshine is however finally convincing me summer is getting here. The proverbial May flowers we are hoping that will bloom over the exam period in Key Stage 4 and 5 are heavily revising and preparing themselves with their teachers and parents for the intense exams ahead. I am counting how often during the day I am hearing "it's a pinch point" at the moment. When is it not a pinch point in a school when you are entrusted with the educational futures of young people? I was asked about the parental boycott of SATs this week in primary schools being a parent of two children in primary school and one in pre-school. There is an awful amount of testing that goes on in schools, and it is important that parents and educators debate this fully and frankly especially as young people are being put under enormous pressure to succeed from a very young age. Knowing the profile of a learner is crucial to how we teach and see clear progress and attainment but to forsake the very art of instilling a love of learning in a student that is lifelong is detrimental to the individual and society. Many educators, parents, governors, and students will be pleased to hear the U-turn today on the forced academisation proposal in the Education White Paper. The National Schools Commissioner, Sir David Carter writing in the TES today said *"...I am certain that there is a place in our education system for successful, sustainable stand-alone academies"*. Wyedean School will work with networks like Challenge Partners so we are not isolated but as a school we are deciding what is right for our students.

I sat along with our parents and staff and watched the outstanding Sixth Form team here on Wednesday evening celebrate the academic year by honouring the success of Wyedean Students. It is at those moments that the worst of days can diminish into a hazy blur as the real sum total of all the effort invested speaks from the heart about achievement both academic and personal. I had the honour of being invited by the Chepstow Rotary Club to hear our Head Boy, Tom, speak about his experience of the Rotary Club's leadership programme for young people. Not only was it a good dinner but it was a great way of working with our local community. My thanks this week to the Chepstow Lions for their very kind donation of a defibrillator for the school. We all echoed the same sentiment at the presentation handover; let's hope we never have to use it.

I am looking forward to next week when my A Level Politics class will be talking to their counterparts in Gar-Field High School Virginia over Skype about the presidential election. I am trying not to focus too much on what a possible Trump v Clinton election battle will hold but with no disrespect to the Assembly and local elections in the UK this week for a student of politics America is fascinating right now. My Year 10 Critical Thinking class have to be steered away from Donald Trump regularly and even the most abstract of our topics seems to lead back to him. At least young people are interested and keen in the World around them.

I know it has only been a four-day week with the Bank Holiday but it feels a lot longer. I am hoping that the weekend is at least a time for some rest before another week of "pinch points" to come. And the study leave dates get closer and closer. I know there are a lot of good sites out there and revision support such as our own GCSEPod but I like a lot of what is posted on The Student Room site especially this recent one on revision:

http://www.thestudentroom.co.uk/content.php?r=14029 -How-to-set-a-study-goal-the-Grow-your-grades-February-roundup

I still think one of the best pieces of advice when it comes to revision is making sure you get rest, exercise and fresh air in between revising. Sunshine really does make flowers bloom.

6th June 2016

"Change is the end result of all true learning." Leo Buscaglia

"I've cried so much today but just want to thank everyone in Wyedean Class of 2016. It's been 5 great years honestly so sad to leave." Emily@emily_bufton

"Big thank you to everyone at Wyedean who made the past 5 years of my life such a great experience." Jess@JessCooksonxo

"@WyedeanSchool Class Act. So glad my kids go to a school with such great staff." Liz Kayll@madmadmadmadmum

I'm not sure what has been more difficult: to get my thoughts around that the summer seems finally to be here or that we have less than 7 weeks until the end of the academic year. The last few weeks seem to have flown by and the exam season is now in full swing as we said goodbye as a school to Year 11 and 13 just before the Whitsun break. There are lots of times in this role when some days feel harder than others but I have really

45

enjoyed reading comments and thoughts from our students and parents about the experiences and sentiments towards Wyedean School. The two assemblies I saw for school leavers in Years 11 and 13 on Friday 27th May made me appreciate the importance of school and the marking of the passing of this time for young people. It is a real boost to morale and energy as staff have worked tremendously hard in getting students through the academic year and ready for exams. The education climate has remained constant throughout the year; less funding, uncertainty over new measures of progress & attainment, and whether all schools should be academies in Multi Academy Trusts. In Wales MAT stood for "More, Able and Talented", how I wish this was still the case. The education Bill in the Queen's speech backed down a little from the contentious aspects of the March White Paper but professional associations are still looking to take national action in protest.

This is still though my favourite part of the academic year. The structures for the next academic year in September are already being planned for such as staffing, timetable, and the calendar but it is also a time for more holistic learning experiences in the curriculum. We have experienced a huge surge in numbers for Years 7 and 12 from both sides of the border starting in September, and we have a number of transition events to prepare our future students into Wyedean to commence the next part of their educational pathway.

I was able to Skype with my old partner school in Virginia, Gar-Field High School, for my last A Level Politics lesson before the break. The Year 13s spoke to their counterparts in the US on a range of topics ranging from Donald Trump and the election, Obama's legacy, America's place in the World and the British EU vote coming up in less than 3 weeks from now. There are some moments in this job when you know this is the absolute best job in the World. It happened watching an incredibly compassionate head of Year 11 and a dedicated director of Sixth Form say goodbye to kids they had stewarded through good and bad times but always together. It happened on that Thursday afternoon in my study as students who can vote this year engaged in a lively discussion across the Atlantic using the best of digital media to make their learning and understanding of the World much more meaningful and compelling.

The recruitment and retention crisis in education occupies a lot of column inches and social media space these days. A recent TES poll said only 52% of teachers would put their kids into the school they teach. Over half term, a family member who had been a very good primary school teacher told me he was giving it up this summer and had enough. This is an appalling situation to read as an educator. We need outstanding teachers firing up students with limitless ambition and noble aspirations. At times like these I re-read what our staff, students and community say about Wyedean and take a lot of strength and heart knowing that what we are doing here in extremely challenging times are the right things for our young people.

1st July 2016

"We cannot change the past, but we can change our attitude toward it. Uproot guilt and plant forgiveness. Tear out arrogance and seed humility. Exchange love for hate, thereby making the present comfortable and the future promising." Maya Angelou

I am not sure about politics but a week is a long time in education. Last Friday I sat with South West Heads and Principals at Bristol Met' Academy to listen to Sir David Carter as part of his UK roadshow speaking to schools as the new National Schools Commissioner alongside Rebecca Clarke who now fills Sir David's SW RSC role. The very palpable elephant in the room was the result announced on the EU referendum in the early hours of Friday morning. Whichever side people voted I haven't met a single person who knows what will happen next following this historic moment in the history of the UK. On Thursday, my Year 10 Critical Thinking group held one of the most refreshing discussions I have heard in this long campaign about Britain's future after this vote. Today we will be honouring another significant moment in the UK's past when we attend the commemoration service in Chepstow for the 100th anniversary of the Battle of the Somme. A timely reminder that in the grand scheme of things history is bigger than all of us.

I spent a really enjoyable afternoon at my former school, Royal Wootton Bassett Academy, last week as I met old friends and colleagues from there and old colleagues from the visiting American school, Gar-Field High School Virginia. The students from the States were as engaging and interested as they have always been and just happy to be in a different country interacting with British students. Naturally the EU vote came up as a topic of discussion as well as the US presidential election this autumn now gearing up between two quite different candidates in Trump and Clinton. It reminded me again, as I drove home along the M4 to Bristol, the absolute value of students having a global dimension underpinning their education. Whatever happens over the next two years in negotiations for the EU, one thing is as certain as death and taxes, the World will experience more globalisation not less, and our young people need to be educated to face this challenge.

It is hard to believe the academic year is just a couple of weeks away and we are in July already. As a "newish" Head now I am in the process of reflecting back over the year as well as planning forward to the new term starting in September. I know my colleagues and students are ready for a well-deserved rest over the summer, so I am amazed at the energy and enthusiasm still going into events like next week's Creativity Festival, the summer picnic we have today, and especially for the Year 6 induction week we have just had, where it has been a pleasure to see our future students from our primary partners in Gloucestershire and from Wales spend time getting used to the change. We have record numbers of Year 11s with us next week for Sixth Form induction as they begin their next stage of education now the exams are over. I understand from tired but happy colleagues how successful the Year 11 Prom was on Thursday.

There is a new book out on educational leadership by Andy Buck called "*Leadership Matters*" and he is a huge advocate of the idea of "discretionary effort" - colleagues going the extra mile. If I was to look at anything that stands out for me as a Head it would be the willingness of Wyedean's dedicated staff, parents and governors working tirelessly with our students to make the school a success. I see it daily and it has made all the difference to me as a Head this year ensuring the school is going forward for the students we have in our trust.

I am not sure I can watch the Wales v Belgium game but whatever happens, it has been an incredible achievement in the Euros already by this team. Chris Coleman's greatest success for me is making all those individuals from the World's most expensive player to the plodding journeymen from the lower leagues into this one team. Stronger together. A valuable example to say a headteacher, educational policy maker or even politicians struggling to give clear leadership when it is most needed.

Cymru am byth!

8th July 2016

"Culture eats strategy for breakfast every day of the week." Sir Kevin Collins

I spent Sunday afternoon on the eastern side of the Severn looking across to Wyedean from Old Down Country Park as my kids ran around in the sunshine. Apart from feeling exhausted at the end of this academic year and my first year as Head, my thoughts on a summer's day were on the week the school had just experienced in terms of witnessing the positive culture in action we know will take the school forward to where anyone involved in and supporting Wyedean knows it can aspire to.

The PE department celebrated their successful girls in sports at the start of the week with their awards ceremony and Lily Crawley has been representing Gloucestershire in the U15 High Jump at the English Schools' Track and Field championship in Gateshead. I sat in a very stuffy hall in central London on Tuesday with other heads listening to Sir George Berwick and officially beginning Wyedean's partnership with Challenge Partners, the network that grew from the highly successful London Challenge. This is where Wyedean School needs to be right now in terms of an effective network of over 300 outstanding schools across the UK committed to school improvement, leadership, and compelling teaching & learning. The Head of Bradley Stoke School and former Wyedean Deputy Head, Steve Moir, spent a morning with us on Thursday. Steve was impressed with the progress the school has made especially in terms of positive school culture and as we walked around we saw many good examples of challenge in learning of all students. Global Learning has been at the forefront of learning innovation for us as a school this year and it made me very proud as Head to see the school awarded Global Learning Partners "Expert Centre" status by DfID this week. There was a very interesting article in the TES from the principal of UWC Atlantic College, John Walsmley, on the importance of global learning, echoing the belief and commitment we have to it as a school.

http://www.telegraph.co.uk/education/2016/06/29/brexit-shows-how-much-we-need-international-education/

With a week that started with American partner schools marking the 240th anniversary of the American Declaration of Independence, a national NUT strike on Tuesday, Year 10 IT students visiting the Fairford air show, and new Year 12s in for their induction week, it was a pleasure to see the Creativity Festival week in Wyedean School as a central part of the school's culture and belief in creativity in the curriculum. We were really fortunate enough to have had a performer from the West End musical "Wicked" spend several days with students in Masterclass sessions leading to a stunning performance on Thursday afternoon. All week long the school production of "Blood Brothers" ran and I got to see the final performance on Thursday evening. It was a mesmerising production and illustrated how much confidence and ability students in this school have in the creative arts. My thanks to Drama colleagues for their hard work on producing this play. The Creativity week finished on a high with the festival here on Friday evening and our community coming into school to celebrate with us wonderful learning and work their children produce. My thanks to all colleagues, students, governors, and parents involved for making this festival happen. The Wyedean school picnic the previous Friday had already brought a summer feel to school as we entered these final weeks. A huge thanks to Angharad, Sara and Layla for these events. Lots of photos on our school Twitter.

I sat in my final Full Governors meeting for the academic year on Tuesday as we reviewed an extraordinary year in the life of the school as we move forward. This has lingered with me hence my thoughts drifting back to Wyedean on a Sunday afternoon across the Severn. My thoughts approaching the end of my first year as Head are that I am definitely pleased to see the culture of the school is one where everyone is valued and can contribute to improve all the time what we are doing to give our young people the very best in education. Still more to do though, and we are planning for the next academic year around, continuing to raise standards as part of our strategy; but without the right culture in a school any plan remains dusty and abstract on a shelf. This week alone illustrated the power of the right culture and the right strategy working in tandem for the benefit of the students.

20th July 2016

"A Smooth sea never made a skilled sailor." F.D. Roosevelt

"But to go to school in a summer morn,
O! It drives all joy away;
Under a cruel eye outworn,
The little ones spend the day
In sighing and dismay."
William Blake

I'm not sure I would agree with Blake having experienced school enrichment opportunities in these last two weeks but this week in particular the weather has been too hot and the impact on staff and students is very noticeable. As my Year 8s reminded me in the canteen this morning: "I bet it rains when it is the holiday". The Sixth Form spent the night sleeping out in the school grounds as part of their work with Shelter Cyrmu. They certainly had the right weather for it although lots of bleary eyed and tired Year 12s this morning as I walked past them at 7am. One day starting, theirs beginning with sleep. One of my Year 10s this week said his summer holiday is largely based around sleep. The school has really had a wealth of experiences to enjoy these past two weeks with Sports Days, curriculum enrichment days, Year 10 Work Experience, the annual Fun Run, guest speakers in school, master class workshops, the list goes on. I definitely think Blake was wrong. Well, applied to students at Wyedean anyhow.

51

A number of parents have asked about ideas to make sure their children don't get too bored and what they can do over the summer as a way of keeping their learning topped up. As a former Head of History I used to always make sure my students, not just exam classes, had a decent reading list to plough through over the summer. Much easy with say a Kindle these days, than a suitcase full of AJP Taylor and Alan Bullock being dragged to the Dordogne. Anyhow, there are some websites below that may be of use. I am not recommending Pokémon Go, largely because I don't understand the chaos seen say in Central Park in New York last week. My own kids love geocaching and spent last Sunday chasing clues around North Bristol.

25 ideas for students in the summer holidays:
http://www.educationworld.com/a_curr/profdev073.shtml

Geocaching:
http://www.schoolfamily.com/school-family-articles/article/10829-geocaching-101-family-fun-for-all-in-every-season
http://www.readingrockets.org/article/get-ready-summer-ideas-teachers-share-families

In education, in wider politics, we seem to be in more uncertain times as we go into the summer and look ahead to a new academic year. The appointment of Justine Greening by Theresa May as the new Secretary of State for Education was largely welcomed by the profession especially because of her own comprehensive school background. Frankly, I just want an Education Secretary committed to education with the highest aspirations for all students no matter where he or she went to school. Having worked in both the independent and state sectors, wanting the best for students tends to be the same. The reported focus on new grammar schools as a first announcement isn't the most pressing issue in education right now for many school leaders and teachers. The new Prime Minister did seem to offer a focus on supporting all sections of society in her first speech from the steps of 10 Downing Street. Time will tell. Our kids will still need an education full of skills, values, knowledge and understanding that will allow them to take their place as global citizens in a globalized 21st Century society.

I had a full experience of this on Monday when we took the Year 10 Critical Thinking students to the East End of London to work with Newham North Mosque community and the staff and students of Forest Gate School. My deepest and heartfelt thanks to all those who organised this event and hosted us especially one of our Wyedean parents, Mr Mike Peckham. It was a pure privilege to witness the dialogue and discussions between these two very different communities living in the UK. Days like these make you so glad you are an educator and in the job you do as groups of Gloucestershire/ Monmouthshire and East London teenagers deal with the senseless nihilism of say the recent Bastille Day-Nice atrocity or the daily violence in Iraq and Syria. I am so proud of the students and staff of Wyedean School and cannot thank parents and governors enough for their support of what we do to allow days like Monday to happen. This project will continue into next year. Moldova next summer for these students too as we aim to finally visit our partner school in Chisinau.

My first year as Head appears to echo FDR's famous words and to continue in a nautical theme we also don't develop ourselves by hugging the coast line afraid of sailing across the sea to discover new worlds. There have been challenges to face in my first year but as I told staff in briefing last Monday, in my twenty-second year of teaching this has to be one of the best. I am exhausted but have driven home every day across the Severn to Bristol already looking forward to the next day in school. I work with some extraordinarily talented students and people every day. I have a holiday with my family planned and certainly lots to read over the next few weeks (a biography on Theodore Roosevelt - distant cousin to FDR) but with August exam results, UCAS clamour for places and then the 1st September return I am excited about the new academic year and the promise of what is to come.

Have a great summer and see you in the autumn for the new academic year.

PART 2: SEPTEMBER 2016 - JULY 2017

9th September 2016

"Everyone must take time to sit and watch the leaves turn." Elizabeth Lawrence

Hard to believe it is Friday already and the first week is out of the way. The Year 7s I have been speaking to this week, especially the ones at lunchtime today, appear to have had a really good first week. And they like the new dress code! All the year groups seem to have grown taller over the summer and speaking to students in the various assemblies as we welcomed them back to school, all seemed ready for the challenges that lie ahead in the new academic year. Year 11 are appreciating the trust of a new common room and when it is finally finished the Sixth Form have a brand new cafe/coffee bar in the Sixth Form Centre.

Driving around Bristol this summer, I did seem to get stuck behind the same bus advertising Sidcot School and their slogan "We are more than an exams factory" which made me think for the latter part of August about what I would say to my colleagues on the first day back. Qualifications are extremely important, especially as they are the means to access the next stages of education and a way into careers as well as proof of a student's attainment. The best schools do this but much more and I haven't met an educator who doesn't want aspirational educational opportunities for all the students in their care. The two of the most joyous days in the school calendar, even allowing for the disappointment tears, are the ones in August when staff, parents and governors get to share and see the success of the students. There are some wonderful photos on the school's website from this August and I am very proud of the achievement of the students of

Wyedean School in my first year as Head. I used various social media quotes in my welcome back talk to all staff on the 1st September that illustrated the appreciation of our students and parents for the hard work of the staff at Wyedean School. As I sat in my cabin study this summer, thinking about what I would say to staff on the first day back and the Sidcot bus quote floating around in my mind, I also put together a collection of some of the photos from the school year just gone, to show we are also definitely more than just an exams factory at Wyedean School, and educating the whole student is a core purpose here. We need education to be celebrated more and often.

I have been asked several times over the summer what I think about the proposals, confirmed today, about the Prime Minister's roughly outlined Green Paper on allowing all schools to become grammar schools and select their students if they wish. I am starting my 23rd year in teaching this autumn, having experienced a fair few secretary of states for education and five prime ministers. All I know is there has always been a lot of capriciousness in educational politics, and always will be, but the basics remain the same. Schools need to be places people can be proud of to attend and say "that's my school". Strong identity, culture and ethos is way more than a uniform or a slogan. Schools also need to be a safe learning environment that allow students to be nurtured, challenged, and ultimately to grow in their wider knowledge and understanding through compelling teaching and learning in order to take their place as citizens and in 2016 global citizens at that. If educational policy allows educators to achieve this with the right funding and framework and to get on with the job then as with most political debates, along with my colleagues, I will wait to see what emerges in the detail. The last educational White Paper was launched only in May 2016, a month before the Brexit vote. That now seems to have been largely shelved. It's fair to say 2016 has been a seismic year for the UK so far which is why more stability is needed in fundamental areas such as the educating of our young people.

The school has its Open Evening on the 29th September and again this gives Wyedean School the opportunity to showcase to our community the success and achievement of the educational experience at Wyedean. The summer exam results in GCSE, BTEC, and A Level are some of the best in the history of the school but there is so much more as well to this school to see.

Today the school said goodbye to Dave Burgess, the business manager, who is retiring after 13 years of fantastic service to the school. Dave leaves a very big hole as a colleague and a friend. Dave epitomises the dedication and passion in all staff at the school who only want the very best for the young people in our care. Wyedean School wishes Dave, Jean and his family a long and happy retirement together and thank you for everything you have done for the school, not least for this rookie Head helping him navigate the challenges of his first year. May the wind always be at your back and the sun shining on your face.

So we made the weekend and even with the sun shining it feels autumnal. "Last Night of the Proms" this weekend, so it is definitely the end of summer. Instead of ploughing through the T.E.S or my ASCL briefing paper to try and fathom educational policy that can wait; for now I am going to take the kids and the dog out walking to find the leaves turning. A much better use of time.

16th September 2016

"Enjoy the little things in life because one day you`ll look back and realise they were the big things." Kurt Vonnegut

Well the first signs of the new academic year are manifesting at the end of only the second week back – coughs and colds. I have had a sore throat this week but I am fairly sure that it is the amount of talking I have been doing after a near monk's like silence in comparison through the summer holidays. I am sure I read once that in the course of an average school day an educator will speak and interact with around 200 people. It is one of the absolute pleasures of the job to be able to speak to students, staff, and parents daily so I am more than happy to risk a sore throat for the weekend. Besides my children will be pleased as it means I can't nag them to tidy their rooms on a Saturday morning. Walking around the campus this week I have seen great learning across the school although slightly disappointed at missing the smells and explosions in Science as I dropped by. Early days in the autumn term yet though. I have seen a lot of parents over a number of issues and I do need to say thank you to the parents who have donated sofas for the Year 11 common room. More still needed please. This week we also saw the school's case study for significant improvement and excellence in the annual "Parliamentary Review" report on education published.

In school, the new Year 7s and 12s seem to be more than established at the end of the second week of the academic year. The Learning Areas, when they are not involved in the day to day of teaching are preparing their analysis reports from the summer results ahead of the meetings with the Leadership Team over the next two weeks looking at what went well and what we need to do to improve as part of our school improvement plan. I had a really good meeting with one of our new art teachers as we discussed ideas for the next phase of developing Creativity in the school and I am pleased to finally see flags of the World up in the school's assembly hall as we continue to develop as a centre of excellence for global learning. As a part of our digital learning strategy, "Show My Homework" is now the online platform for all home learning. In conversations with parents, the overwhelming consensus is they absolutely love Show My Homework. Homework can be seen that has been set, if it has been undertaken by the student, and it also allows more stretch and challenge as well as independent learning. To the Year 10 boys who had a moan to me this week about it meaning they now have to do their homework and can't "get out of it" – in the words of Socrates "tough".

The "great debate" in education rumbles on following the Green Paper last week and the proposal in introducing more grammar schools and allowing schools to select. One education leader has asked, *"What happens when all schools can select? What happens to those students not selected? Where do they go?"*. It was commented upon in Parliament this week that as a policy proposal it has united more or less the teaching profession including the ex-Secretary of State for Education, Nicky Morgan, but not Michael Gove. And was it coincidence that David Cameron quit Parliament on the same day as the announcement? I am curious to see where the debate will develop following the new incoming head of

Ofsted, Amanda Spielman's signalled intentions to consider scrapping the top inspection rating because she was *"quite uncomfortable"* about *"some of the effects I see it having in the system"*. How many schools, including this one, have set their aspirations to be "outstanding"? For Wyedean School this label always means "high performing" in all that we do for the best possible outcomes and opportunities for our students. Hopefully we are always aware that the little things are the big things right now – especially in our school.

23rd September 2016

"It takes a whole village to raise a child." African proverb

My room here at Wyedean often witnesses a whole range of interesting conversations, meetings, and dialogues through the course of a week and I can only imagine what has been said between these four walls over the decades from my four predecessors. It wasn't my first choice of location for a Head's study when I was first appointed but in a very short space of time I couldn't imagine where else it should go especially as it is located on the main corridor with the windows facing straight out onto the school yard. Basically, I get to see the school daily at work and play. I remember a school in Bristol I worked at a long time ago where the Leadership Team housed themselves down an isolated corridor with a coded door. Not sure what the intended message to staff or students was from that gesture but definitely the wrong one. My Year 11 Critical Thinking group, over tea in my room, tackled the concept of "forgiveness" this week; inevitably, Donald Trump managed to get a cameo in the debate. This morning I hosted Year 11 sports ambassadors over tea and cookies as they individually spoke about the sports they had represented their area in and in some cases their country. Achievement like this never ceases to amaze. As there were several female international footballers in the room and my 7-year-old daughter has just started with her local club I did manage to get a promise of a coaching masterclass in the near future.

Next week the school holds its Open Evening on the 29th September throwing open the doors to all our prospective students and their parents to come and see what makes Wyedean School so special. The school essentially has open day every day, and it is one of the best features of Wyedean School that parents and children are around the school visiting all the time. I have been invited by old friends and colleagues from the British Council to visit Abbeyfield School in Wiltshire next week as we celebrate some of the best practice in international learning in the UK at a special event on Tuesday. I spoke to colleagues in Stryn, Norway this week about the possibility of their leadership team coming to Wyedean next year to look at teaching & learning, pastoral care, and other aspects of school life. This is a school I worked with over 10 years ago, and to be able to share and swap ideas with educators around the globe is one of the best things for me about international education.

I was very impressed to see the student leadership from Year 10 boys as they took control of the other half of the old pastoral block to turn it into their common room. The plan is to have a dedicated Key Stage 4 area on that side of school for Years 10 and 11 to look after. Hopefully there are plenty of sofas on Freecycle to go between them and Year 11. The 6th Form café has been up and running this week and it is the student leadership driving the initiative that is impressive. Plus a lot of hard work from Mrs Lewis and her team.

My Norwegian colleague made a comment that made me really think about what's at the heart of a "good" school – relationships. She mentioned the old African proverb about it takes a village to raise a child and how in a small town like Stryn tucked away in the mountains of Western Norway it is the whole community that ensures an effective partnership between home, school, and the community exists to benefit the child. This week I spoke with a parent about what we had to do to ensure that their child gets through a difficult patch in life right now and it was the willingness to work together that made me drive home back across the Severn Bridge knowing the child will come out the other side and be fine. We have good relationships working here at Wyedean between school, home, and the community and the more engagement we have the better for the student.

7th October 2016

"Small minds are concerned with the extraordinary, great minds the ordinary." Blaise Pascal

The follow up to our school Open Evening on the 27th September has been overwhelming and there is nothing ordinary about choosing your child's next secondary school even if for them it feels as such. I have spoken to a wide range of parents over the last week on their follow up tours around the school with Wyedean students, and I have been immensely proud of the feedback comments about our young people as ambassadors for the school. We are currently working on the "Taster Days" from the 10th October to welcome for the day Year 6s from schools like The Dell, Thornwell and Undy to come and see the school working on a normal day. There is no such thing as a "normal day" in any school and they should all be extraordinary in the very ordinary things they do. I have had a number of extraordinary moments at Wyedean just in the last few days and none more so than being invited by the English Learning Area to have a celebration lunch with the Year 9s who were successful in their summer IGCSE examination. I am going to speak to the NPQH cohort of senior leaders at the Cabot Learning Federation on the 12th October and will certainly be using the examples of this half term alone of some of the great moments in this job as a Headteacher.

Thank you for all the emails and conversations about Show My Homework. As a school we are more than surprised already at the impact in learning, stretch and challenge, individual organisation, and home support it is having as a key element of our approach towards effective digital media. The first half term of this academic year is nearly through and it is astonishing to think we are only a week and a bit away from the break. There are many things students can be doing to extend their learning, and if it incorporates a walk outside in the autumn air even better. Living in the Forest of Dean and the Wye Valley, as many of our staff and students do, this should be the perfect excuse for a walk. There are a lot of studies around at the moment looking at well-being and mindfulness of both students and staff, and the conclusions are not surprising about rest and work/life balance. As a parent, I am very keen to ensure my children use technology in a constructive and positive way even if it does mean reminding them not to be using an iPad when we have a meal together. A report out this week looked at how teenagers were suffering from lack of sleep because they were addicted to mobile devices receiving messages and updates throughout the night. The technology cannot be dis-invented but we construct ways we can avoid the distractions of modern life and balance how we live with our phones and tablets.

I met with the school's LGBT+ group on Friday to discuss some of the issues they would like to see addressed in the school this academic year. I know I am getting older (wiser?) because I reminded them when I first started teaching it was still the era of Section 28 when educators couldn't even discuss LGBT+ issues. It was nice to see there is progression in society even if sometimes it didn't feel as if there was. The leadership of students on issues like LGBT+ always impresses me, and it has been commented upon constantly by the parents visiting Wyedean to see the school over the last few weeks.

The grammar school debate rumbles on with the Green Paper out for discussion and apart from a few emails asking me as Head about things like a House system introduction, there are probably more important things to pay attention to in staffrooms and leadership teams up and down the country right now. I will leave the last word to former Head girl and Wyedean alumnus, Joanne Rowling. She tweeted recently in response to an article from education correspondent, Nicola Woolcock, supporting the reintroduction of a "grammar school ethos" in state schools: "Just for the record, the comprehensive (state school) I attended had four houses, too". We did and it works very well still in schools like Redland Green Bristol where it supports students. Which is why we would look at re-introducing a possible House system at some point on the basis of a system of wider student community support and enrichment opportunity rather than an attempt to revisit yesteryear. And as an "ordinary" part of school life. Elvis aside, the 1950s were very overrated, according to my father.

21 October 2016

"Why do we commemorate so many things? Because we are a people who remember." Father Michael St.Clair speaking at the anniversary of Aberfan.

I walked my children to school this morning in the bright autumn sunshine. I dropped them off, hugged and kissed them, wished them a good day in class and watched them skip into school with their friends to be greeted by their teachers. It's hard not to weep reading or hearing any of the testimonies from the tragedy that happened to the Welsh mining community in Aberfan fifty years ago today, as raw now with emotion as it must have felt then. I read about one rescuer who had found the body of the deputy head teacher, Mr Beynon, *"He was clutching five children in his arms as if he had been protecting them"*.

My father was a coal miner and I came from a coal mining community. These communities were always particularly resilient and supportive as communities go and if there is hope in such a tragedy it was to read and hear about how the community of Aberfan have supported each other constantly for 50 years despite having had a generation wiped out. Some of those who lost children and family members only now being able to speak about their loss in 2016. When I first started teaching and I worked in a school in Bristol there was an old Welsh Maths teacher, Nigel Bowen, who told me with tears streaming down his face, that he was one of the first on the scene. All they could do in the mayhem of the avalanche of coal waste slurry that had engulfed Pantglas school and the surrounding houses was dig frantically with their bare hands and hope to find someone alive buried below. The fact that the now defunct National Coal Board refused to acknowledge until 1997 responsibility for the waste tips they had piled high above the village makes this injustice hard to take. The people of Aberfan had to use the money kindly donated from around the World to clear up their town, rebuild their houses and bury their dead. The then Welsh Secretary of State, Ron Davies, did the honourable and decent thing and changed this finally in the first year of the Labour government under Blair in 1997.

The minute's silence was observed across Wales and other parts of the UK linked to mining like the Forest of Dean this morning at 9:15. I know in my old school of Crickhowell, where the sense of community and the school's part in the community is one of the strongest I have known, the school came together to remember and commemorate the awful events of Aberfan 50 years ago.

In 2004 I remember the events in Beslan particularly as I had just started working in Russia with schools in Siberia when that southern Russian town should have been celebrating the first day of an academic year and instead gunmen and gunwomen took the school hostage. In the resulting chaos hundreds of young and innocent lives lost for no reason. My French friend told me this week they had just had the first of their "terrorist lock down" drills in her Lycée in southern Paris, and it didn't matter how many times I saw it in the IB schools I worked with in Virginia, heavily armed school security and police guards in high schools with airport style security frisking students was something I could never get used to as a person or an educator.

I was very fortunate on Monday to be invited to take part in a unique forum at St George's House, Windsor Castle, at the kind invitation of one of Wyedean's parents, Mike Peckham, and the CEO of Virgin Money, Jayne-Anne Gadhia, who had sponsored the conference. The theme is something Mike has been working with the school on since the summer when we took the year 10 critical thinking group to East London to work with the local mosque and Forest Gate school in Newham. The conference had a range of participants from all spheres to talk about the impact of recent events such as Brexit, radicalisation both religious and political as well as the impact of globalisation on communities across the UK and the World. Having watched the US presidential debates this autumn, and reading about the situation in places like Mosul and Aleppo, it is hard to find at times the optimism to explain these situations to your own children let alone your students. The conference on Monday was inspirational for me to not only hear about how people have remained optimistic and focussed from a range of examples from the Troubles in Northern Ireland to ethnic minorities combatting racism but also made clear there are alternative narratives to challenge what often appears a spiral of despondency in the World.

Schools have always been and always will be places of incredible hope and optimism. I gave my Year 9 assembly on Wednesday with this being reflected in what I need to be able to offer the young people in my care as their headteacher. I followed this straight after with the opening ceremony of a special event for the whole 6th Form organised by the assistant director of 6th Form, Sam Bishop, and Gloucestershire Road Safety, called "Drive for Life". There are moments in life when you can be really humbled, and on Wednesday the dignity and courage of a mother who had lost her 18-year-old in a road traffic accident was immense as she spoke to the entire 6th Form. The job of school is to teach a curriculum, to be able to pass exams, and to obtain qualifications recognising that process. But holistically education is and should be so much more than this and on Wednesday at Wyedean this is what the young people in the 6th Form experienced. My thanks to all visitors and organisers who put on this unique event for the school and as ever there are photos and links on our Twitter feed. Staff have very kindly given up their break to take students to visit Auschwitz in Poland and the WWI battlefields in Belgium. On Monday the school held an inset/twilight training around building leadership and why staff go the "extra mile" for students. Wyedean has the best teachers and support staff I have known for both aspects and I have worked in some pretty good schools.

The school broke up for half term on Wednesday and we held a non-uniform day to support the local foodbank in Chepstow with donations and food to deliver for Harvest Festival. We return on Monday 31st October with darker and colder days to face and the long slog until Christmas. The school is hosting a Challenge Partner Review team in November for several days as we bring in external verifiers who can look at what and where the school is doing well. Also what we need to do to be even better and a way to improve the school to continue to be a high performing beacon of excellence for our communities in the Forest of Dean and in Monmouthshire. I will let parents know the date for the school's first "coffee morning – town hall meeting" in late November as part of this dialogue.

I am looking forward to a few days away in mid Wales with my wife, kids, and dog Dylan at my family's place in the middle of nowhere near Llanidloes. Possible trip to the sea and Aberystwyth for fish and chips as well as long treks up mountains with the dog and my daughters. And no wifi for their tablets there as well! I wish all our staff, students and families a very good rest and break.

11th November 2016

"I pray heaven to bestow the best of blessings on this house and all that shall hereafter inhabit it. May none but the wise men ever rule under this roof." John Adams

When Founding Father and second US president, John Adams, entered the newly built but largely undecorated White House in 1801, it is alleged he said these words as he walked around the executive mansion of the very young republic that had come into being as the United States of America officially in 1787. It was a quote beloved by a lot of subsequent US presidents and it was President No 32, Franklin Delano Roosevelt, who had it inscribed on the fireplace in the state dining room of the White House. For many, it gave people not only something to think about in the caliber of their president but also the sense that the White House, unlike say a Head of State's residence such as Buckingham Palace, was their "House". Well, as with the British people with Brexit in the summer, earlier this week "We the people..." the American people had spoken as the Founders intended them to every four years. And very much like Brexit, at least sort of spoken. But did politicians understand what they had been trying to say? I fell asleep around 1am trying to stay up for the results on Tuesday into Wednesday, and then my American friend started messaging and calling around 3am so we talked over the couple of hours as it became clear that the "blue firewall" was not holding and when Pennsylvania was called for Trump it was all over. I am sure its C17th Quaker founder, William Penn, would have loved the irony. People discuss the idea of "leadership" all the time in all sorts of contexts; business, political, educational, sports etc., but on Wednesday morning leadership was visible in all the major players involved and that is why there is also hope. There is always hope and every leadership theory has that in it as a component as well. "Reservoirs of optimism" I was once told, is a key element in the mindset of the school leader. You can say that again.

John Dunford, the pupil premium champion, has written a very timely helpful article in the TES on the back of the US Election results for educators: *In these troubling times, teachers have an essential role in countering prejudice and hate.*" John is right. Part of our role as educators is not only developing understanding and reasoning alongside society's liberal values in young people, but it is also to allow a forum where dialogue with students allows them to make some sense of their World. This week we had the school being reviewed by a team of fellow school leaders as part of the improvement network we are a member of, Challenge Partners. It went really well, English Learning Area was rightly confirmed as an "Area of Excellence" and the reviewers validated the changes, the positive culture at Wyedean, as well as the things we need to do to continue to be a high performing school moving to "outstanding".

On Wednesday morning a group of my Year 11 Critical Thinking group turned up at my door desperate to talk about the US Election and President Elect Trump. If I hadn't been on my way with the lead reviewer to watch my colleague Julie Smith teach Year 12 English Literature I would have stayed and spent the morning analysing the results and the likely consequences. This is probably the most important event of their lives and they are ironically the generation sandwiched between 9/11 and 11/9. I was fortunate enough to be on a History trip to West Berlin as a student when the Wall came down, and standing on the Wall by the Brandenburg Tor as the DDR crumbled and people hugged and sobbed as they were soon to be united Germans, the strength of that emotion has never left my mind. Will Trump turn back the clock and start building his Wall? When I did meet my Critical Thinking group officially on Thursday morning for discussion over tea we were finally able to let rip as they say. It's interesting the significance of the 9th Nov in German History: the day the Kaiser abdicated in 1918; the Munich Putsch in 1923; Kristallnacht in 1938 and of course the Wall coming down in

1989. And now Trump. And his family is German on his father's side. Make of that what you will.

Standing in the silence in Tutshill this morning with the local community, as we all were remembering those who fought for our freedoms, I did think about how events are caused as I questioned in my mind; do we appreciate at the time the consequence of the moments like the shot at Lexington "heard around the World" or the fateful one in Sarajevo 140 years later. Did the lads of Tutshill or Sedbury understand this when World events impacted their small corner of the Forest in 1914 or 1918 or 2001? Right now, there are a fair few people wondering about the magnitude and potential consequences of the events of 2016. I know a number of people will be much happier when 2016 is over. With Halloween and Bonfire Night gone the run down to Christmas is certainly on, and the cold and shorter days are definitely apparent. I'll say it again, we should adopt "Thanksgiving" at the end of November in the UK. Even just for the cornbread. I have been very lucky to have spent a few Falls in North America and taken part in some very special Thanksgiving events with American friends. It's the America I adore and is still in the Founders words "The shining city on the hill".

Wyedean held its Academic Mentoring Days yesterday and today, and it was a real pleasure to talk with parents and students about their progress and how to support students further in their learning and development. Year 11 Mocks are at the end of the month and our Sixth Form Open Evening is on the 1st December. I have my assembly ready for Monday on the theme of "Time" hopefully not to send Year 11 to sleep with. But first, after the week of Challenge Partners, Trump's election, Wyedean Staff at Gloucester TeachMeet (Julie Smith doing a brilliant job), Beachley Barracks to close in 2027 and Academic Mentoring it's time to at least enjoy a quiet weekend. Can I go weekend without reading/listening/watching the news? I blame the rise of social media. For a lot of things.

25th November 2016

"Following a period of turbulence when the school was in special measures and staff felt very pressurised, the new Headteacher has worked tirelessly to develop a culture of openness, transparency, and trust. In particular, leaders have been empowered and are enjoying the freedom to innovate. As a result, the school now has a clear vision and is a harmonious place where everyone feels valued. This is helping to drive school improvement because all stakeholders are pulling in the same direction." Challenge Partners Review Report: Wyedean School, Nov 2016

"Really enjoyed my conversation with sixth form @WyedeanSchool on Friday. Confident, articulate youngsters, we didn't always agree - healthy." Baroness Royall after her visit to Wyedean 25th Nov

The progress markers of the school year are flying by right now as this long term suddenly starts to show an end in sight with the glitter of Christmas holidays starting to infect a lot of conversations in hallways and classrooms. We have our Sixth Form Open Evening here on Thursday 1st December. As much as this is the evening to show our community just how good Post 16 Education is at Wyedean, I also have a sneaking thought that it is also a good excuse to get Christmas trees, real NOT fake, from the Forest of Dean up and decorated around the school to remind us the holidays are not far away. For the Year 11s this probably cannot come too soon and they finish their two-week formal mocks at the end of the fortnight. I would say most of Year 11 are already in the mind-set of looking at life beyond GCSEs and have spent most of the autumn term looking at schools and colleges for their potential post 16 futures. We were very fortunate to host Baroness Royall on Friday as she spoke to Sixth Form and upper school students. Lady Royall was Labour Leader of the House of Lords under Gordon Brown. In a "post-truth" World, it is refreshing to know young people are debating issues with politicians like Jan Royall, disagreeing, having debate but all engaged in respectful dialogue.

The question I gave to my Year 10 critical thinking group this week was "does the means justify the ends?" I thought about this as like all schools we received our data analysis (RaiseOnline) for the Key Stage 4 2016 results. This is the first year of the changes on accountability measures with all English schools being measured by "Progress 8" as schools no longer report on how many students received five GCSEs above C including English and Maths. The current Year 11 will also be the first cohort in England to undertake English and Maths qualifications using the new numerical grading with other GCSE subjects to follow. It's been a difficult one for all schools to plan, implement, and undertake some of these fundamental changes especially if you include KS3 "assessment without Levels" changes. Don't get me started on education funding. The Chancellor, Philip Hammond, said nothing about increasing education funding in the Autumn Statement, with the Institute of Fiscal Studies reporting earlier this year that education has suffered a real terms cut of 8%. When I meet other school leaders as I did the other Friday at a meeting at Royal Wootton Bassett Academy, the only conversation around the room is about where are you saving money and which further cuts will you have to make? In all of this the demands on more from the education system grows. It will be interesting to see the PISA findings next month as England is compared to other leading education systems. For Wales, it is predicted PISA will only show even further decline in key standards of English, Maths and Science.

For Wyedean School, the report from Challenge Partners on our school has been a fantastic validation of the work we have done to make sure not only is the school fulfilling its core function, meeting DfE requirements, balancing the budget, but we are also being innovative and creative in the educational outcomes and opportunities for our young people in Monmouthshire and the Forest of Dean. I will be sharing the report with all parents and will put this on the school website. This review/inspection by Challenge Partners is a way of making sure that even though the school can expect Ofsted in 2017, the school still knows where it is and what it has to do to be even better. I found it very odd when I worked in Powys that an inspection could be over 6-7 years between inspections, to the day, and no such group of school improvement network like Challenge Partners exists west of Offa's Dyke no matter what Cardiff has tried to emulate. It is not the original Challenge Partners that grew out of the highly regarded "London Challenge" group.

A group of senior leaders here met with a senior representative from the International Baccalaureate Organisation (IB) to talk about how Wyedean potentially becomes an "IB World School" offering programmes such as the IB Diploma and MYC. One of the reasons why being an academy is a good thing is precisely because it is the school that gets to lead on areas such as what type of curriculum and education philosophy it should be offering rather than following the diktats of the local authority or a narrow national educational agenda. The principal is a leader rather than a manager of somebody's agenda remote from the school. Wyedean sits on the confluence of the Wye and Severn and looks out to the wider World. This is increasingly reflected in the World Class education we have in this corner of the borders. And best of all it is what our parents and students know is the right education for the 21st Century. If statisticians want to measure education by calling it "Progress 8" then that is fine but when visitors judge students as "confident and articulate" and staff as "committed and innovative" then we know Wyedean School is doing the right thing for the communities it serves.

16th December 2016

"My idea of Christmas, whether old-fashioned or modern, is very simple: loving others. Come to think of it, why do we have to wait for Christmas to do that?" Bob Hope

A week ago, I spoke to a group of colleagues who seemed to sum up my own feelings about this term; so much good has happened over the last few months at Wyedean School that we don't want the term to end, but at the same time staff and students are exhausted and cannot wait for the break for Christmas to re-charge batteries ready for January 2017. Both the Year 6 and Year 11 Open Evenings this term have been opportunities to again show off Wyedean School at its best to our local communities both sides of the river Wye. The huge increase in student applications is testament to the excellent teaching, the educational opportunities, and the nurturing/caring learning environment at Wyedean School. This was validated completely with the Challenge Partners Review visit over 3 days in November as they looked at all aspects of the school. My English and Latin colleague, Julie Smith, contributed a significant article in December to the Times Educational Supplement (TES) on the development and approach of ongoing teacher training here at Wyedean. Baroness Royall, the former leader of the House of Lords, came to speak to students a few weeks ago and complimented them for being *"confident, articulate and could challenge in a good way"*. This incredible model of developing student leadership has been evident in a range of ways this term from the BTEC students who have set up and are running a commercial café in 6th Form, to the students who took part in creating the study/learning garden at the start of December, to the critical thinking students who have debated Brexit, Syria and Trump with students in schools around the World over Skype, and sat in Windsor Castle alongside eminent business and academics for the day in October debating a positive narrative for their generation.

The various Wyedean Warriors sports teams have enjoyed considerable success this term and you can read more in the school's Dec 2016 newsletter on the website. The Music Dept has been heavily involved in the community supporting a range of concerts and events with their choirs and bands. I sat and watched them in St Mary's Chepstow this week and was just amazed at the depth of talent and confidence the young people of our school have. Hearing John Denver's "Country Road", a particular family favourite of mine, being performed beautifully on the harp in that beautiful church will carry me through the cold and winter gloom of the January and February days when we return in 2017.

I know a lot of people who will be glad to see the back of 2016 for various reasons, a few reasons already referenced above. The national education picture both in England and Wales is probably one of the worst I can remember as an educator in terms of the funding crisis, PISA results in Wales, and the recent green paper on education for England to name but a few. But I only have to walk around the school and see the energy and optimism of the staff and students. I know that the focus will continue in 2017 to be on giving these young people in our care the best educational environment to support and nurture their development to take their place in the World with hope and confidence. I invite you to see some of the things that your children have been doing this term in the December 2016 newsletter to see what I mean. We also post on Twitter, Facebook, school website, etc. daily the learning and enrichment that together with the curriculum makes Wyedean a beacon of educational excellence. In early January, I have been invited to a special meeting with the National Schools Commissioner, Sir David Carter, to talk about the experience of Wyedean and at the end of January, I have the huge honour of being asked to speak in London at the invite of the British Council at the Education World Forum which is the world's largest gathering of Education Ministers and policy makers. There will be plenty to talk about at both. We all need a positive narrative for 2017.

I wish you and your families a restful, enjoyable Christmas and a hopeful 2017.

10th January 2017

"January, the Monday of months..." F. Scott Fitzgerald

"Write it on your heart that every day is the best day of the year." Ralph Waldo Emerson

It's not even close to the supposedly worst day of the year, Blue Monday, which takes place on the third Monday of January. Personally I have never had too many issues with the month of January and the first day back after the break students and staff seemed fine with being back in school and picking up where we left off just before Christmas. Year 11s have just completed their Sixth Form taster days in school and Year 12s are beginning their formal mocks. This term sees a lot of reporting and follow up consultation evenings and it is a great opportunity to meet and discuss with parents the progress of their child as well as what we can all do to work together to further support students.

I was invited to a meeting in Bristol on Friday with a small number of principals and CEOs across the South West to talk with the National Schools Commissioner, Sir David Carter, and the SW Regional Schools Commissioner, Rebecca Clarke. Sir David is an astonishing educator not just because of his work at Cabot Learning Federation or as the RSC for the SW but also for the work he has done at a national level on school improvement. Someone told me recently that Sir David was "the smartest person in the room". As I listened to him make sense of current education policy in a very honest but positive way on Friday I thought to myself he is probably the smartest person in every room. It was a real pleasure and privilege for Wyedean School to be invited to this round table dialogue. As I left the busy Friday afternoon city centre and drove home up the M32 to North Bristol the thoughts in my head from the dialogue kept echoing around how much we are doing the right things at Wyedean to improve education and life chances for all of our students.

My colleagues in the Music department were phenomenally busy the whole of December participating in events throughout the community and this week they are involved in a special ten week masterclass course for Year 8s through the music hub initiative based in Gloucester. It is sad to hear of schools where the curriculum has been reduced really to a set of basic skills and no real breadth of curriculum in exciting and creative subjects because they no longer exist for that school. Students need all sorts of intellectual challenges and wider curriculum exposure and I am proud to say that Wyedean School has been asked to speak about its global education and learning at the World Education Conference in London on the 26th January. This is the largest gathering of education ministers and policy makers from around the World at a special event sponsored by the British Council. On the 1st Feb we will be speaking at a Classics/Latin conference at the University of Bristol about the development of the subjects in the curriculum at Wyedean School – not a normal thing for a state school and my colleagues, students, and parents know the enrichment and intellectual curiosity this has brought since we started the initiative. On Saturday 7th January Y12 student Joshua Hicks competed in 'Champions of Tomorrow 2017', a national Latin and Ballroom championships in Blackpool's Winter Gardens. Year 12 student, Joshua Hicks, and his new partner, Sophie Hayward, competed in the U35 Novice Latin and Ballroom championships – winning both. To win both disciplines at national championships is a huge achievement - something that hasn't been achieved for a decade. Joshua and Sophie were the youngest competitors in the U35 category, aged just 16, and from score sheets they were unanimously the judge's champions. As a result of their achievements Joshua and Sophie are now part of Latin and Ballroom history – Roll of Honours. To add to this triumphant achievement Joshua and Sophie, who are part of the Dance Associations National League (NL) are currently top U35 Ballroom and Latin dancers in the league. Due to this, Joshua and Sophie will compete in the National League Championships in July, hoping to take the NL title. This is by invite only – top 12 in the country will compete.

I have Spanish friends from a school I work with in Barcelona who have a tradition as the clock strikes midnight on the 31st December to eat as many grapes (or olives) as possible within the bongs to gain as many wishes for the coming year. I was very tempted to try this one out this New Year's Eve looking at the prospect of 2017. My wife nearly bought "I survived 2016" t shirts. The long walk with the dog, family and German visitors on the first day of the year made me think more however about what I hoped and wanted for 2017. Trump and Brexit are two things that we are going to live with and get used to so I have decided not to dwell too much on this. It was the words of Michelle Obama that gave me hope as an educator in her last public speech as First Lady when she said: *"Lead by example, with hope not fear"* and she urged young people to work hard and get a good education. Abigail Adams and Eleanor Roosevelt, add another to the Pantheon. Over to you Ivanka.

I know education funding will get worse, not better, and that education policy will continue to be confusing as schools and educators try to see the strategy around MATs, academies and grammar schools. I hope we really do see the development of a "shared society" as the UK goes forward. But leading with hope and not fear means continuing our day to day education in this small corner of the borders that challenges and equips our young people effectively to deal with their ever changing complex World. That's my 2017 resolution. Have a great year ahead.

23rd January 2017

"We must accept finite disappointment but never lose infinite hope." Martin Luther King Jr

The words of MLK could apply to any number of situations not least a strong resonance to anyone gearing themselves up for the start of the Six Nations at the start of February. Wyedean Warriors have enjoyed some New Year success with the Year 10 Boys football team winning the district football tournament last week. Netball, Badminton, and hockey teams are in action this coming week. I spoke to Year 7 on Friday morning about this time being a moment in history with the inauguration of a new president as well as the UK government's position on what sort of Brexit becoming clearer ahead of Article 50 being triggered in March. These momentous World events are providing an interesting back-drop to the everyday life of the school but it is precisely the everyday that is moving us forward. The Year 9s went through their Options Evening on Thursday and this coming Thursday Year 11s have their consultation evening. The Sixth Form applications closed formally, even though we are still taking more applications, and we topped over 200 applying to come to Wyedean for this September. Linked to the recent news on nearly 200 first choice applications for new Year 7s this autumn, it is a strong endorsement from our students and community in Gloucestershire and Monmouthshire that the curriculum, learning, achievement, and education at Wyedean school fits in with their aspirations for what they want from their school. As I walk around the school daily I see this in every classroom and how hard my colleagues are working to deliver quality education for the young people in our care.

Part of the strategy for Wyedean School over the last couple of years is not just re-engagement and strengthening the ties with our community, but also as an academy being able to develop our own partnerships for school improvement, transition, and developing further compelling learning opportunities. We are pleased to have become a strategic secondary school partner in the West Forest Primary Group of schools and last week, Martin Jenkins, vice principal for pastoral, attended the regional conference for Challenge Partners with our fellow CP schools in Portsmouth. The Music department has been involved in an incredible collaboration project with the Gloucester Vocal project that is currently running a special masterclass stretch and challenge programme with Year 8 throughout the next 10 weeks. The wider enrichment of music in this school and our commitment to music in the curriculum is sadly something disappearing in so many schools with the ongoing budget cuts.

I have the huge honour of speaking at the World Education Forum in London on Thursday at the invite of the British Council, to talk about the curriculum, community involvement, and global learning work of Wyedean School to an audience which will include education ministers and policy makers from around the World. Getting the opportunity, in the words of Quaker George Fox to Oliver Cromwell, to literally speak truth to power.

The DfE released official figures last week for the 2016 summer examinations using the new accountable measurement of Progress 8 and Attainment 8. This is also the summer where English and Maths are undertaking the new specifications with the numerical grading. Wyedean is in a fairly unique position because only around half of our Year 11 are included in the figure because of a sizeable chunk of our students coming to us from Monmouthshire. Statistically we did fine, still with room for improvement but interestingly a lot of the debates between educators and parents on social media focussed on the magnitude of the Government reforms now hitting schools linked to the real term spending cuts of around 10% associated to a perceived confused DfE strategy for education.

I did highlight this to my leadership team as we discussed at length the curriculum model for September 2017 onwards against this backdrop and actually trying to keep true to what our students need in terms of skills, knowledge, and education for the 21st Century. Wyedean School is working with the International Baccalaureate with the aim of offering IB programmes linked to the school vision of global education. Education in schools at all Key Stages has to be much more than a narrowing set of foundation skills being offered in state schools. If Theresa May's vision for Britain is to be more "global" as she said last Tuesday, in a fragmenting multi-polar world with economic power shifting eastwards, then a dynamic knowledge economy is the way schools should be developing their curriculum, to allow a breadth and depth of skills and knowledge to equip young people for the challenges their generation will face in this century.

I even shared with my Leadership Team an overlooked paragraph in the DfE's circular this month on Progress 8 which I will share in full here:

"The performance measures are designed to encourage schools to offer a broad and balanced curriculum with a focus on an academic core at key stage 4, and reward schools for the teaching of all their pupils, measuring performance across 8 qualifications...Schools should continue to focus on which qualifications are most suitable for individual pupils, as the grades pupils achieve will help them reach their goals for the next stage of their education or training."

The great champion of Pupil Premium, John Dunford, wrote a great article in the TES on the 17th Jan extolling schools to remember; *"Despite the avalanche of change, it is still possible for schools to develop a curriculum fit for the 21st century"*

https://www.tes.com/news/school-news/breaking-views/despite-avalanche-change-it-still-possible-schools-develop-a

I heard John speak to Gloucester Heads last year and he is always worth listening to especially on this issue. I think the infinite hope has to be that despite some despondency and disappointment in what has been allowed to happen to education under all colours of recent governments, we can still ensure the curriculum and education excites, captures and grows the minds of our young people as they progress long after their school days are over. But by then they have become lifelong learners and good global citizens in the process.

3rd February 2017

"The greatest danger for most of us is not that our aim is too high and we miss it but that it is too low and we reach it." Michaelangelo

I had quite a humbling moment last Thursday at the British Council in London when I got into a long conversation with the Education Minister from Ethiopia, Dr Tilaye Gete Ambaye, just before I was due to speak at the World Education Forum. We were talking about the general concerns that I faced as a principal of a school in England and of course I went through the TES's standard Friday issue list of articles from funding cuts, Progress 8, MATs, grammar schools, new qualifications this summer in English and Math, and so forth. Dr Ambaye then responded by talking through the issues schools in Ethiopia face. When I spoke to the very distinguished audience, my focus came back to the comparative nature of education around the globe. The similarities in terms of engagement of learning, technology, pedagogy, stretch and challenge, are all there whenever you talk to any educator from anywhere in the World. The differences become apparent when resources and finances come into the mix. Dr Ambaye certainly "closed shut" my TES list as he went through what schools, communities, parents, teachers, and students face daily in Ethiopia. But he made sure I got his last point that education was valued above all else and all had high expectations and aspirations no matter what the classroom looked like or how many students there were to one teacher sharing so few battered text books.

One of the sights that still stays with me from my time in Bandung, Indonesia is the bamboo shack accommodation at the back of one of the schools that housed dozens of 14-16 year old students being looked after by a "nanny" because these students wanted to continue with education after compulsory education finished at 14. They were away from their families and villages in the hills around Bandung, and were enduring this situation because they wanted to learn so desperately and they needed to continue their education to break their cycle of poverty in West Java. I cannot think of anything more humbling as an educator when I think back and it certainly left its indelible impression on me as a teacher when I think about the duty of care and responsibility we have towards our young people.

I sat in the Gloucester Heads meeting the next day after the conference in London listening to the various discussions and one of the most pressing discussion points for the county schools is the government's proposals on the national funding formula. I want to say now no school leader wants to take money off a school struggling in another part of the country. It has been raised by school leaders and organisations this week that about the £385 million allotted in May 2016 to developing more MATs has suddenly disappeared back into the Treasury. When schools across England are struggling with real term funding cuts of 10% over the last few years and reducing quality education in their schools back to the minimum, why can't this money be found to fund a World Class education system? Surely the reason why China, South Korea, Singapore, Canada et al. fund their education so well is to ensure that the next generation are not only good citizens but they are building the skills for the economic wealth for the future prosperity of society.

My Monday this week started off as it normally does, with answering emails at 7am at my desk in my study in school, writing up the weekly briefing for staff for the 8:35 meeting, holding the daily operational meeting at 8:10 with the leadership team, say good morning to sleepy (eager to learn...) students starting school after the weekend, and on with another week. This week, same routine only at 9am the Lions Club of Chepstow came into school to present Trinity Jones in Year 11 a special award for her recent exceptional progress and a £75 Amazon voucher. As we had a photo taken at the front of school I noticed she was beaming. Rightly so. Her school principal was bursting with pride at the same time. I was also extremely proud looking at the tweets from the University of Bristol on Wednesday as Lucy Roberts, our Latin and Classics coordinator, spoke to a special conference in the Wills memorial building about the developments and huge impact here of the subjects. The Wyedean Warrior sporting success also goes from strength to strength and earlier this week the badminton teams in the county finals in Stroud acquitted themselves well. I have invited them to have a celebratory lunch next week to mark their success. Nice to be a proud principal.

In the week the British Parliament voted to allow the government to trigger Article 50 next month and start negotiations to leave the EU, I held a wonderful Skype Classroom talk with staff and students of partner school Gheorghe Asachi High School in Chisinau, the capital of Moldova. My thanks to the brilliant educator and eTwinning Ambassador, Tatiana Popa, and her wonderful students who spent over an hour talking about their favourite books, President Trump and his first actions in the White House, the EU and Brexit as well as Moldova's own delicate relationship as a former USSR republic with Putin's Russia. There are moments in this role when you occasionally question your sanity and what you are doing and there are moments when you are engaging with young people like the students 3000kms away on the other side of Europe, and you are just bowled away by their hope, intelligence and their faith in education. I need more of these opportunities in global learning.

One more week until we break up for half term. I know this is a shorter term after Christmas but it is astonishing how much work gets accomplished and how many important decisions get taken now that have a huge impact later in the school year. Henry Adams once said: *"A teacher affects eternity; he can never tell where his influence stops"*. Lucy and Tatiana will no doubt be enjoying a deserved rest this weekend but despite being on the opposite ends of Europe in two very different countries they have both given opportunities and compelling learning to their students that will resonate and influence long after this particular time in February at the start of the year has been forgotten. As Dr Ambaye said in London to me, the hope he has for his country whatever the state of the world, lies in the optimism of education and its transformational power of good in the lives of ordinary people.

13th February 2017

"We had simply the best day ever with your BARK team of students, thanks for all your preparation and all help to date. It was lovely to work with you and share ideas for the future. On our initial brainstorm meeting we did think your chosen group were mature, enthusiastic and were about to bring a great deal of creative skill along to this project.

Today I could say that their behaviour was exemplary, but that simply would not describe all that they were! We witnessed a desire to learn with complete engagement from the start. Autonomous learning was evident in all students, which resulted in Tom our artist commenting that it was brilliant to see young people able to make their own progress working independently where possible but also being able to communicate development needs in a clear way asking all the right questions at the right time.

Students worked in teams well but it was remarkable to see the whole group support each other as a complete unit. Any individual who was not as confident was soon scooped up by the group and mentored in skills and made to feel a part of it all. Artistic skill aside for a moment, your young people are a huge credit to Wyedean full of empathy and consideration for others in such a positive and encouraging way. And boy did they all have fun in the process with confidence and energy all channelled in the right direction."
Email to Wyedean School, 7th Feb, 2017, Susan and all at JGC BARK Team

It's actually difficult where to start to describe a "typical" week in Wyedean at the moment. It's the end of half term, the middle of February, still cold and gloomy, Friday was an INSET for the students and staff working on key school priorities and all were waiting for the end of the day when the half term break began and colleagues can then enjoy a well-deserved break with their families. My colleagues in MFL, led by Beky Simpson, have just touched down in Barcelona for their KS4 visit to that amazing Catalan city as part of their Spanish studies and the annual Ski trip, led by Dai Thomas, are off to Austria with students to catch the winter slopes. My thanks to colleagues for giving their holiday time to ensure students of Wyedean get these opportunities to enrich their learning and build their experiences. There are already some really lovely Tweets on the PE, MFL and Wyedean Twitter accounts.

We had Ritsumeikan High School, Japan, with us all week topping off an unusually rich global education week even by Wyedean's standards for compelling international learning. The staff and students from our partner school in Japan have really made themselves at home in our school and some of the events and opportunities over the last few days have been just wonderful days in learning. As it should be. Again, pictures and videos of their visit to Wyedean are on the school social media sites. I had a fair few Japanese students come and join us for tea and coffee on Thursday for Critical Thinking with Year 11. We had a really interesting discussion about well-being for young people and whether or not a "finishing line" exists anymore as pressure intensifies on students to achieve. It was interesting to talk about the experience of the Japanese education system compared to the English one and I remember from my own time working with schools in SE Asia the long hours, the endless assessments, and overall pressure young people seemed to be under in these education systems. A well-being balance needs to be found somewhere and I used the American movement "Beyond Measure" and the recent book-film by Vicki Ableles to illustrate how this is changing.

Israeli and international jazz musician, Asaf Sirkis, very kindly came into Wyedean to deliver masterclasses to music students and my thanks to colleagues Pat Allard and Brian Ellam for arranging for students to get this unique exposure to a global performer in music. I was very encouraged to see the engagement and confidence of Year 9 students presenting in the FameLab school finals for Science-STEM and I look forward to having tea with all the finalists after half term to celebrate their success. This is a great way of building self-esteem and getting students involved in science and just wider problem solving. This is the future of education serving C21st needs and my thanks to my colleagues in Science especially Stuart Motson, for organising these events. The work and creativity of Wyedean students in Art with the BARK team, the feedback I have quoted at length at the start of this blog, illustrates again what a rich and broad curriculum should be doing in schools. Nick Gibb MP, the education minister, has recently released a DfE paper on the importance of the Arts in a broad holistic curriculum for all students, and yet at the same time the funding is being severely cut in education and even Andreas Schleicher, education director of the OECD, warned the UK that not investing in education would damage the future prosperity of Britain. Let's hope someone listens. On Thursday we held a non-uniform day collecting for research into prostate cancer and what was unusual about this charity collection is that it came from one Year 10 student's leadership, Amyleigh Brice, motivated because of a close family member's battle with this cancer. The future is in very good hands with students like this showing exactly the sort of skills, empathy, and leadership needed for a successful global society and economic.

I had a very interesting conference last week at Cheltenham Race Course for Gloucestershire school leaders focusing on a "Road Map to Outstanding" which wasn't exactly how the Regional Schools' Commissioner for the SW, Rebecca Clark, much to the consternation of school leaders in the room, saw the county right now and said so in her speech. In fact, we also found out the Forest of Dean is a priority area in the South West and we discussed at length at the West Glos' School Group a couple of days later what this actually means for education in the Forest. I think we all agreed that a strategy including further collaboration, partnership, sharing of good practice, and professional network support was the way forward for students and families of the Forest of Dean. Simon Rowe, Ofsted HMI for Gloucestershire spoke at Cheltenham and was the lead inspector last time for Wyedean in November 2014. When I spoke with him he did point out *"Wyedean must be due soon"*. All I can say for Wyedean School is we can be looked at by anyone at any time and as Challenge Partners found in the autumn, the quality of education and the high standards continue and every member of staff is committed to the very best educational experience and outcomes for all of our students. At the regular Full Governors meeting before the break this is what we shared with governors and also reflected on how being involved in the school improvement network Challenge Partners had significantly impacted Wyedean's journey to outstanding as a high performing school. Looking forward to showing Ofsted this in the autumn or potentially any day before. In England, the inspection system is a lot more rigorous and is not geared up to allow schools 6 or 7 years to the day until they are seen again.

I am speaking at the annual ASCL conference in March for the British Council showcasing the work we are doing at Wyedean and I am now involved in a special weekly TED global education conference lasting until May. This is through the University of Illinois and involves a small group of educators in Europe and North America working collaboratively online each week looking at comparative education systems and essentially what it is that we need to be teaching students so they are learning the right things for the C21st and how we should be doing that. It really is a privilege to have been chosen to represent Wyedean and our school community in this global education forum and I took part in the opening session this weekend.

I am looking forward to time with my wife and kids, not walking Dylan, my dog, at such an unearthly hour for a week and getting away to see family in mid-Wales in Llanidloes. I am not even going to mention the rugby at all in this blog after Saturday. I know all exam groups are starting to feel everything moving up a gear or two but hopefully plenty of rest and downtime this break to prepare for the next few months ahead. There is a finishing line in education and it is the responsibility of all of us; educators, parents, and students to make sure we don't lose the essence of meaningful and effective learning in the race to get to that line. More weeks in education as we enjoyed in Wyedean last week. My great Canadian leadership hero, Michael Fullan, once wrote a book about "*What's worth fighting for in education?*". A week such as last week and many others and the education system being allowed to focus on teachers and support staff providing these opportunities. Students coming home to tell parents, unprompted "*Guess what we did today in school?*". That's what is worth fighting for in education. Have a good break.

6th March 2017

To: Headteacher - Subject: Thank you - Sent: 21 February
2017 14:48

*"Dear Mr Ford; Please can you pass on our thanks to Mr
Thomas and all those involved in organising another
brilliant ski trip. It amazes us how your teachers & support
staff continually go above and beyond. Not just the ski trip
but the music tour and all the other opportunities you provide
the students. Just about every week something exciting seems
to be going on at Wyedean. As parents & a family we so
appreciate this. Thank you and your inspirational staff. Kind
regards, Lindsey & Alan Tyrrell"*

I read this weekend an article in The Leadership Project by a
writer called David McQueen entitled *"Leadership isn't
about being great, it's about enabling others to be great"*. It
resonated strongly with me not least because of the kind words
from the Tyrrells in the email they had sent me after half term
echoing exactly this idea. I think I have been very fortunate to
have worked in schools and with school leaders who practice
this approach daily. In fact McQueen goes onto say in the
article two important things all education leaders should note:
1) Success will follow if you believe in the 'possibility' of
people.
and quoting Aristotle:
2) *"excellence is not an act, but a habit, we are what we
repeatedly do"*.

I was really fortunate last week to be part of a team of
Challenge Partner reviewers led by a very wise and able Ofsted
HMI, David Powell, reviewing Hove Park School on the south
coast. Having reviewed schools for Challenge Partners before
you never lose the sense of privilege it is not only to work with
a school leadership team on self-improvement, but also to
observe colleagues teaching, and to meet with support staff
and students. In the conversations we had with the leadership
team over the three days, it was obvious that this underpinned
the culture and ethos of Hove Park School. One of the greatest
things I love about being in Challenge Partners is this
opportunity for collaboration across a huge network of some
of the best schools in the UK. There are always lots of things

to bring back to your own school but also plenty of other things to make you appreciate what your school is doing.

All school leaders want to enable their staff to be great educators because that means the opportunities and learning of students goes exponential. Wyedean staff and governors have worked tirelessly to ensure our school communities across the borders of Gloucestershire and Monmouthshire have a school committed to compelling learning, stretching, and challenging the mindset of all students. Wyedean School is now officially oversubscribed with Year 6 parents receiving the news last week of their first choice secondary school. It is astonishing but not unsurprising based on the number of parents and potential students we have had through the door over the last year wanting the education we are offering them.

On Saturday, the Sixth Form College at Wyedean hosted a "taster morning" for close to 100 external Year 11s looking to undertake their Post 16 at Wyedean. ALPS have just confirmed the "outstanding" success of progress in Sixth Form results at Wyedean as the school has been consistently in the top 25% nationally for three years running. The range and scope of global learning at Wyedean goes from strength to strength and the visits before half term and last week of Japanese partner schools re-enforced that commitment to global learning and languages. The Spanish MFL visit to Barcelona was such a rich cultural experience for our students in that lively Catalan city. I presented to transatlantic educators through a TED and University of Illinois forum on the 26th February about the development of global learning and critical thinking at Wyedean. This job has some very proud moments but when a group of educators in the mid-West of the USA ask you if your students are specially selected and the school must be private you know we are doing something right in this corner of the World. I have the British Council Ambassadors' conference in Manchester in two weeks and will certainly be sharing this one with colleagues.

The school celebrated World Book Day on Friday and there are some great photos on Twitter from the event. I know social media has seen debates about the expense of costumes but spending a lot of money to dress up is unnecessary and the homemade affairs were brilliant. At the heart of World Book Day is the idea of getting students aware of and more into reading. Even I donned my D'Artagnan costume (I can live with the jibe about Oliver Reed and Athos but Henry VIII really?) and talked about why Dumas' "The Three Musketeers" had caught my imagination as a young avid reader. The Science department at Wyedean never ceases to amaze me with their incredible STEM work and Year 9s were absolutely captivated by the talks on Friday in the Colston Hall Bristol by Robert Winston. My colleague, Katie Macer Wright, has been working with local primary schools through transition, developing young enquiring and analysing minds for the future. The Wyedean Science Twitter account has some of the best clips I have seen of a whole range of experiments and students just enjoying their learning. Year 11s have mocks before the end of this term and a group of them recently visited Cardiff University Law School to look at study and careers in Law. My whole hearted thanks to a great day planned and prepared for the students by Cardiff University Law School.

ASCL and other teaching unions are asking schools and educators to trend on social media under the hashtag #whatwouldyoucut to highlight the breaking point schools now face with reduced funding and falling budgets. I sat with a colleague over lunch at Hove Park School one day last week, a MAT CEO from somewhere in the South East and I spoke about the approach to curriculum, holistic education, and 21st century learning at Wyedean we take with our aim of becoming an IB World School in the next couple of years. She seemed a great leader but snorted at what I was describing in her words as "bells and whistles". I kept my own counsel and thoughts because there wasn't a great deal to gain arguing what she thought was the right approach and no doubt operates in her schools to what I know is working for Wyedean. When I read the emails from parents like the Tyrells, talk to our fantastic students, see the great leadership from individual staff, and see daily the compelling learning going on here which is why we are oversubscribed, "bells and whistles" are definitely not unaffordable "add-ons" or frippery. A commitment to languages, creativity, arts, music, history, maths, science, literature, sport, technology, computing, etc. are what makes up a meaningful education that stretches, challenges, and engages students to prepare them for their next stages. Excellence isn't an act at Wyedean it has become habit.

23rd March 2017

"Bad things do happen in the World but out of those situations always arise stories of ordinary people doing extraordinary things."

"The flower that blooms in adversity is the rarest and most beautiful of them all."

"You have to be at your strongest when you are feeling at your weakest."

Quotes taken from the daily signboards at various London Underground stations the day after the Westminster attacks; 22nd March 2017

Last weekend, I had the privilege of being asked to speak about international education in Manchester at the annual British Council Ambassadors' conference which was centred on the concept of "cohesion". The relatively new Holiday Inn hotel in the centre the conference was held at over the weekend spoke to my younger 1990s student self as it was themed around the music scene of "Madchester" and as several people commented, spending a Saturday night in the Hacienda was a dream come true. The room rather than the club I am afraid. As my eight year old daughter Evie, gently reminded me a few days ago, I am more "male, pale and stale" than ever. Choosing a room named after The Stone Roses rather than the actual seminar theme probably wasn't the wisest thing to base a decision on though. The train going up from Bristol was absolutely packed with revellers on the way to the Cheltenham Festival and continuing up to Birmingham and then towards Manchester, where it was raining of course, people were getting on and off after finishing work or going for the evening in the city after a long week. Carriages were also full of students going home or visiting friends. Ordinary people going about ordinary lives.

As I walked around Manchester on the weekend, I remembered one of the last IRA acts of terrorism was the bombing of Manchester centre in 1996, just before the historic Good Friday Agreement finally brought a peace and an end to The Troubles. One of the architects and classic terrorist turned statesman, Martin McGuiness died only last week. I was a very young teacher back then and had started to make my history lessons less abstract by using "revolutionary" video conferencing with schools in Germany and Russia in the late 1990s and saw the learning power of international education even then. What happened in London on Wednesday was another random and senseless act of terror where people were going about their daily lives; tourists walking across Westminster Bridge, a mother running late to pick up her children, an American husband celebrating his wedding anniversary with a trip to London and a policeman, with a wife and young kids, doing his duty to the very last. My theme for the Year 8 assembly on Thursday was already based on "Tolerance and Understanding". Just as my generation grew up used to the acts of terror from the IRA, this generation is also sadly growing up in such a world. What inspired me in Manchester, what always inspires me, is talking to and listening to people who continue to work hard in classrooms, in society, and in their homes to ensure that the narrative for our kids is one of hope and that the World contains infinitely a lot more good in it than it contains bad. As a school, we held a reflection for the victims of Wednesday and in tutorial colleagues discussed the events with students.

I once worked in a school where non-uniform days and specific charity days like today's "Red Nose Day" were symptomatic of what a group of researchers from Groningen University in Holland called "blind activism". Students paid a pound but had no idea why. I am happy to say I walked around the campus at break and lunchtime today, and saw Wyedean students enjoying the Red Nose Day events in the sunshine, and being aware of why we are working together in a cohesive way to make sure we understand issues and why it is a key part of our values to assist and support other people.

Another area of community activism has been the national and our own school campaign to stop the current proposal on the Fair Funding Formula especially as Wyedean would be the worst off secondary school in West Gloucestershire despite being one of the most successful. My thanks to parents, staff, and governors who have contributed to the national consultation. I have been in correspondence with our local MP, Mark Harper, and Mark kindly agreed to visit the school on the 7th April to talk with leadership and governors on this issue and wider school funding. Wyedean School does not advocate taking funding away from any school to "fair fund", but it seems completely irrational that the Chancellor's budget this month found several £100 million for Free Schools and Grammars, when the Institute of Fiscal Studies, the OECD, all professional associations and others predict that nearly 100% of state schools will be in chronic deficit by 2020 with an average of a £300k deficit to fund. This will equate to 6 teachers being lost on average, larger class sizes, a narrowing further of the curriculum and for some schools being only open for 4 days a week. Wyedean School is exactly a beacon of educational excellence and opportunity on both sides of the border needed in this area. We are over subscribed for September for new Years 7 and 12s and we are being invited regularly to national and international conferences and fora to showcase the work that goes on here. I think it is called a no-brainer. I'm hoping eventually the DfE see it that way too.

I was really encouraged as a school principal to hear the new chief of Ofsted, Amanda Spielman, make curriculum one of her priorities as she spoke at the ASCL conference:

"We know that there are some schools that are narrowing the curriculum, using qualifications inappropriately, and moving out pupils who would drag down results. That is nothing short of a scandal where it happens. Childhood isn't deferrable: young people get one opportunity to learn in school and we owe it to them to make sure they all get an education that is broad, rich and deep."

Reading that makes my educator's heart beat just that little bit faster. This is why having the resources to realise it and less capricious fads from the DfE is vital. Over the next few months one of my key priorities at Wyedean is to look at us becoming an IB World School and offering genuine aspirational and challenging World Class 21st Century learning to the communities we serve on both sides of the border. The school's social media and new website continues to show daily the quality of the compelling learning that is the hallmark of Wyedean School and our commitment to outstanding education for our students. This week alone, the work of our Duke of Edinburgh scheme was recognised with a substantial grant to allow it to expand further, Joshua Thomas in Year 9 was runner up in the FameLab finals in Cheltenham, the gospel choir performed and competed in the Somerset Music

Festival, and our sports successes for the Wyedean Warriors in Netball and Football in particular add to a great year for our sports teams this year. I am particular proud of the school's partnership work on LGBT+ and it is a focus for our priority meeting as a staff next week as we continue to work with Jonathon Charlesworth and Stonewall on challenging homophobic and transphobic behaviour as we aim to be a trans-inclusive school under a collaborative partnership with the DfE.

Next week the South West's Regional Schools' Commissioner, Rebecca Clark, is speaking to Forest of Dean/West Gloucestershire school leaders about the area being one of the SW RSC's "priority areas". As an oversubscribed "Good" school we already work with a number of schools through partnership to ensure we have excellent education across the area. I am speaking at the same meeting about Wyedean's school improvement network with Challenge Partners as a model of good practice. It's also Full Governors Board meeting next week where I present the half termly "principal's report". The Core Year 11 mocks have just finished this week and I am really pleased to see how the Year 11s have been preparing themselves for the summer exams. Not long for them or Year 13s now, and we have been ensuring that we focus on good well-being for the students throughout this time.

The last weekend in March is always the switch to better months as the clocks spring forward and we celebrate "mothering Sunday". It's my wife's godfather's 80th birthday this weekend and we are celebrating with him on Saturday. He was the former chief engineer on Concorde so he always has a few good stories. I don't mind spending a Saturday this way but unfortunately being away I missed the family outing to the cinema last weekend to see "Beauty and the Beast". My TED-University Illinois forum continues on Sunday and last week it was looking at immigration and education. Fascinating to hear from colleagues in Southern California, Texas, and Armenia about how they deal with related issues to ensure these kids get stability and an education. It's a privilege and it is humbling to work with such educators. I think we definitely do need to remember we are at our strongest when we are at our weakest.

24th April 2017

"These boys and girls are to be asked to wield the royal sceptre; we must therefore give them the souls of kings and queens. Otherwise it may be said of us that we took the ordinary person from the shadows of history and set them in the fierce light that beats upon thrones and they were blinded and ran away". Nye Bevan

"THE COMMONWEALTH OF MASSACHUSETTS REQUIRES THE EDUCATION OF THE PEOPLE AS THE SAFEGUARD OF ORDER AND LIBERTY" Inscription on Boston library, the first publicly supported free municipal library in the world.

It feels good to be starting a new term this morning and seeing colleagues and students back to school. When I first heard the announcement by the Prime Minister in the Easter break that she would be seeking a general election in June my first thoughts were probably similar to most educators along the lines of concerns that education would actually lose the attention it needs so crucially right now in national political consciousness and debate. The secretary of state, Justine Greening, only the previous week had caused a huge furore through a major speech outlining further details on the government's proposal to allow more schools to select students and for the further establishment of new grammar schools. The public consultation on this green paper and the national Fair Funding formula were supposed to be made known soon after Easter. However, due to the civil service purdah during the election period, both these announcements have been delayed with the possible likelihood of a new secretary of state at the Department for Education; if Mrs May wins the election and, as she hopes for, an increase in her party's parliamentary majority. As a keen lifelong student of politics I am acutely aware of the seismic impact of last summer's Brexit decision on the future of the UK. However, at the same time something as important as the future of education and the very real problems schools face right now cannot be allowed to slip down the policy agenda of any political party, especially during this important general election.

Over Easter I was asked a number of times my thoughts on selection and grammar schools. I repeated what I tell everyone that the question is not a very insightful one to ask. There are too many false dichotomies and binary arguments in the debate around educational structures in England. Having worked in and with many varying types of state schools and in and with many varying types of independent schools, in the UK and abroad, the question really should be asking what type of education, access, inclusion, and learning should we have in our schools for the future of our young people whatever we end up calling the school. I have worked with some pretty poor independent schools and a fair few outstanding state schools in my time. The label doesn't mean anything if teaching is mediocre, the curriculum is narrow and dry, and the well-being does little to develop and nurture the individual in an overall negative school culture. I honestly don't believe the rose tinted nostalgia that often accompanies the debate on grammar schools is helpful in examining how education has got to where it is in 2017, based on a personal perspective of an individual's school back in say the 1950s or 1960s.

The original 1944 Butler Education Act created a post-war tripartite system based on the assumption and belief that a worthwhile education is about the best in culture not accessible to all. I love the public library in Copley Square Boston and the very American/Founding Fathers notion that an educated population is the key to a stable and functioning free society. In 2013 the then education secretary, Michael Gove, quoted the Italian Marxist Gramsci in a speech to the Social Market Foundation. Gramsci had made the argument in his *"Notes from Prison"* of the need for "emancipatory education" and for everyone to have the access to "powerful knowledge". Gove also quoted the educationalist E.D. Hirsch and the idea of education being about "cultural literacy". I believe Gove was right to cite Gramsci and Hirsch in developing an education policy that makes sure education is worthwhile for all students. The reality over the last few years unfortunately has been an education policy that prioritises a standardised narrowing curriculum, rigid disciplinary rules, and an authoritarian pedagogy. Not exactly a framework to develop critical self-consciousness in the learner let alone an ability to pursue TRUTH in any way, shape or form.

My own rose-tinted view of my own schooling in a comprehensive in a former mining town in Shropshire has obviously played a formative part on my philosophy towards education. Fairly similar to Justine Greening's comprehensive school in Rotherham in the South Yorkshire coalfields in the 1980s, but a world away from Jeremy Corbyn's fee paying Salopian grammar school in my former county; or even why Diane Abbot chose to send her children to a selective school than a non-selective state school. My state school had a very broad curriculum that included lots of cross curricula learning, a development of critical thinking, a strong emphasis on creativity and technology, was global in outlook, full of committed student centred teachers who pushed all students to learn more and access "powerful knowledge" through exposure to higher culture. I have never forgotten the fantastic educators who developed in me and my contemporaries a love of learning that has never gone away and has only grown deeper. My teachers instilled in me the ability to think critically, to question, and to want to know more. I don't care what the school was called or what category it came under but it allowed for my social mobility and a coalminer's son to become the first in his family to go to university, and eventually the privilege of working in education to hopefully give back something that had been given to me.

When I first read the quote on education by Nye Bevan it resonated with me immediately. This is what we need to aim for with all our students. We will only be able to do this if we allow access to a broad and rich curriculum. Where all subjects are seen as vital and important for the future well-being of society. Where the curriculum develops the learner's skills as an individual to access the future economy and society. A curriculum that places student well-being at the centre. I believe the current debate on education needs to break free of the tribalistic echo chambers of the respective protagonists. Successful societies such as in Scandinavia, Singapore, and Canada have placed World Class education for all high up on the list of policy priorities and funding. What would be incredible in this general election campaign being fought over the next 7 weeks would be an education debate not stuck on grammar versus non-selective, but a debate that went back to the question "what is a worthwhile education? "What are we teaching the next generation? Is it preparing them well for the future? We need to make sure all our students are given the souls of kings and queens and none of them run away from the light as they take their places in society as the next doctors, teachers, lawyers, engineers, nurses, builders, plumbers, and so on. That they can not only cope with modern life but it allows them to enjoy that life. I know that is what my colleagues and the parents of this community want for the students of Wyedean. That is what we work towards every day.

2 May 2017

"Today is another opportunity to change the trajectory of your students." Blunt Educator Twitter Post, April 2017

"The terminology of 'a culture of high expectations' is in itself complex and problematic, but any opportunity to explicitly raise expectations should be seen as a moral imperative." Julie Smith, Director of Teaching and Learning, WyedeanSchool
https://ukedchat.com/2017/04/29/creating-culture

It's always good to have a long weekend with the Bank Holiday we've just had, but also it's hard to believe we are now in May already and the countdown for Year 11s and 13s to go on study leave has entered the final few weeks in earnest. The sun shining today certainly gives a summer atmosphere around the campus. The focus on our commitment to compelling teaching and learning for all students at Wyedean School gets shared again this evening in Cardiff; at the kind invitation of South Wales TeachMeet our director of Teaching and Learning, Julie Smith, is presenting to Welsh colleagues on the innovations here at Wyedean. Julie's recent blog contribution for UK Ed Chat highlights the drive and strategy we have to keep raising standards and expectations for all of our students. I am a huge fan of the Blunt Educator's Twitter feed, and coming across this quote from April reminded me how important it was for all educators to remember it's their moral imperative to use every opportunity every day to positively influence the pathways for all the students in our schools. It really doesn't matter if it is a sunny Spring day in May or a wet Wednesday in gloomy November, the core purpose of a school is to ensure there is always a culture of high expectations to inspire students to learn more, to understand and access their world further, and to develop all potential in a nurturing framework. That is the culture of Wyedean. For example, since the start of the new term last week, the brilliant Wyedean Gospel Choir have just won the regional competition to go forward to the national finals in Birmingham. This places Wyedean Gospel Choir amongst the 30 best nationally. Imagine the pride the whole staff took in hearing that this morning at the end of staff briefing.

It was a pleasure to have former Wyedean student and local entrepreneur, Neill Ricketts of Versarien, in school today at a careers event for Year 10 talking about his success in business, and inspiring students to think about where the skills, knowledge, and understanding they are learning now could possibly take them in the future. Education is often erudite for good reasons but it cannot be in abstract and the best schools bridge this gap. I spent part of my day today working with the Assistant Principal and Director of Sixth Form, John Lane, on the enrichment programme for Post 16 and the careers developments for Sixth Formers. It is no wonder the Sixth Form is inundated with applications, and the curriculum is not narrowing down or excluding subjects for students to study post 16 such as Music or Maths.

The Wyedean Adult Community Learning programme gets underway this evening for the summer programme and this is such a rich element of not only supporting the local community but also the commitment to lifelong learning we have as a school.

Last week I was impressed with the commitment of the student leadership team, led by student president Matt Grindle, who represented the school in Chepstow at the WWI commemoration for Chepstow Victoria Cross hero Able Seaman William Williams who was killed at Gallipoli. A poignant reminder of what previous generations of people of this community have given to ensure young people today can enjoy the freedoms we often take for granted even in this uncertain world. These are the same student leaders who have continued to raise money and collect for Chepstow Food Bank this term. I often feel confident about the future knowing such strong moral leadership exists in our young people.

The school's participation in the Carnegie/Greenwood reading scheme has got underway this week inspiring greater numbers of young people to read and develop further their passion for literature. There are two astonishing GB climbers at Wyedean, Finlay and Lyall Wood, who will represent the UK at four international climbing tournaments across Europe this summer. It is incredibly inspiring and both brothers epitomise the very best of our young people. The culture of WyedeanSchool makes you so proud as an educator every day.

Gwennan Jeremiah, the Vice Principal for the academic side of the school which includes teaching and learning as well as the curriculum, attended an ASCL conference in London looking at exciting opportunities for the future curriculum at Wyedean. Wyedean School is seeking to become an IB World School in 2018 and to offer International Baccalaureate programmes to our students. There are many reasons for any school to look at the IB, not least its global learning and curriculum, but my central reason is the premise of IB, to look at what the student will become as a result of studying the programme at the end. How refreshing is that for an idea in education, and how exciting for educators, parents, and students to look at education this way instead of through the narrow national prism of a politicised curriculum model. The IB learner profile is below. If only politicians were debating the merits of education from this perspective in an election campaign. You have to be an eternal optimist in education.

Finally, the English Learning Area are trending with "#whyreadwyewrite" throughout May, promoting creative and imaginative writing opportunities that don't normally exist or happen in the confines and constraints of the formal curriculum. On the day that a former famous inspiring Wyedean student apologised to her fans on Twitter for killing Professor Snape, it seems appropriate that the next generation of writers are given the opportunity at Wyedean to alter their own future trajectories. I love this job.

23 May 2017

Jane Elson@Mousegirl2502 May 12, replying to @WyedeanSchool, @WyedeanVP:

"We are so happy we chose Wyedean, it has been a fabulous 5 years. Hopefully grades will be good enough to return for 6th. Thank you all. I always wonder how teachers feel about seeing another group move on."

Wyedean School@WyedeanSchool May 12, replying to @Mousegirl2502, @WyedeanVP:

"Good question. Like a parent; proud they are moving on but sad they are changing and things won't be the same again. Great kids we have here."

Last week I gave an assembly to Year 7 on the idea of "Home" and the notion that this was more than just a place to live drawing upon the more powerful meaning in the German word "heimat" and especially the beautiful Welsh word "hiraeth". Almost upon hearing the word, it makes me want to put my hand automatically towards my heart. I went back to Shropshire last weekend to celebrate my sister's birthday. On the Sunday morning, I took the dog and my kids along with my niece's family and her dog on a long walk through the Ironbridge Gorge and my childhood haunts. On the way back we came past the site of my old school now just a pile of hardcore rubble awaiting use for a new housing development. It was a shock. Ironically, it was a "Shropshire Lad" (even more ironic because he was from Worcestershire to the south), AE Housman, whose famous lines came instantly into my head:

"Into my heart an air that kills From yon far country blows: What are those blue remembered hills, What spires, what farms are those?

That is the land of lost content, I see it shining plain, The happy highways where I went And cannot come again."

I wish I had quoted my favourite lines of Housman to my Year 11s when I spoke to them and wished them well for their exams and their future at their last assembly in mid-May.

Essentially this time will not come again and when Mrs Elson tweeted to the school her thanks and asked how we felt about such moments as educators, I conveyed that they were a mixture of sadness at the change but also joy at a pivotal moment for these young people in their lives. They are an exceptional year group and watching them today go into their first English exam, the first time with the new changes and numerical grading awaiting them, I felt proud of the people they are now and the people they will become.

There is a lot of pride in the achievement of our young people at Wyedean and we are fortunate as educators to play a small role in helping to shape this success. It was a privilege for me last Tuesday to sit with the two Year 8 music classes as their video from their "Journey to the Heart" project was shown officially for the first time. There is a link to it here and on the school website. The confidence and passion demonstrated by the students as they sing is very clear when you watch the video, and my thanks to the Songwriting Charity for their work with Wyedean staff and students producing this song. Although the weather was against us last week, the first rain for a long time, the BARK Street Art project came into school again to continue their project with Year 9s and creativity and History came alive with the Year 7 model castles. Not all based on Chepstow Castle I should add. Last Friday evening Year 10 student, Amyleigh Brice, was a finalist in the "Pride of the Forest" awards where she narrowly missed winning the award for young community activist. The Forest of Dean community rightly recognised her dedication, leadership, and initiative in raising money and awareness for cancer charities.

Year 13 will leave this Friday as we break up for half term. Many of them have been at Wyedean seven years and once the small matter of A levels or BTEC exams are out of the way, they should have a long summer to rest and enjoy some freedom. The next generation of Wyedeaners are getting ready to join us from Year 6, as transitions are starting to take place soon for our primary partners in Monmouthshire and the Forest of Dean. The day Year 11 left, we were holding appeal panels for those parents who have not been able to get their students into Wyedean School. It is a nice position to be in, to be oversubscribed as a school, because that means the education and the ethos at Wyedean is right for our communities, but it is not a nice position when so many families are left in limbo because they cannot get into Wyedean as their school of choice. We are about to see the same for Year 12 with record applicants this year, because the present Year 11 here and in other schools want the quality education, breadth of curriculum choice, and wider opportunities our Post 16 centre offers the area.

Not many of the Year 13s would have expected to be in the position of voting right now in the upcoming general election. On Thursday in school we have a hustings in the J.K. Rowling library for all parliamentary candidates standing in the Forest of Dean constituency. I think the school community is looking forward to this unique event and judging by the questions submitted there are a fair few on Brexit, also a whole lot more on education, health, tuition fees, taxation, transport, fracking, rural deprivation the list goes on. Hopefully a lively participatory debate and dialogue to come, and I am grateful to the candidates for agreeing to come to Wyedean School in what we believe will be the only time all will be debating together on the same platform in the Forest seat campaign. I had a strange email from my French colleague who said that such an event in her school would be unthinkable, and the education system there would not allow politics to enter the school in this way. Whereas the French and indeed Europe breathed a collective sigh of relief the other Sunday, for me as an educator it is only through these opportunities and events that we get young people engaged in politics. We also develop how to debate and get used to a dialogue with one another in a democratic respectful forum. I know the French are far from apathetic when it comes to societal issues but if education is abstract from the real world, our students do not have the skills or ability to question or put forward or even challenge arguments; then for me we would be failing as teachers.

I will finish with the lovely event from this Sunday just gone, at my daughter's primary school where they held a family day to support Syrian refugees. The various communities in this part of north Bristol including eastern Europe, the Middle East, and even Staple Hill, got together to raise money and awareness of the awful tragedy taking place daily at the eastern end of the Mediterranean Sea. For many Syrian refugee families' home is now just a diminishing concept and not a place at all. Let us hope the young people we are setting forth into the wider world this summer are the next generation of leaders who can make better-informed decisions and build far more bridges than walls than the present generation. There is always hope and optimism in this World. Our young people carry it forward.

Wyedean School and Sixth Form Centre, Year 8 - Journey to the Heart videoWyedean School Hustings programme – 25th May 2017

25th July 2017

"It's the curriculum stupid"

"History says, don't hope...
But then, once in a lifetime
The longed for tidal wave
Of justice can rise up
And hope and history rhyme"
Seamus Heaney

"Every day children, young men and women who live and breathe multiculturalism, who demonstrate in all that they do and say that for them it is the person that matters not the gender, nationality, skin colour or faith, surround me. You might take the child out of Europe but you cannot drive him or her out of the wonderful, diverse global society we are all privileged to live in today." Brian Christian, Principal of The British School in Tokyo

It is nearly the end of a very long academic year here at Wyedean School with staff and students ready for their long summer break. Reflecting over the year it would be hard to pick a particular moment out of so many inspiring and compelling educational opportunities that take place at this school daily. There have been a number of audiences in June and July I have found myself talking through the narrative of Wyedean's academic year including Parent Voice groups, the Full Governing Board, and visitors from the South West Regional School Commissioner's office as recently as last week. The hard work and dedication of all the staff here are the obvious foundations of the success and what has been evident this year is the exponential growth of leadership everywhere around the school from the students, the support staff, and the middle leaders, especially those without the titles. They have all made the school not only move significantly forward but also allowed a C21st approach to education that had provided so many compelling learning opportunities daily. The platform of the new website linked to the school's responsive daily social media outlet of Twitter and Facebook means the school is communicating constantly what we are doing to our community and beyond. For me as principal I think this has been one of the successes of the year as we constantly demonstrate the school's vision and commitment to World Class 21st Century learning.

The sword of Damocles hanging over all of us in schools and in education continues along with the uncertainty and lack of national leadership around school funding. I know some of the very difficult decisions my leadership team and the governors of the school have had to make in order to ensure the very difficult balancing act of ensuring high quality education and an enriching curriculum all links tightly to a very efficiently balanced budget. The General Election in June did not give any further certainty about the direction of national education policy other than the Conservative's loss of their parliamentary majority meant contentious issues such as grammar school expansion were stopped. The "confidence and supply" arrangements with the DUP raises particular issues within education from the Secretary of State of the DfE down to the classroom teacher because the DUP's stance on certain social issues. Even the recent announcement of school funding in July came with the caveat that this would not be new / additional money but £1.3billion of savings within the DfE. The long-awaited results of the consultation on the Ebacc were published in July with significant changes to the percentage of students entered at Key Stage 4 for the Ebacc as well as the timeframe now pushed to the 2020s for possible implementation. As a few commentators have pointed out the UK may have experienced more than one new government by that time. From a personal point of view as an educator, the fundamental flaw in the Ebacc was the narrow definition to the detriment of the arts and creative subjects.

At the end of July Wyedean held its annual Creativity Fair and this year we linked it to Careers and Guidance. It has not been an easy task to ensure the curriculum here is as rich as it can be with a range of subjects interconnected and giving meaning to learning and wider knowledge for our students and their daily experiences of education. However, this is what leadership is about and such decisions made have these sorts of consequences for the longer-term curriculum. I believe strongly that in this current state of education flux, educators and schools should not wait for a convoluted national picture or direction to emerge after a series of political compromises and capricious fads to keep basic power. Sir David Carter, the National School's Commissioner has said often; "it is about the outcomes not the structures". In May 2016, the then White Paper committed all schools to becoming academies by 2020 with the preferable model of a Multi Academy Trust. After the Brexit vote, last June, and Theresa May became Prime Minister, educational policy centered on the expansion of grammar schools and free schools. Since the June 2017 election that manifesto commitment disappeared. What has come as a relief is the remarkable speech by Ofsted's chief inspector, Amanda Spielman, in June at the Wellington Festival of Ideas. It is worth repeating the key passage below illustrating how refreshing that a body like Ofsted, of all the major players in education, now making a clarion call for schools to be refocusing on what is it we are teaching in schools and for what purpose?

https://www.gov.uk/government/speeches/amanda-spielmans-speech-at-the-festival-of-education

One of the areas that I think we sometimes lose sight of is the real substance of education. Not the exam grades or the progress scores, important though they are, but instead the real meat of what is taught in our schools and colleges: the curriculum. To understand the substance of education we have to understand the objectives. Yes, education does have to prepare young people to succeed in life and make their contribution in the labour market. But to reduce education down to this kind of functionalist level is rather wretched. Because education should be about broadening minds, enriching communities, and advancing civilisation. Ultimately, it is about leaving the world a better place than we found it. As Professor Michael Young wrote in his article,

'What are schools for?':*"Schools enable young people to acquire the knowledge that, for most of them, cannot be acquired at home or in the community."* Yet all too often, that objective, that real substance of education, is getting lost in our schools. I question how often leaders really ask, "What is the body of knowledge that we want to give to young people?"

The curriculum has been at the heart of education debate in England at national policy level for a long time even before the inception of the National Curriculum in 1988. Until recently, schools felt that the direction of travel was only to follow the Ebacc proposals with little room for maneuverer or freedom even for those in academies where curriculum freedom was one of the reasons to convert from a maintained school. The Ebacc measurement is not a "baccalaureate" (a collection of subjects interconnected through skills and a joined approach towards curriculum such as through a learner profile) and if the government does persist in wanting 90% of students to take the Ebacc then this will damage arts and creative subjects.

It is the intention at Wyedean that we fulfil the curriculum statutory requirements as a basic given but we need to do something much more meaningful and relevant for ALL students that prepares them for life and positive well-being beyond school. That is why we are looking at how we design curriculum pathways for vocational, academic, the unsure, etc looking at curriculum programmes like the IB. We have to be about more than foundational learning skills as our "selling point" as a school. We are the only school in our area, both sides of the border, that are going to do this for our education offer. I am curious with the curriculum changes in Wales, "Successful Futures", and the pioneer schools under the Scottish education professor, Graham Donaldson, especially as his "Curriculum for Excellence" in Scotland has come under heavy criticism for its dirigisme approach and a focus too much on skills. Our approach here at Wyedean is that we want the curriculum to be a broad and balanced model. Students will not be attracted here just because the basic skills are covered effectively as would be expected from a school rated "Good" with our learner profile. The post 16 model especially in niche Post 16 academic subjects plus a new approach to sixth form enrichment means the whole status of Sixth Form is the aspirational engine of the school. We need much more into KS3 that hooks all students into learning for KS4 as part of our wider holistic approach towards the curriculum both in the informal and formal curriculum.

The vision for the school is to continue to allow initiatives like the Duke of Edinburgh scheme to develop, and for curriculum subjects like Classics/Latin to be supported especially by accessing external support and funding. This has been particularly successful with Mandarin and our Confucius Institute partnership. The growth and lead of MFL subjects is almost completely against the trend of most languages in state schools nearby. The school's commitment to the arts and creativity is in the incredible enrichment and profile of those subjects attracting students, parents, and visitors to the school and we have staff who are putting this at the core of the school. Digital learning and STEM subjects are vitally important to develop this further. The work of Applied, Science, DT, and Maths in these areas gives the school an exceptional base for STEM. Underpinning all of this is support of the curriculum through the skills development of the individual through the strong PSHE programmes exceptionally led by the Heads of Year as the senior middle leaders of pastoral in Wyedean. Our core subjects from the Challenge Partners "Area of Excellence" in English to the solid Social Science subjects in Humanities means we have a rich and challenging curriculum in place already with outstanding educators. We have a very admirable and niche curriculum at Wyedean already and one we are proud of especially through the way individuals have led this in a deficit budget such as the Food Tech students and the café initiative and the work with BTEC and vocational. All have a rightful place in a broad and balanced, cost effective curriculum. It is an exciting development and key priority of the school to ensure we have a World Class 21st Century curriculum to offer students linked to developing life skills and careers beyond.

I was asked to contribute in early July to an OECD report and was interviewed on Skype by the report's author in Washington, Richard Colvin. It was a great way to end a long week on a Friday afternoon talking to someone as eminent as Richard about the importance of global learning for international education. I was reminded of this as the Year 10s here took part in an incredible video conference last week with

Syrian refugee children as part of their MFL lesson as they trialled this project with the British Council. There have been many powerful moments over this academic year and this certainly was one of them. Our young people need to be able to think critically about their World and ask the deeper questions as they work to solve global issues as the next generation of leaders. The World is not going to get smaller and globalisation in our economy, our society, our environment, and our politics is not going to diminish. I will address this theme in Poland as I have been asked to speak at a conference of international educators in Cracow in September with the British Council looking at the impact of Brexit, educational leadership, and what we should be doing with our curriculum in schools.

The next logical development of the curriculum is to look at outstanding and exceptional curriculum models such as the International Baccalaureate as a possibility for Wyedean. There is a movement in England to develop an "English National Baccalaureate" based on the IB model but we are committed to international and global learning and the IB is one of the strongest gold standard brands in education in the World. Already we have looked at a number of successful IB schools and spoken to the IBO as we are investigating this model further. Wyedean will continue to develop a holistic, broad, joined up, and rich existing curriculum model that allows all of our students to flourish, achieve, and access a C21st economy and society. We have the opportunity to offer something exciting and World Class in our education here that similar state or even independent schools will not offer, as they are constricted by their education model or their narrow educational leadership. This is a very exciting initiative to continue to develop in the school over the next few years and the more people that are involved the more we can question, challenge, and develop what is right for Wyedean School.

PART 3: SEPTEMBER 2017 - JULY 2018

1 September 2017

"If we cannot change the World ourselves, we might by creating leaders who can through education." Kurt Hahn

As I look out of my cabin window where I sit writing this first blog of the new academic year, it seems summer and autumn are battling to see who will prevail as the day feels like any traditional summer's hot day in July, but the dead leaves from my Siberian birch are all over the lawn, and most plants are now beginning to die back ready for the change in season. It definitely is the first of September. In Russian and Eastern European countries, this day is celebrated as the "Day of Knowledge" and is a great way for students, educators, schools, parents, and entire communities to recognise and acknowledge the vital importance of education; not just for the future prosperity of those societies but it is about empowering the next generation to pick up the baton and carry it further forward. I am speaking at an international education conference in Poland in a couple of weeks' time with the British Council on the themes of global learning, educational leadership, and influence/impact in the classroom. I have thought all summer about what I am going to say to this prestigious audience about the impact and influence of beliefs and approaches of education on our students in the UK, Europe, and across the globe as they step up to take their roles shaped by these systems and philosophies.

I was reminded of the torch being passed onto former students of mine when an old IB student and now a very successful vet got in contact recently to offer her assistance with current students who may be looking at going down the veterinary science route. Another former IB student of mine contacted me at the start of the summer to let me know he had been awarded a place at a prestigious forum this autumn to represent young business leaders at an international conference, looking at the knowledge and skills needed by young leaders as the challenges of the 21st century continue to unfold, and a common and global approach needs to be devised. As I reminded him, not bad for a lad from Mozambique who barely made it through the school gates for the first three years of secondary school, written off by so many of his teachers until he took the IB and now he has a phenomenal career at Apple. What these two former students epitomise for me is what I have known for my entire career to date, 24 years this year as an educator, that there is a natural cycle to education which is about people who do trail blaze putting something back to ensure there is a solid conveyor belt moving forward, but more importantly, to inspire the next generation onto greater ambition. And this goes way beyond the dogmatic narrowing of the curriculum and the slavish adherence to exams that so many schools have chosen to focus on.

I have mentioned it before here in this blog, but it is worth mentioning again as I seem to be behind the same bus around north Bristol this summer; Sidcot is an IB school in Somerset and they have the very simple but thought-provoking message for their open day advert for this month "We are more than just an exams factory". Summing up a simple but brilliant holistic approach to educating the whole of the individual so that they are not just leaving school with relevant qualifications but also skills ranging from critical thinking to resilience that will help them navigate their next stages and life. There is something about a holistic educational approach that a few schools are still brave enough to offer, despite the onslaught of the current education ideology, and the students leaving these schools have far better well-being and a growth mind set to cope with the challenges and complexities of this globalised world. All education should be about this and all educators should have this in their core beliefs about why they want to work with young people.

This August my colleagues, students, parents, governors, and our local communities got to celebrate again the remarkable achievement of the A Level, BTEC, and GCSE results at Wyedean. I will never lose the sheer emotion of these two days as students (and staff and parents) nervously anticipate and find out their results from their hard work for over two years. This August the two cohorts were the guinea pigs of educational reforms in qualifications and curriculum dreamt up by a secretary of state long gone from the scene, but schools are coping with the legacy of the sheer amount of reforms across the whole of education impacting so many areas with such a short time of implementation. My colleagues have been nothing short of heroic in their determination and resolution to ensure the students have not suffered in all of this. I look at the challenges for the new academic year and the crisis in school funding fills me with trepidation as a principal. Knowing what my school has had to do to attract increased numbers, develop a broad and unique curriculum, retain the best staff, and deal with ageing infrastructure because of public finances and the wider crisis of the domination of the Brexit decision at the heart of current national governance.

So as I watch the autumn creep slowly across my garden on the sunny 1st September, the Day of Knowledge, and I finish my "state of the union" address to deliver to my colleagues this coming Monday, I look very inwardly at finding the optimism as a school leader to be able to look to better times, and to make sure the new academic year is rich in what we want for our young people to nurture them, and for our young people to enjoy and experience a year, to make sure their lives are better permanently for being in our educational care. It's the tough challenge of anyone in education and the reason why this job is a vocation. I would like to add personally though, I never really expected the sports car or the playboy lifestyle when I picked up my first piece of chalk. I will tell my colleagues on Monday what an incredible job they did in the academic year 2016-17. I will share with them the success and the moments we create and celebrate daily at Wyedean with our community. I will tell them categorically that all school leaders are the lightning rods and it's our job to soak up the fads, directives, whims, and whatever else gets thrown at us to ensure they can do their jobs educating our young people for the future. I will make it clear that we will continue to develop a World Class 21st Century learning holistic learning experience anchored on creativity, digital and global learning because the century is going to need our young people to be able to adapt and change and think and reflect and build a better World for the future. And as this is the celebration of the Day of Knowledge I am going to quote a Victorian Headteacher who was way ahead of his time and still stands true when the point of education is in question. Dr Arnold said education was an introduction to the very best of what has been said and thought. We need to remember that in a globalised, technology complex world, the need for knowledge and wisdom has never been more to tackle the laziness of "google information" on the individual. Today the great Anthony Seldon, one of my heroes, urged school leaders in the TES to be even more ambitious and make their schools even better as centres of education.

"Leave our 19th-century schools system behind – we should all be teaching entrepreneurship and exposing students to the arts, creativity, sport, adventure and challenge. In 25 years' time, we will look back at schools today and ask ourselves if we were stark raving mad to have let them be so narrow and so low-achieving. We need schools for the 21st century but we have a school model designed in the 19th century..."

This may be hard for individuals who have received for several years now nothing but below inflation pay awards, reduced resources, and expectations of further bureaucracy and empty judgements from a creaking system but it is one challenge we must find a way around as educators this coming academic year. The quote from Kurt Hahn has always been on my classroom and study wall throughout my education career because if I do need to dig deeper inwardly to find optimism to motivate my colleagues as their principal on Monday morning then I need to think about the likes of my two former IB students that contacted me this summer. I need to think about their incredible contributions, and countless others because of the influence of decent hardworking educators, that these former students are making to a better society thanks to their education and compassion. That is the educational challenge always and it's not for the faint hearted or the lover of the cheap and quick reward. Hearts and minds the clarion call on Monday, like every year.

2 October 2017

"The function of education is to teach one to think intensively and to think critically. Intelligence plus character – that is the goal of true education." Martin Luther King, Jr.

"Don't be pushed by your problems. Be led by your dreams." Ralph Waldo Emerson

An old Spanish friend from university (or should that read Catalan friend? She claims both labels as well as a European and citizen of the World) is spending the first Monday of October not only cleaning up her school in the northern suburbs of Barcelona today but also making sure her colleagues and school parents are ok following the violence yesterday across Catalonia. As for her students, there are a few hurt following Sunday's events and the response from the police to people trying to vote. As an educator, she will also find the time and words to sit down and try to explain to her students what could possibly happen next for their country. Last Friday here in school just before I left for a meeting of Gloucestershire Heads I spoke with the staff of the Spanish school visiting from Catalonia who are with us for a few weeks with our students, about the possible outcomes of the vote on Sunday. There are often so many moments in school where educators are in the difficult position of explaining difficult events in a way that is not patronising or shying away from unpalatable issues but at the same time students understand and are then left in the position where they can ask the right questions to further that understanding. One of the reasons the Spanish students from Vigo are in Wyedean School now is because we believe as a school our students and school community should be actively engaged and exposed to a wider world. I have a skype session this week with the British Council and some of our Year 10 students are talking to a student from Kazakhstan who has won a STEM competition to come to the UK and meet Professor Stephen Hawking.

I have a number of thoughts as I drive across the old Severn Bridge either home to Bristol or to school at Wyedean. Three that have been floating around in my head for a couple of weeks now since I spoke at an international conference in

Poland. So, in no particular order: 1) The Finnish education system is not as great as everyone thinks it is; 2) Educators are impotent; and 3) Students exposed to internationalism will not necessarily become "global citizens".

The conference in Poland was an interesting gathering of largely Nordic and Eastern European educational academics who have been meeting on an annual basis since the fall of the Berlin Wall. It was also a nice excuse to be back in Cracow especially as in a previous role as head of history I took A Level and IB students there regularly as part of a wider school tour of history and politics.

It struck me on a very warm September afternoon in a Polish primary school watching students my daughter's age perform their national songs and dances to a small group of international educators how political education really is. This moved from theory to fact when I spoke to a number of Polish academics and educators about the hard nationalist movement sweeping through Polish politics and society. In textbooks on history, in hardening social attitudes where it was once progressive, an academic from the auspicious and august host university, Copernicus's own alma mater, Jagiellonian, founded in 1364, said hundreds of school leaders had been dismissed that summer because they did not tow the government line of education.

The keynote speaker on the Friday night in the historic senate room of Jagiellonian, Professor Maria Mendal of the University of Gdansk, warned of the dangers of following the neo-liberal model too far in schools where the focus of education is lost to a business model that treats children and educators as a business commodity. Whereas this has been part of the landscape in the UK and USA for some time, it is a model, with all its faults and excesses, being rolled out across the former Warsaw Pact eastern European countries. I found myself challenging a speaker in one of the lectures to outline precisely when he believed this was "golden age" of education, what it looked like and where it did exist now? It got a good applause as a question but not an answer.

I am not sure I could get an answer to that question and when we had the Open Evening here for Year 6 last Thursday I tried to answer my own questions from Poland just before I spoke to parents. I mentioned there were three questions I carried home from the conference and I was very fortunate to have had a short but illuminating conversation with Eeva-Kaisa Ikonen, superintendent of education from Helsinki. Eeva's talk was fascinating because it started asking, "How do you improve a system that works?" in relation to Finland who tops OECD studies and PISA rankings regularly. The challenge for Finland, Eeva told me, is to anticipate the changes in skills, pedagogy, leadership, society, neurology, and technology that are happening now and almost future proof the education system even if that means dropping down the PISA rankings and suffering short term politically. My heart beats faster just to contemplate the leadership and vision involved in such a farsighted ambition. I am definitely taking Eeva's invitation to go to Helsinki to see what her and her colleagues are planning for in their vision of education.

Then in another talk looking at the Anthropocene era we are now in, I did come away feeling very pessimistic as the speaker loudly boomed in what can only be described as a Polish-East Ridings of Yorkshire accent, "educators are impotent" in the face of these huge societal challenges and preparing young people to lead on them. Which brought me to my own talk on the Saturday afternoon on global learning and what we are doing at Wyedean School. Besides the fact I spoke too fast for the translation and used far too many Americanisms, it really made me think when I was asked in the Q&A about whether exposing students to international education made them any more of a global citizen or less. I did think of 101 examples of when I was on the British Council's International School Award panel and I would cringe at the clumsy but well intended global learning opportunities in schools around the UK. We live in a very global society in 2017 but this very globalisation and fast-paced change linked to the extraordinary advances in technology has left so many communities and societies around the World grasping to make sense and keep up or simply to dis-engage. My dear friend in Moldova wrote to me this morning, on WhatsApp of course, about the horrific shooting at a concert in Las Vegas following the dreadful violence in Catalonia, the floods in the Caribbean, the removal of the Muslim population of Myanmar and the murders at Marseilles train station on Sunday. She is a wonderful optimist but she wrote, *"The World seems to have gone crazy"*.

115

It does seem that way sometimes and yet last week I sat with a great friend and parent of Wyedean School, Mike Peckham along with his son Ashraf, to plan the South West and Wales conference we are holding here on the 9th December entitled "Making Sense of the World now". I am a little bit worried that the aim of the conference maybe promising too much on the back of this weekend's events but at the same time the line-up of speakers and workshops for 16-19 year old students are tackling a range of topics from fake news and the media, religion in the C21st, to identity and democracy. It made me feel hopeful and think of the MLK quote starting this blog about giving students the opportunities and ability to question and think critically. I wish I were at the University of Bristol this week as Wyedean School Year 12 debaters Matt Ward and Hannah Purcell have been selected to take part in a special event looking at the implications of the Brexit vote and process, and what the future of the UK may well be according to the young people who will lead it one day.

Emerson was right to warn of not being pushed by problems and sometimes it is all too apparent the barriers and problems we face along the way. As we get further into autumn and the weeks of this term are ticking by until half term break I want to be focused on and led by dreams and ambitions more as a school leader. I get it from the buzz in the corridors; the Wednesday teaching and learning briefing; my school teams; the kind emails from parents; the energy of the kids out in the school yard at break and lunch; seeing the school showcased at open evening and the daily flood of pictures on Twitter highlighting compelling learning with the knowledge we are in the best job in the World to face the future with confidence. We are educators in the business of education after all.

28 October 2017

School Improvement through Challenge Partners, the enormous impact of peer review.

"Back in Devon after three brilliant days @WyedeanSchool meeting passionate staff and great students. Fantastic leadership." Jamie Wordsworth @jamiew23 Oct 18

"Lovely and inspiring couple of days reviewing @WyedeanSchool with @ChallengePartnr What a fab place, and such great kids." Jane Werry @JaneWerry Oct 18

Tweets from two of the reviewers from Challenge Partners who reviewed Wyedean School 16-18 October 2017.

Hen Coleg is the oldest part of the University of Aberystwyth and sits right on the sea front facing the winds and sea spray head on from the Irish Sea. It is a fascinating Victorian gothic structure that started life out as a railway station and grand hotel for visitors in the 1860s. It never got that far, and instead became the centrepiece of the first university college for Wales, of which a significant proportion of the funds raised came from Welsh worker subscriptions to ensure that their children could receive a university education. I think it is that fact alone that has always made me look at these buildings with awe at the power of foresight, aspiration, and education. The university at Aberystwyth has certainly grown significantly since the 1860s and now sits proudly all the way up the very steep Penglais Hill. Hen Coleg's future is uncertain as a building but I was very fortunate over twenty years ago to not only heed the advice of a wise colleague from Bootham School to get my PGCE and leave York but to also return to Wales. I have always considered the year I spent in this atmospheric university town by the sea the most important year of developing in me the love of teaching and learning in a much more formal way. My interview was an awful January day having travelled down from York on the train through a snowy and cold landscape to arrive in what I can only describe as a desolate and icy windswept place. Whenever I heard Dylan Thomas say, "bible black" in "Under Milk Wood" at the start of the play I think of 'Aber' on that day it was so bleak. The head of the History course was the brilliant Dr Gareth Evans, sadly no longer alive but generations of educators were inspired by this great pedagogic Gog (a Welshman from the north). It's fair to say I have had a few interviews in my time with some tough interviewers but the yardstick has always been the day I sat in Dr Evans' study staring out to the freezing black/brown waves and sky for several hours being genuinely grilled on why I wanted to be a teacher and why I loved history. He referred to me throughout as the "Man of the Marches", they have long memories in north Wales, especially Corwen, and at the end of the meeting, I was happy to go back to York and carry on working in a private school but as an unqualified teacher, when he surprised me by very generously offering me a place on the course there and then. I may have had a beer on the train home back to the north of England. The rest, as they say, was history, but I owe a lot to this place and individual as a teacher and school leader for the example it set and taught me for my career in education.

These memories came flooding back to me this half term break, as if they had only just happened last week, when I walked around an empty and quiet Hen Coleg showing not only my wife and kids the wonderful lecture theatre, halls, and library but it was also in the company of my old teacher and mentor from my own school. Life has a funny way of coming back to starting points when you least expect it, and I sat in the old lecture theatre, in the front seats where Dr Evans' referred to the group of us as the "Pontypool front row" and amongst the reminiscing I hoped that I have lived up to the high aspirations, service, intellectual ambitions, and dedication as an educator which were the hallmark of the ethos and culture of the education department at Aberystwyth. I even remembered the inscription of the first book my old teacher gave me as a 14-year-old to read, "The Road to Wigan Pier". It read; "Carry the flame and defend the weak". I have it here in front of me now as I write, and it still resonates deeply within me when I think of the role we have as educators in schools. Ironically on my shelves it is next to Orwell's other classic from the 1930s, "Homage to Catalonia".

Wyedean School had its annual review from Challenge Partners just before half term. This consisted of a three day visit by five colleagues who work as senior school leaders or with Ofsted, and came into school to look at the leadership, the school improvement plans, the standards, and data all centred around the quality of the learning environment and the teaching and learning. The two tweets at the top of this blog are the comments from two of the reviewers.

I will say it again; I am so proud of Wyedean School, the students, the community, and above all my colleagues who I work with. The review for me is how we should be raising standards and improving schools not just in England but in the UK and other countries. The review team essentially do it "with the school" not "to the school" using the language of "What Went Well – WWW" and "Even Better If – EBI". Challenge Partners is a school improvement network that came from the London Challenge and now has 400 schools in its national network. At the heart of the collaboration, support and critical friendship is the desire to improve education and schools. It is a model that will deliver the 21st century learning schools so badly need.

The growth of leadership and teaching in Wyedean from being a member of Challenge Partners is astonishing and this was further evidenced this summer with the amazing results in Key Stage 4 and 5. The review is very thorough, but it is a conversation and I know as principal the time I spent with these external reviewers from other schools and Ofsted was invaluable in how I lead the school and take it forward. It is also an opportunity to validate the hard work of the last few years and there was no prouder moment than the Thursday before half term standing in the staffroom for a special briefing reading to colleagues the first initial feedback from the draft report.

My colleagues in the Applied Learning Area under the brilliant leadership of Emma Williams were chosen this year to be put forward as an "Area of Excellence" for Vocational Education and BTEC. This is an area of the school that is not only a real strength of Wyedean in terms of teaching and results but their innovations to learning are something I am fortunate to have in Wyedean School. They more than smashed the review over the three days and this year we have a working group looking at the IB Career related programme to implement at the school in the next couple of years. Last year it was the fantastic English Learning Area, validated as an area of excellence, a judgement reinforced from the review

119

again this year. The wider picture for education seems so gloomy at times nationally especially on funding but sitting in Full Governors just before the break reporting back to the trustees on the success of the school and the things we still must do to become high performing felt as if a milestone had been reached for Wyedean School. There is so much hard work, passion, and dedication from the entire school community driving this remarkable institution forward I pinch myself at times.

Looking ahead to the next 7 weeks and the run up to Christmas with the clocks going back and colder, darker days to come, the vital and valuable daily work continues for the school. Year 11 have their mocks to face, the International Christmas fair is being planned for December, the Awards Evening being held in St Mary's church for the first time on the 6th December will be a phenomenal celebration of our students in all fields and capacities, and we have the Open Evening for Sixth Form on the 30th November. I must make mention of several individual student successes we celebrated this autumn already. At the Cheltenham Festival, Year 13 student, James Robertson, was honoured with an award from the playwright and author Alan Bennett. James has ensured that the local library in Bream has stayed open serving the community in the central Forest of Dean. Words fail me as a principal to describe the pride I feel for James' work. Year 11 student, Finley Wood, continued his incredible climbing success in becoming British national champion at the British Lead climbing championships. When I spoke to him he was as modest as ever, but it is some trajectory this young man is on. I had tea in my study with Ollie Moss and Milly Connor just before the break to congratulate them on their national successes respectively in golf and dance.

The incredible work of the school's LGBTQ+ group has been recognised as a national case study by the Department of Education this month and staff and students have shown real leadership and transformative education in their work and support of LGBTQ+ in the school. I am encouraged whenever I hear the head of Ofsted talk about the importance of the wider and richer curriculum for all students and how we should be broadening educational opportunities not narrowing them. That evening the geography teachers were taking their A Level students to a special lecture at the

University of Bristol. The lead reviewer of Challenge Partners, came to see my Year 12 critical thinking group in full debate (female equality and glass ceilings the topic that week) in my room during the review and afterwards we both agreed completely that schools should be offering as much as we can to give these young people skills, qualifications, opportunities, life chances to develop and take them onto their next path as leaders in society. This is one of the reasons Wyedean School is working with Mike Peckham to put on a special conference on the 9th December for young people entitled "Making Sense of the World". There are details on the school website and social media and this is a free conference for young people. There is a very strong line up of national speakers and I am really honoured that Baroness Royall and the Rt Hon Mark Harper MP, as Forest of Dean senior political figures will be there to open and close what should be a rich conference full of ideas and ways forward. I can live with the annual reports on the unfairness and perceived bias of Oxbridge colleges because I know the education at Wyedean School is based around the old maxim of Dr Arnold of Rugby *an introduction to the very best of what has been said and thought"*. Still applicable 170 years later and even Malala jokingly said this week winning the Nobel Peace prize didn't get her the head girl role of her school or help her with her Oxford interview.

I have a clutch of assemblies this half term coming to give for all year groups but hopefully none of the "traditional" beloved of some school leaders of the work harder, do your ties up and tuck in shirts variation. I am also lucky to be attending an EU-eTwinning conference this weekend coming up in of all the glamorous places my adopted home city of Bristol. I feel very honoured to have been invited to this conference as an ambassador for the British Council but will also get to meet and work with my partner school from Moldova.

On the 17th November, I have been invited to give a talk to a special British Council conference in London about the development of international education in the current climate of a more inward-looking nationalism around Europe and the world, and how global education can counter this narrative. I have contributed two pieces for books on international education and leadership for a Canadian publication from the University of Toronto and one on the impact of neo-liberalism on education for a book from the University of Gdansk. Both books are out this December. I am fortunate to be visiting and spending time at UWC Atlantic College as a guest of the principal Colin Jenkins this month. A pantheon to the very ideas of international learning and the IB if ever there was one.

I have teased my Vice Principal Academic, Gwennan Jeremiah, that I too was seen during the review with my Year 12 critical thinking group, she doesn't buy it either, but I think integrity and heart as an educator is something Dr Gareth Evans was getting from me as a "Man of the Marches" all those years ago. I have an incredible director of Teaching and Learning at Wyedean in Julie Smith, and we constantly talk about ourselves as learners and how we need to exemplify this always. Education is no ordinary job and it is far too important to see as a mere process. It is also something that happens over a long period of time and nobody is ever sure what they may discover about themselves on the way, what they might learn, and know or who they might become because of the influence of a good educator and education. This is what makes the role so daunting but so exciting. I still feel the same as I did when I stood on the platform at Aberystwyth station clutching my letter confirming me on the PGCE course knowing that I was in the right place, at the right time, and with the right people. A feeling not changed as I type this blog nearly 23 years later.

8 November 2017

Turning strategy and leadership into a positive culture and climate.

"The strong man holds in a living blend strongly marked opposites. Not ordinarily do men achieve this balance of opposites. The idealists are not usually realistic, and the realists are not usually idealistic. The militant are not generally known to be passive, nor the passive to be militant. Seldom are the humble self-assertive, or the self-assertive humble. But life at its best is a creative synthesis of opposites in fruitful harmony. The philosopher Hegel said that truth is found neither in the thesis nor the antithesis, but in an emergent synthesis that reconciles the two."

A tough mind and a tender heart, sermon by Martin Luther King Jr.

Despite the fact, I have lived in Bristol for just over 20 years it is to my shame and embarrassment that I have never once been inside the mighty St Mary Redcliffe church. From the harbour, it seems more like a cathedral with its soaring spire looking down at the same Bristol docks and the Welsh Back from where the likes of Cabot sailed from in 1497 to discover Newfoundland; five years after Columbus, Cabot's fellow Italian sailor, first sighted land and claimed the "New World" for Spain. By chance, last Friday I finally found myself inside one of England's largest parish churches during the lunch break of the European education conference which I was attending in Bristol; the hotel and venue was just opposite on the other side of the road. I am hoping my Moldovan school partner, Tatiana Popa, didn't mind the excursion either but it did seem a good opportunity for a visit.

My American friend and colleague from Virginia, was also in the UK with his IB students. Looking at the photos of their trip on Twitter reminded me of a comment he made to me years ago when we first started to work collaboratively as global educators, back in the days when we were young idealistic trans-Atlantic IB coordinators together. He told me he loved Britain simply for the fact there was so much history packed into such a small space. Which made sense coming from an American and most of his country's history is packed into just the Old Dominion itself where he hails from. I have always appreciated his remark and thought about it when I came across the armour, memorial, and tomb of one Admiral William Penn. Penn died in 1670 but King Charles II still owed him a huge amount of money. Charles Stuart handed over to Penn's son, also called William, a huge tract of land from the Americas, which is now modern day Pennsylvania, and Delaware. I have always been more interested in the Mid-Atlantic States and have spent many hours walking around the Quaker capital that is the city of brotherly love, Philadelphia. Not necessarily for the run up the "Rocky Steps" or the impressive visit to Independence Hall and not even for the Liberty Bell, but definitely for a Philly cheesesteak in South Philly at either Geno's or Pat's. I have never been able to decide which of the original claimants to this hot sandwich I have preferred, but I am always struck by the sign at the counter window at the Italian-American, son of refugees

Geno's that reads *"If you can read this sign, thank a teacher. If you can read it in English, thank a Marine"*.

To find Admiral William Penn buried in Bristol struck a real chord in the history student in me, especially as it is a sort of place of pilgrimage for a certain type of American visitor. His son, William Penn, is definitely worth reading up on. As is the son's remarkable second wife, Hannah Callowhill Penn. A Quaker from my part of Bristol originally and one of the first female leaders in the colonial period only really being recognised now for leading and building Pennsylvania for six years after her husband's death. The colony of Pennsylvania that was developed by William and Hannah as a tolerant Quaker colony in contrast to the slave colony of Virginia and Puritan colony of Massachusetts, served as the inspiration for the United States constitution. Unfortunately, infamous Bristol sons like Edward Colston and the city's heavy involvement in the slave trade of the C17th and C18th is a more unsavoury connection between the city and the southern colonies and Deep South. It was also no coincidence that Pennsylvania became one of the most prosperous colonies in the British Empire and the place for the fledgling USA to declare independence, commencing one of the most fascinating experiments in modern government. Geno's counter sign and President Trump being very much part of that democratic pluralism the Founders envisaged. I have always liked the Welsh connection with Pennsylvania too and there was a time during the 18th century when there were more Welsh language newspapers and books printed in Philadelphia than actually in Wales. One of the oldest Welsh language societies established in the city in 1729 is still going very strong to this day. Penn's vision, leadership, and strategy for Pennsylvania is nothing short of inspirational and so I felt humbled to be staring at his father's tomb in a Bristol church last Friday, having spent the last 24 hours in a conference of several hundred European educators from all across the continent.

The conference was over several days and it was an opportunity to listen and talk to a wide range of educators and policy influencers from across Europe. I think the main thing that struck me throughout as I reflected on Saturday night in a field in Wiltshire watching with my family and Moldovan partner a huge bonfire and fireworks display, was the optimism that exuded from so many different school stories. I listened to a remarkable teacher from a small village school in the mountains of Croatia describe the leadership and vision she had to ensure the students of that school connected to others from across Europe as a meaningful and regular part of their education. The school barely had heating or materials and the local farm animals would come and drink out of the school's pond during the day, but this educator's strategy ensured she engaged her community with the education of their children. Because of her tenacity, this tiny mountain village school had won European awards and was being showcased in Bristol to hundreds of European educators. There were many similar examples throughout the conference.

After four years of working with Tatiana Popa, I finally got to meet this remarkable Moldovan educator who is one of the most inspirational teachers I know. Showing her proudly round Wyedean School on Friday morning where she was able to spend time with another remarkable educator Wyedean is fortunate to have in Lucy McManus, the Year 10 English class were able to meet the teacher they have been speaking to over Skype and reading poems to their Moldovan counterparts in Chisinau. Tatiana believes passionately in the transformative power of education, languages, and learning. Where she teaches, in one of Europe's poorest countries she sees it as vital that the students in her care are able to use their education to improve their opportunities and life chances. The culture and climate of her classrooms resonate this aspiration and it is very humbling to work with such an educator. She epitomises hope and a positive role model for young Moldovans. I found myself in several debates around the future of Europe and whether or not the opportunity for the UK to engage in such a European forum would exist in the near future.

I am currently working on my talk for the British Council policy forum and dialogue in London on the 17th November. I have been asked to speak to policy makers about global learning and leadership in schools in this uncertain educational and political climate. I know what Wyedean School's ambitions are for World Class 21st century learning, but it is even more clear following the weekend's conference and my discussions with school leaders that I am fortunate to be able to determine to a large extent this direction for the school as principal with the support of governors, staff, and community. Although having seen a few posts on social media from colleagues I worked with on the weekend from Greece, Bulgaria, and Croatia I did have to point out that I am not "the principal of the Harry Potter School" and I don't have the powers to change what is already the fine school name that is Wyedean. Hopefully no governors were offended or even our most famous former student, JK Rowling. I did twitter this in response immediately.

In this context, I was looking at the draft Challenge Partners report from the Review Team for Wyedean School that took place a few weeks ago. My eyes focussed immediately on these lines below as I thought about the leadership and strategy that had developed the positive school culture and climate in the school.

"There is an uncompromising drive by school leaders to improve and maintain the highest levels of achievement and personal development for all students.

Evidence of the impact of leadership at all levels can be seen in the school's impressive recent performance, especially in the enhanced rates of progress for English and mathematics.

The principal is passionately committed to the school and ensures that the well-being of staff and pupils is at the heart of the school's work.

The principal and staff place a great emphasis on the importance of a sense of community.

The school has a shared vision of where it wants to be and how to get there. This is regularly articulated and re-visited so that all staff understand the importance of continuous improvement.

The school has a strong moral purpose, which is clearly and passionately articulated by all staff. The school's ethos is rooted in strong values and high levels of mutual respect amongst all members of the school community.

The very positive relationships that exist between leaders, staff, and students ensure that every student has the best opportunity to achieve. Evidence of these warm relationships were manifest during learning walks and observations throughout the review.

There are new senior and middle leadership teams in place after a period of uncertainty and significant change. School leaders confirm that they feel fully empowered to make decisions and that they are listened to.

The enhanced role of middle leadership is integral to the school's success. Middle leaders have been given very helpful support, training, and coaching. As a result, the middle leadership team is now successfully driving the school's quality assurance process forward. All leaders are reflective practitioners who are constantly striving to improve their own leadership skills, teaching ability, and learning outcomes for students.

The focus on strengthening teaching and leadership capacity across the school is demonstrated by the very strong commitment to continuing professional development (CPD). Wider networking is a significant strength of the school and staff talk confidently about the projects that they have led on within school as part of this process."

The gala meal for the conference was held on Friday night in the wonderful Bristol City Museum, my own children's favourite museum, and the scene of many a good Saturday afternoon after a burger and milkshake at Rocotillos opposite on Queens Road. This Victorian museum donated by the tobacco magnate Henry Wills, which houses so many eclectic collections with all sorts of artefacts and exhibitions looted, stolen, borrowed, and bought from across the old Empire and the wider globe, hosted a dinner of several hundred forward looking European educators, all passionate and committed to the power of learning and education. It was hard not to think of the words about Wyedean from the Challenge Partners report, and the hope that this conference has given me in terms of optimism looking forward in education. What MLK referred to as the "creative synthesis of the realists and the idealists" can be seen on how we use leadership to turn strategy into a positive educational climate and culture and therefore there is always hope where educators and education is concerned. I watched a few Danish and German teachers dance rather too enthusiastically to Abba's "Waterloo" under the 1910 Bristol Boxkite hanging from the vaulted ceiling of the museum. I also witnessed less "fruitful harmony" in the groovy Nordic moves but at least they were letting their hair down in a foreign city which even teachers are allowed to do now and again. The fact they did not fall over proved there is always hope with educators.

22 November 2017

Trying not to sweat the small stuff in leadership and knowing when a hill is worth taking a stand on as a leader.

From: Lynes, Rob (British Council) Sent: 21 November 2017 08:23 To: Robert Ford

"Dear Rob, thank you. It was a pleasure to meet you and thank you for your excellent contribution to the discussion. I would love to visit Wyedean at some point. Colleagues speak very highly of the fantastic work you do there. Best wishes, Rob" Rob Lynes | Regional Director UK, British Council

Email regarding the British Council Policy Forum dialogue in London on Friday 17th November:

"Dear Rob and all staff at Wyedean School, ...I wanted to send a short thank you note for your hospitality and time through your Challenge Partner Review. I thoroughly enjoyed the experience and left feeling proud of Wyedean and the journey it is on. Wishing you and your team the very best for the future – I am keeping up to date on Twitter." Jamie Wordsworth, Deputy Headteacher, St James School, Exeter, Nov 2017

Like many school leaders in England today I am anxiously waiting to hear what the Chancellor has to say in the budget statement regarding any increase in school funding from the chronically underfunded situation schools have had to cope with now for too long. I know I will not ask already hard-pressed families in my school community to contribute to school funding to assist in buying the very basics, as I know a number of school leaders have been forced to do already. We completed the 2016-17 annual appraisal cycle a few weeks ago and I know of some of my school leaders are not taking their

128

well-deserved and thoroughly merited pay progression awards because of the current financial situation in the school. Linked to a national public service pay cap that has been kept at 1% and way below inflation for over 7 years now means real term incomes have kept falling. The additional high costs that schools have to meet are making already delicately balanced budgets for the year without a reserve to help when colleagues fall ill or a boiler breaks in winter tip dangerously closer to an abyss that too many schools are now facing. This is why there is huge momentum around a national campaign for fairer funding in schools and only last week headteachers' marching to Downing St with a letter calling for fairer school funding supported by 1000s of schools.

Wyedean School has a strong projected financial trajectory over the next few years because of all the hard work and necessary difficult decisions undertaken in making cost efficiencies and savings as well as the strong promotion of the outstanding education. This has grown the school back to being oversubscribed with nearly 1100 students in two years from a low of close to 900. This is in an official falling roll area as well. Innovations in the curriculum such as Latin, Classics, and Mandarin have come about because we have been very proactive in bidding for these specific funds from outside agencies and we believe strongly in broader and unique educational opportunities. However, every time a colleague tells me they have personally paid for their classroom posters or provided prizes for a competition or not claimed a travel expense or contributed personally to make an educational visit viable I wince at the damage being done fundamentally to this noble profession and vital sector of our society and economy. In no way is this sweating the small stuff and educational funding is definitely a hill many educators, governors, school leaders, students, and parents are making a stand on now. Education is not attracting enough of the next generation of teachers needed to take the sector forward into the new ways of learning, new technologies, and the skills challenge we are facing as a society over the coming decades. If they do make it into teaching, they certainly are not staying long as the demands of the role and the often poor work-life balance in difficult educational and financial conditions becomes all too apparent. There is an interesting recent article in the Guardian worth a read about what we should do to convince teachers to stay in the profession:

https://www.theguardian.com/teacher-network/2017/nov/16/to-stop-teachers-leaving-the-profession-lets-help-them-make-a-difference

By extension the high calibre skilled school leaders sorely needed are not emerging in nearly enough numbers to take on the very demanding role of taking educational learning communities forward with hope and making sure educational opportunities and standards are the very best we can offer our young people and keep so many communities hopeful for the future. This is definitely not the small stuff in educational and national leadership.

I spent the other weekend in Bristol with my old and dear friend from Prince William County Schools in northern Virginia, Brian Bassett. Brian is one of the most inspiring advocates of the International Baccalaureate in the Americas and an exceptional school leader and IB coordinator. As we walked across Brunel's Clifton Suspension Bridge, with thankfully one of his students ensuring my three young daughters were not being too silly, we talked about the difficulties schools face financially in the UK and USA. We also spoke at length about the increasing difficulties in the relentless, often pointless educational initiatives that school leaders try to grapple with whilst balancing the very core of education with a focus on compelling learning, all very well intentioned, but still capricious and short term depending on the office holder. Even over fish and chips in my kitchen on Saturday evening, we still could not believe how something as inspirational and necessary for 21st century education & World Class curriculum like the IB has all but disappeared from UK state schools in the last ten years because of government short sightedness and short termism. We did break off as we got the fish and chips from Downend chippy as I pointed out where W.G. Grace once played his cricket – the English version of Babe Ruth helped make it clearer for Brian. His IB student, originally from El Salvador, coped admirably not only with her first battered haddock but was very polite about the bright green mushy peas. She did point out this was not something common in Latin American cuisine. My four-year-old singing John Denver's "Take me home" as we drove back along the M4 to their hotel late on a Saturday night before their Sunday flight home made the frustrations with education disappear for now. Brian has been a champion of international learning for so long now and has been recognised by the British Council for the developed work around IB curriculum he and his colleagues have undertaken with a number of UK schools over many years. Educators like Brian give us all hope in these times. I found his tweet @ibatgf, his school IB Twitter, for Thanksgiving, worth a read especially when we waste time sweating the small stuff:

"I am thankful for...the taxes I pay because means that I am employed; The clothes that fit a little too snug because it means I have enough to eat; A lawn that needs be mowed, windows that have to be washed, and gutters that need fixing means I have a home; All the complaining I hear about our government means I have freedom of speech; The huge pile of laundry and ironing because it means my loved ones are nearby; The alarm that goes off early in the morning because it means that I'm alive".

The hills I have decided to make a stand on as school leader are the ones I believe worth fighting on... This is simply ensuring that the students, staff, and community know that every day at Wyedean School we are focussed on our core purpose of supporting our young people, delivering compelling learning, exciting education, and that we are preparing our students for the future as global citizens. Even an uncertain one. After all, this is a job far too important for a process driven technocrat who is more concerned with salary and status rather than the transformational power of education a good committed leader can wield effectively that can change societies for the better.

If I look through the last few days alone to illustrate what has happened at Wyedean to develop our positive culture: Friday I skyped in the morning with staff and students of Heritage International School, Chisinau for international education week; the Christmas International Card competition delivered outstanding entries from students from across the school; The students and staff raised over a £1000 for Children in Need and Chepstow Foodbank; the year 10 students who help on a Thursday at the Forest of Dean Baby Bank have been commended and will appear on a BBC news story; we started our approved Erasmus + partnership with

MFL and Spanish schools; MLF started working officially with Ecuadorean students this week; Year 7 students came 5th in the British Schools Orienteering Championships on Sunday; our Oxbridge applicants are going up to Cheltenham Ladies' College to work with them on interview techniques as we work together as two schools; the PE dept. played fixtures against various schools and took the teams to watch Newport County play in the evening; we held a safeguarding peer review with a local partner school, Dean Academy; one of our students, Pip Winter, finished just outside the top ten of 50 in the show jumping championship; Sixth Form Open Evening on the 30th Nov; The International Christmas Fair on the 4th Dec; Celebration Evening on the 6th Dec ...and on it goes on top of the day to day incredible learning seen in every classroom as I walk around this wonderful school daily.

Leadership is not only about inspiring others but also finding ways through the problems and breaking down the barriers. I always think of the outstanding school leaders I have been privileged to work with and I remember what characterised their leadership style and approach and for all of them it was not that they sweated the small stuff. Ian Small, Rob Gibson, Lindsey Hewson, Eric Lyne, Pat Firth, Norman Lowden, Chris Montacute, Bill Bixby, Cherif Sadki, to name but a few. I read an article this week where a school leader said they had looked at their three-year financial projection and it was just dire. That is what we also experienced here in December 2015 and we used our leadership to shape the future for Wyedean. As Obama once said, *"Our destiny is not written for us but by us"*.

Last Friday I had the honour to sit in a room at the top of the British Council in their London HQ in Spring Gardens, overlooking the whole of Whitehall through an incredible picture window. I was the first speaker opening up a policy forum dialogue between academics, school leaders, policy makers, and related organisations. All participants discussing ways on how we keep the importance of global education at the forefront of education in the UK and what that would and could look like over the next few decades. The paper I presented used my experiences as Wyedean principal and my experience as a school leader heavily involved nationally and internationally in global education for a number of years to advocate the importance of global learning providing a meaningful and relevant basis for education and to enhance engagement and compelling learning. I referenced two particular influences I had read in the last few months; the chief inspector of Ofsted's speech at Wellington around a broad curriculum and an article from Professor Bill Lucas of the University of Winchester. Dr Lucas is responsible for developing creative thinking for PISA and he not only warned about educators being caught up in the "false dichotomy of knowledge v skills" but also suggested we needed to stop referring to future educational aspirations for curriculum and learning as "21st century learning" – something I reference a lot. He made the valid point that we are 18 years now into a new millennium and Professor Lucas suggests it means we still have not worked out what they are and what is needed. Perhaps we have not and that is one of the fundamental problems in education right now. My Finnish colleague in Helsinki is leading a policy dialogue with school leaders there brave enough to break some of the more binary thinking on curriculum and learning and I am hoping I never meet another narrow minded school leader who believes the education diet in the average state school is about literacy and numeracy predominantly and everything else is frippery from arts to music to sport to languages.

I finished a long day having a glass of red wine in a plush law firm speaking to an eminent member of an international education group about exactly what exceptional World Class education should be about, what it looks like, and why social mobility should be at the heart of it in a global society. Food for thought on the late train back to Bristol and walking around post-Industrial Coalbrookdale with my children looking at the UNESCO site where the Darby's changed the World in the C18th as I visited family on Saturday back in my home county of Shropshire. I concluded that the best leaders know to avoid sweating the small stuff and which hills to stand on. My friend Brian will be with his family in the Appalachian Hills in West Virginia celebrating Thanksgiving this Thursday. I know he will be putting aside the trials, tribulations, and very real problems we have to find decent solutions to in our roles and responsibilities as educational leaders no matter what our context. At the same time our effectiveness is about how we see the problems and what we do working with others to solve them. This is how we intrinsically develop the ability as leaders to avoid sweating the small stuff and see the right hills to make a stand on.

18 December 2017

A school is not a school without its community.

"Alone we can do so little; together we can do so much." Helen Keller

"Life's most persistent and urgent question is, what are you doing for others?" Martin Luther King

"Tomorrow the morning will be clear and happy. This life is beautiful. Heart be wise." Anna Akhmatova

The "nine men of Madeley" story is rarely known outside of my own Shropshire village and certainly in terms of numbers doesn't compare to the loss of life in similar mining disasters in towns such as Gresford in 1934 or Senghenydd in 1913. What they all have in common though is the impact and response on those tightly knit mining communities when the feared loss of life dreaded by all families at the start of a working day confirmed wives, mothers, and their children's worst fears when the colliery hooter sounded, or the shouts of people could not be ignored any longer and there had indeed been a pit accident. In 1864, in the small Salopian mining town of Madeley, nine men and boys, the youngest was only 12 and the eldest 52, were being lowered down the 220-meter shaft of the Brick Kiln Leasow Crawstone Pit by a crude rope and hook system when at half way down, about the height of Big Ben, the central hook came undone and all nine men plunged to their death smashing to the bottom of the shaft below. The nine men were laid to rest side by side by their families and their community in the churchyard of Thomas Telford's imposing Madeley church. I remember as a child seeing the communal victim's tomb and being fascinated with this story, especially as my own father was doing pretty much the same job 120 years later in the same mines that had been the mainstay of the area since Medieval times. The deep coal mining industry has long gone in Britain and the few ex-miners left like my father are all happily and safely retired, and deservedly so. The communities in these areas that are left from Lanarkshire, Durham, Yorkshire, Lancashire, the Midlands, Kent, the South Wales valleys and our own Forest of Dean, where coal is an integral part of the story of the Forest, still contain something of the spirit and ties that made these places pull together so strongly and effectively when times were good and not so good.

I can't remember anything or anyone referring to the importance and strength of support of the wider community to schools when I undertook my Masters in educational leadership, and certainly nothing about the positive impact it could have from when I studied for my NPQH as I wanted to move further up into school leadership. No current research or any particular academic were recommended and in fact the whole shift in English education with the academy programme/Multi Academy Trusts (MAT) away from the local authorities in the last decade has seen a strange hybrid local education relationship develop where governance and school leadership often have very little in common with the very communities they are supposed to serve.

Interestingly enough my NPQH was through the Cabot Learning Federation which originally served as a MAT for only schools in East Bristol and it is the legacy of the now national schools' commissioner, Sir David Carter. These schools work closely with and serve the very communities their young people come from equipping and instilling in these students a sense of pride, aspiration, service, and lifelong learning in order that they enrich their community as adults. More importantly, they can give something back to inspire the next generation of young people.

In the recent December 2017 annual Ofsted report it is in fact these very Bristol schools that are now being applauded and recognised for this very work where once Bristol schools languished at the bottom of most educational tables. I have met Sir David on a few occasions and Wyedean was very fortunate to work with him and be in his "Race to Outstanding" group of SW schools in 2015 when I first started as Head at the school. Sir David is a very inspirational educator who has very much "walked the walk" as a headteacher in Gloucestershire and Bristol. His whole educational philosophy and approach is about raising standards and aspirations in schools to allow their very communities to thrive through this ethos. So much has recently been said about social mobility and the perceived lack of it for so many young people and yet if schools do not offer aspirational education, full of opportunities and a rich curriculum then this educational apartheid will be further entrenched. When I first started looking at the International Baccalaureate (IB) from my then Bristol school back in the early Millennium, as much as I was bowled over by the phenomenal education offered in UWC Atlantic College, it was in fact places using the IB like Broadgreen International School in one of the poorest parts of Liverpool, under the great school leader, Ian Andain, that impressed me most. Ian took the IB, an international curriculum rightly associated with rigour, intellectual development, and holistic education of the individual, but wrongly associated with elitism, and used it to raise aspirations and standards within his community in his area of Liverpool. The IB has always contained the very "community" section in the CAS element that underpins the whole baccalaureate structure of the IB, as much as the subjects, essay, and theory of knowledge components.

I have been very fortunate in my career to only have worked in schools that valued the relationship and support of the local community. I stood with my then Sixth Formers, along with the whole town, on too many occasions on the High Street in Wootton Bassett watching the corteges of fallen service personnel being brought back from wars in Iraq and Afghanistan to RAF Lyneham and their families and communities. In Crickhowell, as a deputy head I experienced daily the wonderful support and relationship the community gave to its school, and this extended to the way secondary schools worked together in collaboration and partnership, wanting to only raise standards and create educational opportunities for the rural communities they served. I have appreciated deeply when I reflect on these experiences the significant role the positive relationship with the local community has played when the school and community are engaged and working together for the common good of the young people and each other. I despair when I hear school leaders talk and openly advocate fewer ties with their local community almost as if the school doesn't quite belong to the very area it is supposed to serve. I have often wondered if the

"Klondike" rush to national MATs in the last few years has encouraged the remoteness in certain school leaders; often the ones parachuted in and parachuted out again as a quick fix solution to deeper educational problems that doesn't appear to work longer term along with the "hero Head" model, once favoured more than it is now in the DfE – thank goodness. I don't think a great deal of educational research needs to be undertaken to show it is obvious that it is the very team of school leaders, plural, and all staff that make the difference in a school.

I have to confess that when I first arrived to take up my post at Wyedean School, I wasn't aware then just how crucial the role of the wider community supporting the school was going to be, especially as we have gone through some very challenging times with the current dire financial situation for schools, as well as the pressures on schools to form or get into MATs. It's easy to start with the governors. As a colleague of mine once said, they are the trustees of the school and are from the very community the school serves and whose children we educate. Wyedean has phenomenal governors who freely give up so much of their time as volunteers to support the school. Their role ranges from sounding boards for leadership, wise counsel, practical support, business/volunteer organisation expertise, and ready to pitch and support everything from the PTA to open evening. We are really fortunate as a school to have such critical friends as stewards of Wyedean.

Over the last few months of this busy term I have had parents contact me to offer a range of support from advice, sofas for the common room, Christmas trees, plants, donations, talking to students from an industry background, flooring for the top corridor, the list goes on. I see it when I sit in the ancient beauty of St Mary's priory church and parents, governors, community members are all there supporting/sponsoring our awards evening, carol concert, careers events, etc.

The recent "snow day" saw the Forest of Dean look absolutely beautiful as it does and even more so in the snow, but it meant students and staff could not get to school because of the ice and snow on the roads. Parents were superb in their support over social media and together we made sure everyone was aware, decisions could be taken with as much full knowledge as possible, and above all our students and staff were safe.

The Year 11s have about 5 months left before the summer exams and have already put their applications in for Sixth Form, local college or apprenticeships. I work with many dedicated colleagues and the Head of Year 11, Claire Rush, as a senior pastoral leader is just incredible in her devotion and support of the year 11s in her care. Claire made sure the mocks were treated as the real thing to prepare the students and even on Thursday morning they had the results given to them as if it was the real thing. When I spoke to them in their assembly with Claire, it wasn't about stressing them out, but building them up. This extended to the parents' evening for Year 11 on the penultimate day of term. So many of our parents are coming into school to work with teachers and students to get the best results for our young people. It made me very proud as Wyedean principal looking around the school gym on a cold December evening with everyone wanting Christmas to get here and yet the partnership between home, school, and community there in action. It is the same year group that has been working with the Forest of Dean Baby Bank since the summer, helping with the donations to families in the Forest to support their infants and young families. It epitomises the school and community working together. Some students approached me this week and asked if the beautiful Christmas trees we had in the Sixth Form café and school hall could be used again and be donated to local care homes. I am so proud of the community and civic minded students we have at Wyedean. These are moments you know the future is definitely not all doom and gloom as some would have it.

We celebrated the wide and varied achievements of Wyedean students in St Mary's priory church on the 6th December and one of those very former young people who once attended Wyedean, Mr Neill Ricketts, came back as our guest of honour. Neill is the founder and CEO of Versarien PLC and his own story as a Wyedean student and the support and influences he had was very inspirational to hear, especially as he was passing that hope and sense of journey as an alumnus of Wyedean to the next generation. Neill announced he is very generously going to refurbish some of the science laboratories in honour of a teacher who influenced him, John Nettleship. John is the acknowledged inspiration for another famous Wyedean student, JK Rowling, and he is the basis of Snape in the Harry Potter books.

As the old year of 2017 comes to an end and most people I know seem to be breathing a sigh of relief after an often tumultuous year at many levels, I personally feel there is so much to feel optimistic and hopeful about 2018. Baroness Jan Royall, Forest resident, former Leader of the House of Lords and now principal of Somerville College, the University of Oxford, wrote to me and other schools wanting to actively create more opportunities for our young people to get exposure to education and experiences offered by Oxford. We also start off the year with the BBC "Any Questions" being broadcast from Wyedean School on the 12th January. For a school that prides itself on its culture of critical thinking, open-mindedness, inclusivity, and holistic education this is a fitting start to the year. My hope for 2018 is not anchored in a meaningless vacuum but in the very real knowledge that we have not only survived extremely difficult years in education, but we have continued to build and develop the right education needed for the communities we serve here in the Forest of Dean and the Wye Valley, which allows these young people to develop into adults and access successfully their global World and society, proud of where they are from in their community.

8 January 2018

An effective school's ethos and values are in true alignment with its every day positive culture and practices.

"I'm advocating for a new vision for education and childhood. If we truly want to improve the educational experience of our children, our focus should not be hinged on competition with other nations; it must begin with conscious parenting and education practices that address the development of the whole child – their intellectual, emotional, and physical well-being. They centre on developing creativity and critical thinking through project-based learning and fostering student engagement through collaboration. They support a model of parenting and education that encourages children to discover their individual talents and pursue their true passions. They don't demand perfection. They don't involve assigning more homework, prolonging the school day, or increasing

139

assessment tests. Our schools need to be community institutions that nurture and inspire children."
Vicki Abeles; writer, producer, and director of "Race to Nowhere" and "Beyond Measure"

A few days before Christmas, I had the pleasure of hosting a Skype Classroom session from my cabin study in my Bristol garden for Canadian teacher Julie Mackenzie and her class at Mildmay Carrick School in Ontario. The class asked me a whole host of questions about the UK, which taught me a lot about Canada and some were even surprised that in Britain we shared the same Queen as Canada. It is a nice role to have as a Microsoft Educator and Skype Classroom facilitator not least because it is a unique window through digital learning on classrooms all over the World. During the whole session with Julie and her students, despite the cold and snow outside their school and the end of term hours away, the class were lively, inquisitive, and engaged. They exuded everything their school and local school board states, about the vision and values of the education in their various mission statements and policy documents. Julie herself came across as one of those teachers you wished and hoped all students would have the privilege of being taught by. No one seemed to be struggling to get to the end of the term, it made me think about the last few days in school at Wyedean, and how positive and engaging the school learning environment seemed, despite how long the term had been since the start of September, and the seemingly permanent dark cold days of December. I am now looking forward to working with Alexandra Nedbalskaya and her students in Minsk, Belarus, before the end of January.

One of the other reasons I am fascinated by working with schools around the globe is there is such a huge variety of school cultures, educational priorities, organisational structures/systems, values, ethos all reflected in a myriad of school mottos. I think there is a gap in the market for someone to just simply collect and publish school mottos. One of my personal favourites is a school dear to my heart, Gar-Field High School in Virginia: "School of Champions". Taken to another extreme a school I worked with in Tomsk does not even have a name, it is simply School 56. The motto is almost as stark: "Students come to learn". Here is the thing about these two examples about mottos aligned to ethos and culture in these two very different schools, in two very different countries. In Gar-Field HS, students believe they are actually champions. Teachers believe it and so does the community. The celebration of learning and success is the best in any school system I have seen. There is an incredible culture of coaching, partnership, support, and high aspirations for all. It is infectious. Similarly, when I spent time working with the staff and students of School 56 the commitment, importance, and transformational value of an engaging learning culture pervades everywhere. Siberia is a tough place especially in winter as I well remember. It is in schools such as these you see the integrity and authenticity of a school's ethos and culture permeating everywhere in the whole school community. In Thailand, I saw in many of the schools I worked with not so much an individual school motto but the Buddhist mantra repeated, "No happiness surpasses peace of mind". Two things struck me about the school culture I saw in Thai schools; firstly, their progressive approach to LGBT+ issues was way ahead of anything I had seen in a UK/Western school at that point, this was 2007-9. Secondly, these Sukhothai province schools were huge, often averaging around 3500 students, yet they all practiced the most effective well-being and self-discipline I have seen in any school system. The strong influence of Buddhist culture of balance and harmony had a tremendous impact on these school cultures and despite their huge student population, they were really joyous and happy campuses to be on as a student or staff member. The positive and supportive school environment also linked naturally to engagement in learning and achievement for the students.

I went into the Christmas break impressed with how my colleagues responsible for exam cohorts had planned the mock examinations, supported the students, ensured the importance and value of the mocks, and prepared students effectively. It demonstrated how important at Wyedean we believe in our own motto and school culture of working together to achieve. I told all my colleagues going into the break to switch off from school, enjoy the rest with their families and friends. Human beings are not machines. I am more and more convinced of the French approach to banning emails outside of work hours. Promotion of a positive work/life balance has entered mainstream workplace culture to the point that even Ofsted now rightly question school leadership teams what they are doing to ensure a healthy work/life balance culture in schools.

At the start of 2018 figures released by the DfE showed the significant drop in teacher recruitment and at the other end retention of teachers is at crisis level. Pay has not kept pace with inflation and the standard of living, but the main reason teachers are leaving the profession is the poor working environment, the unrealistic accountability, the burdensome bureaucracy and frankly, the very love of learning and shaping young minds is just not the daily experience of colleagues in schools across the country. Many school leaders will say loudly they believe in good staff well-being and at the same time find it impossible to speak to staff without mentioning Ofsted or inspection. The cultures of these schools become full of fear and inspirational leadership disappears to be replaced by reactive process driven management.

The late, great education writer and academic, Ted Wragg, in his weekly TES column, had fictional "Gradgrind Academy" as the school where all the dreadful practices took place, full of poor school leaders, oppressed teachers, out of control stressed kids and capricious fads on a weekly basis. Back in the early noughties, Gradgrind Academy was then only fiction and at least did what its name and motto promised. It continues to concern me when I come across as a school leader, unfortunately all too often about the enormous pressure on young people to succeed through endless assessment and the subsequent exponential increase in poor mental health issues for our students. Last week when we returned from the Christmas break, I asked the Head of Year 11 what theme she wanted me to talk about for her first Monday assembly in 2018. I actually suggested two choices – examinations or motivation. She chose the latter, which is why she is an outstanding pastoral leader and Wyedean is lucky to have her.

I have thought a lot about the work of the inspirational parent and educational campaigner in the USA, Vicki Abeles, which I first came across a few years ago. One of the comments that struck me from American teenagers in her interviews in schools was this: "there seems to be no finishing line anymore". In the extract, I have quoted here from Abeles at the start of this blog I would find it nearly impossible to find a school leader, education policy maker, governor, teacher, parent, or anyone who worked in education to disagree with the vision she sets out about learning, skills, and curriculum. Schools around the globe, but especially in this country, have this vision set out in some form or other, and believe this is what the everyday culture of their school actually is when it delivers curriculum, learning and education to students. The reality unfortunately is the latter few sentences of the extract in too many school examples where the focus is on an increase in assessments for their own sake, the longer school day, a reduction of the curriculum, and a reduction in genuine support of an individual. There was even a report in the TES last week suggesting that actual student well-being will now be measured as an accountability measurement like attainment and progress data.

I did come across one education writer who said this week, "You don't grow taller just because you take a height measurement". What Abeles and others are campaigning on now is how we approach the pressures that we put on young people at home and in school. To look at the reasons why we are assessing a student and how we are assessing. To look at the balance in the curriculum, the educational experience, and the culture of our schools in how we develop our young people to cope and succeed as young adults as they leave schools. How we get them to use technology in a wiser, balanced, and less addicted way. As a school leader, I do not want to pay lip service to a school culture that suggests it is about the individual and progressive supportive development of a meaningful education when the reality is the day-to-day experience is gradgrind and intolerable unnecessary pressures for staff, students, and home. Therefore a resolution for 2018 going forward into a new year is to continue working on the positive school culture we have created at Wyedean, and to continue innovating to ensure compelling and engaging learning is not only what we believe in but it is what our students experience daily. Delivered by their teachers and support staff who believe in the power of transformative holistic education with supportive and collaborative leadership that allows them to do what they came into education for: to work with, and improve the lives of the young people in our care. We need to continue to ensure that we align what we say with what we do as schools and educators, or else we will continue to lose our teachers and more generations of young people. This is what I see increasingly as the challenge in education for 2018 and beyond.

6 February 2018

What will educational success look like going into the 2020s?

"What I enjoyed best at my Any Questions? evening was chatting to the Sixth Formers at Wyedean School. Thoughtful, open to ideas, undogmatic...just at present, I wish our country was in their hands." Journalist and broadcaster, Matthew Parris, writing in his Times column after his visit to Wyedean School on the 12th Jan 2018 for the BBC's "Any Questions?"

"Education breeds confidence. Confidence breeds hope. Hope breeds peace." Confucius

I first need to put a disclaimer at the onset of my blog before going any further. I don't know the answer to the question I pose in my blog title and there certainly isn't going to be any panacea to what could even be agreed amongst educators, academics, employers, parents, students or anyone else connected to education to what "educational success" looks like in 2018. No one of worth wants to be peddling any educational version of snake oil where educational success definition is concerned and like most school leaders, anyone willing to promote as such, in a self-styled moniker of "guru" I avoid like the plague. But sitting here on a cold and grey February day in my study in school, with the snow coming down fast over the Wye Valley and the Forest of Dean, I realise it is something I have been thinking deeply about consciously all of my educational life. None more so now as the principal of Wyedean School directly responsible for the education of 1100 students with essentially young children starting with us at the tender age of 11, to them leaving us to go onto university and careers at 18 as adults. That is a phenomenal amount of growing, learning, developing, maturing, and succeeding for these adolescents in our duty of care. It would be useful for them to know what it is they are all working towards and when they will know they have got there in their educational lives.

I think there are essentially two reasons why this question has come back to prominence in my daily thinking as a school leader for the start of 2018.

Firstly, thanks to my colleague in science, Stuart Motson, we were very fortunate to start the new year and term back in school with Wyedean hosting BBC Radio 4's long standing current affairs programme "Any Questions?" with the brilliant Jonathan Dimbleby as host. As expected in the climate we now live, Trump and Brexit dominated the discussions and the programme was well attended by our local wider community to hear the panel discuss the issues of our age. It is also an important part of the school culture and ethos at Wyedean to be outward looking and hosting such a programme of national and international standing by the BBC was a real coup for the school. It was the after show event on the Friday evening I really enjoyed in the Sixth Form's "Big Bean Café" where Jonathan Dimbleby and the panel members kindly came and spoke at length with governors, staff, parents and of course students. It was Matthew Parris' comments in The Times after the event that has really stayed with me though and I have quoted them here at the top of this blog. This famous journalist, writer, and broadcaster, who definitely has a reputation for calling it as it is, felt generous enough to take time to convey in print such an optimistic view of how our young people at Wyedean are seen and what we should be aspiring to always as educators in terms of how we develop our students. It is often levelled at the state education system in the UK that the accountability and inspection system of standards, favoured by all shades of governments over the last couple of decades, has led to an education system where public examination results have often emerged as the only important benchmark of recognition of educational success. Ensuring our young people have the necessary qualifications is an essential part of the role of schools but it is not to the exclusion and detriment of the holistic educational development of our young people to prepare them for the challenges and rewards of their later young (and old) adult lives. The best schools see academic success intrinsically linked to holistic individual development through wider education. That is what we need to get back to in our schools and educational ethos, to develop further as we approach the next decade. These twin ambitions for young people are not diametrically opposed as the goals of the education system of any country. Therefore why do we let this happen in the name of raising standards when in reality we are continuing to narrow the curriculum, lose good educators, and add to the mental health issues of young people?

The second reason is the very thing all school leaders in England fear the most – the dreaded Ofsted inspection call on a Monday morning. We knew as a school our three years were up in November since we were last seen and rated "Good" for our standards and our safeguarding. Two weeks ago on a Monday morning, just before midday, I had a phone call from Sharon. Sharon from Ofsted. And then Iain. Iain was going to be leading the inspection the very next day. Hard as it is for some of my global colleagues to comprehend, in the English system of school inspection, they really do turn up with less than 24hours notice and your school's future is decided on that one day of intense rigorous scrutiny of the quality, safety, and standards of the education you provide. Your ultimate accountability as a school leader. This was my first time leading a school and I have been through similar inspections in the USA, SE Asia, and even closer to home in Wales with the system under Estyn.

When I first experienced this at my then Welsh school, it was astonishing that this inspection had not been undertaken for 6 years. We knew weeks in advance and the whole thing missed so many things Ofsted would have pulled apart, having just been through the process in England at a school that became the first 11-18 school to be "outstanding" in every category under that framework. Does that make it however an educational success? Well, in the case of both my former schools the level and quality of the holistic education and curriculum enrichment and breadth on offer really does make both schools places delivering an outward looking level of education preparing students for the next decade of the 21st century. They were also places educators and leaders could grow under forward looking and moral leadership. I am pleased to say that my sleepless night on Monday two weeks ago, followed by my routine more than normal contemplative 5am dog walk in the pitch black cold around fields in North

Bristol with my dog Dylan, saw the Ofsted team recognise the amazing work of Wyedean staff and students we see every day. Moreover, we are good to carry on with strong recognition for the leadership, rich curriculum, learning, effective safeguarding, and Post 16 education. A link to the report and my letter to parents is here.

https://files.ofsted.gov.uk/v1/file/2753107

We have been open to scrutiny and challenge by anyone as a key element of our school improvement from Day 1 of me being principal, and that is what any good school does, not only to confirm its educational success, but also how to continue to develop itself further with external verifiers and their advice for improvement. It is why we are on the Challenge Partners school improvement network of over 400 schools of such a diversity and range but all striving for educational success with openness and an outward facing culture at the heart of their ethos. In addition, it is led by the very schools involved and school leaders and not some top down bureaucracy with a "one size fits all" politicised approach against any autonomy. I knew I would be back to snake oil pushers again in this blog.

So what is educational success going to look like going forward and the 2020s not too far away? I believe it has to be similar to days like today. My Year 12 critical thinking group started the morning debating the issues around equality in the C21st as part of the 100th anniversary of women in the UK first being given the vote. I kept thinking of Matthew Parris's words in The Times about Wyedean students as I watched the intensity and passion of the dialogue and debate around this issue in my study this morning. It is about celebrating the sporting success of our students and being proud as I felt when I posted the success of Lily Crawley through to the national indoor athletics championship in Sheffield later this month. It may well be viewed as the Progress 8 and Attainment tables released a week ago in England. It puts Wyedean in a strong light but that is only a fraction of the educational success of this school. It could well be the innovative use of digital learning and weekly Skype Classroom sessions we hold with schools connecting classrooms and global citizens in India, Canada, Belarus, Italy to name but a few. It was great to talk to my colleague Bindiya last week in Genius School, now there is a name for a school, in India. An aspirational educator as any I have had the privilege to work with globally. It definitely is Wyedean's completed and accepted application by the International Baccalaureate Organisation last week to be an IB World School aiming to offer the IB from September 2019. It is so exciting to be joining this incredible family group of several thousand diverse schools around the World developing and delivering the IB and its philosophy in our curriculum and as a key part of our ethos. The IB is 50 years this year and it is hard to think of any comparable education system that has stood the test of time and modelled such an aspirational vision of educational success free from the interference from national politicised policy makers. The IB is so much more than a qualification and I have always designed any curriculum I have been involved with as a school leader or advisor from the point of view of the IB's "Learner Profile". What do we want our young people to become at the end of their school years? Stressed out exam factory fodder or something way more and relevant to develop global society for the better? True international education is the latter always and does not pay mere lip service to the notion either. Educational success should not be trite short termism in the 2020s and will continue to be led and defined by educators who believe completely in the moral purpose and transformational nature of educational success. It was a real honour to be in the landmark OECD PISA 2018 Asian Society Global Competences publication for this type of education launched at the World Education Forum in January – Wyedean is on P31 looking at the importance of school leadership in education:

https://asiasociety.org/sites/default/files/inline-files/teaching-for-global-competence-in-a-rapidly-changing-world-edu.pdf

We need to keep moving the debate on as educators from the narrowness of only defining success through our public examinations. We need to educate the public and policymakers to not only see qualification outcomes as the end result of education systems. I work with an extraordinary colleague in the British Council called John Rolfe. Direct descendent, via Yorkshire, of the John Rolfe who married Pocahontas in the early 1600s at the Jamestown Virginia settlement. John has been a passionate and ardent advocate of global education his entire career as a dedicated public servant supporting schools and in the Queen's New Year Honours list he was rightly awarded an MBE for his services to education. We need more people like John supporting an alternative narrative to a narrowing curriculum and to develop further what a "Global Britain" will mean for educational and career opportunities for schools in the UK in the 2020s. Students will always need knowledge and skills and we should not put these two elements of educational outcome against each other in a binary zero sum way. They are not diametrically opposed but we do need to keep looking at what is compelling and engaging learning in our 21st century classrooms and learning is essentially Socratic even in the 2020s. The age-old question, more than 2500 years later, is how do we keep our students hooked in?

You know your students have had an extraordinary day not just in education but also in their lives when they go to look at Oxford University like mine did today and inspirational Nobel Peace Prize winner Malala Yousafzai incredibly shows them around. This is what happened to my students at Oxford University. I have a remarkable assistant principal and director of Post 16 in Johnathan Lane who will continue to deliver this level of education that will earn commendations like Matthew Parris's description of Wyedean students. This is where the bar has to be when we define as school leaders and educators how our educational success should look going into the 2020s. Moreover, yes, I am deeply regretting not going to Oxford today, meeting one of the 21st century's remarkable and humbling World figures who has done so much fighting for Human Rights and ensuring girls and people in poverty in some of the poorest places of the World just have the right to an education. That in itself is an outstanding measure of educational success through such struggle, and we should not forget the distance we have come in modern education in the 21st century.

28 March 2018

What does an effective learning environment look like in a school?

"Nine tenths of education is encouragement." Anatole France

"The freedom to make mistakes provides the best environment for creativity. Education isn't how much you have committed to memory, or even how much you know. It's being able to differentiate between what you know and what you don't." Anatole France

"When educators model extraordinary passion and enthusiasm for learning, it causes students to value the learning too." David Geurin

I had the privilege earlier this month to be invited to speak at the launch of the Cabot Learning Federation's (CLF) new teacher training and leadership centre at the City Academy in Bristol. Over the last few years a considerable number of aspiring and existing school leaders from Wyedean have matriculated here on the NCTL's national leadership qualifications, and this has had a considerable impact not only on the professional development of those individual school leaders, but also on the change in the leadership culture and ethos of the school. It has also led to an exposure to different school cultures and learning environments along the M4 and in Bristol for so many Wyedean colleagues.

I undertook my own NPQH as I prepared for Headship a few years ago from the CLF and have been invited back on a number of occasions to Bristol to speak to subsequent cohorts of aspiring Heads and Principals about my experience and the impact it had on me as school leader. When I spoke at the launch to an assembled audience of the "great and good" of the South West's educators, school leaders, and policy makers it was with complete belief that my own training, the training of colleagues, and the wider association with the CLF has made a significant impact on the success of Wyedean. We are very proud to be associated with the good narrative around education in Bristol and the South West that is a result of so

150

much hard work by passionate and dedicated people working in education here. One of the most important lessons I have taken away from working with the CLF is their strong belief in an effective learning environment in schools. When I first heard the original founder of the CLF and now National Schools Commissioner, Sir David Carter, speak a few years ago he placed the very strong emphasis on having a purposeful and consistent school culture that sets the effective environment in schools for students to learn. This echoes strongly with a New York City principal's message from a lecture in the States which I attended a while back. She made it very clear to her students when they came to school from all sorts of tough and challenging backgrounds that the one consistent was going to be that here in school they get the chance to learn and gain an education. She was uncompromising on that but one of the most compassionate school leaders I have ever come across. She went on to say how her students were told by her directly that she couldn't change skin colour, or backgrounds or put families back together again, but in school she could teach them how to be confident, have ambition and self-belief and resilience, to be articulate and develop their skills and knowledge that would take them on further out of poverty and into colleges, universities, careers, and to develop into decent human beings with strong values and a desire to give back to the very communities they had left. If I get asked what exactly the "transformative power of education" means, I think about this speech from a New York High School principal and the incredible work of educators in Bristol giving the children of their communities hope. This all springs from an effective learning environment both within the school community and out to the wider community supporting each other in partnership.

Reflecting back over this term all the way back to January with the Easter break just around the corner, I have been thinking a great deal about the importance of the learning environment of school, not just in the context of what the atmosphere feels and looks like in corridors and classrooms, but also about the relationships between everyone associated with a school. I know that one of the significant factors in the way Wyedean has changed is the emphasis on positive school culture and ensuring relationships are positive in school and the wider community. This is not always easy especially when we have such a large community. For example, we were hit this March with an unprecedented two "snow days" due to an unlikely alliance of the "Beast from the East" and "Storm Emma". Deciding to close the school is probably more stressful than the Ofsted "24 hour notice call". Well, certainly up there for school leaders. You are never going to please everyone and the ultimate balance in the decision-making is between not losing precious learning time against the safety of students and colleagues travelling through snow and ice unnecessarily. They certainly do not teach you much about this on the NPQH course. Social media and more immediate communications make the snow day call easier on one level but it also means there are hundreds of messages on Facebook and Twitter when the first flurries arrive. What I appreciated in March when we had to close the school for the snow in the Forest of Dean, South Wales, and even over Bristol was how supportive, patient, and helpful the entire wider school community were as we made the decision not to be open. Digital learning was particularly helpful to extend the learning environment as work was set for all students on ShowMyHomeWork. I am sure all students resisted going outside and playing in the snow and settled indoors to work. Although departments set some really interesting pieces of work, for example Art suggested on their Twitter feed for students to go outside and take pictures of the landscape, whilst Maths looked at the geometry of snowflakes. Much as I wanted to sit in my warm cabin-study at home and read the books suggested by the English department, I took my three young children sledging on Pomphrey hill along with the rest of North Bristol.

We were lucky enough to be asked by the British Council if they could come to Wyedean in January to see the school and hold a photoshoot showing the learning environment and our global learning in action. Unfortunately, our Ofsted call in January meant this was postponed and instead they came on a very bright and sunny day at the end of February. It also coincided with the visit of our partner school from Japan, Reitaku Junior High School, near Tokyo, and a Skype classroom session with our great colleague, Tatiana Popa and her wonderful students from Heritage International School, Chisinau, Moldova. I see the learning environment at Wyedean every day and I see other schools so I know what we have in Wyedean. We do not believe in our students walking in deadly silence down corridors to class or students sitting in rows learning in rote. That isn't an effective learning environment in Wyedean. I stand at the foot of the main stairs in the school, with other school leaders, at the start of the day, lesson change over, breaks and walk around the school and I adore the fact that our students smile, say hello, tell you what they are studying or ask you if you have seen a particular teacher. At the end of the day as the buses, cars, and bikes leave the campus they wish you a good evening or a good weekend. We are an effective learning community because we believe in the transformative power of education and a positive school culture. This was all put into sharp focus to separate the mundane from the profound with yet another school shooting in the States in March. What parent or educator has not been proud and moved to tears at the wisdom, courage and leadership of the students of Parkland, Florida following the senseless shootings of their teachers and classmates a few weeks ago. I know arming teachers in a school is definitely not part of an effective learning environment and these young people are right to challenge the people who make laws and decisions at the national level about the basic fundamental right of being safe in school.

When John Rolfe and his colleagues came to visit Wyedean in February, this is what he had to say about Wyedean and our learning environment:

"…just a few lines to say a huge, and greatly appreciated thank you, for such an enjoyable, interesting, and inspirational day at your wonderful school! It was great to be able to meet the students, visit classrooms, and the wider school environment to learn more about your fantastic inclusive vision for education and to see so much high quality and motivating teaching and learning. Rob, we are all so proud and delighted to work with you and to learn from you and your profound commitment to outstanding and inclusive teaching and learning and we want to warmly thank you and everyone at wonderful Wyedean for being such a great hub of excellent work; it was particularly inspiring to be part of the critical thinking class and the VC with Moldova… Thanks for all your time Rob; and for your commitment, energy, brilliant professionalism and for being such an incredible Headteacher…"

John visits a huge amount of schools in the UK and abroad and was recently honoured by the Queen for his services to education and global learning. We were very flattered and pleased that John saw our community at work, experienced our learning environment, and wrote such kind words about the school. John's words reflect what the Ofsted inspectors saw in January; and the Challenge Partner reviewers saw in October; and what the governors, parents, visitors, and prospective students for Year 6 and 12 see every day they come to visit Wyedean - an effective learning environment in a vibrant inclusive school community. This is what I proudly told the CLF audience in March and how the leaders and leadership culture work relentlessly around the school to make sure students want to come to school, are engaged and enjoying the challenge and the opportunities available in their educational offer. These are the characteristics of an effective learning environment.

I have been reading a lot recently about the Finnish education system and in particular the work of the great educator, Pasi Sahlberg. Sahlberg's work is heavily based around looking at how establishing the right learning environment and culture in schools is not just about linking this to attainment, but more importantly the well-being of young people and our colleagues. Put crudely, if schools get this aspect right then upward trajectories of attainment and progress will naturally follow. Finland's record in education as measured by the OECD/PISA speaks for itself. Sahlberg despairs of the tired educational leadership mantra he has encountered in many school systems as *"...if you push the system harder, it will move"* (1). This is characteristic of the approach towards schools by politicians of all the main parties in the UK for the last 20 years. Sahlberg goes onto say, *"...how many politicians have such a narrow and technical view of education and how to improve it in a comprehensive, systemic way". To go back to another of Sir David Carter's mantras "it's not the structures but the outcomes".*

We have had a very long term through the winter and at last, we have made it down to Spring and a break for the next couple of weeks. I had a look through the school twitter feed as we finished the Spring Newsletter for Wyedean – copy of the link below. The richness of school life just flows and encapsulates a creative, innovative, engaging, and compelling education we are all contributing towards to give our students the best life chances as possible.

http://www.wyedean.gloucs.sch.uk/docs/newsletters/Spr ing_Newsletter_2018.pdf

(1) "FinnishED Leadership" Pasi Sahlberg, (Corwin, 2018)

20 April 2018

Why schools share, partner and collaborate.

"Alone we can do so little. Together we can do so much." Helen Keller

"Most great learning happens in groups. Collaboration is the stuff of growth." Sir Ken Robinson

There are too many moments in this role when a "typical day" is impossible to describe. We returned from the Easter break this week and came back to some of the warmest days in April on record. Probably the earliest moment of the summer term on record as well of the request being made for students, by students, to wear shorts in the heat. Instead of enjoying the very relaxed atmosphere around the Wyedean campus, relaxed and Study Leave for Year 11s and 13s is just weeks away, I found myself at Cardiff Metropolitan University in the sweltering sunshine trying to load heavy chairs, desks and notice boards onto the school minibuses. I am fairly sure the average day of a school principal, or his vice principal business and finance for that matter, doesn't normally consist of doubling up as a removal team but in the age we live in nothing surprises me in education. Cardiff Met had very kindly and very generously offered the school a whole host of free furniture for school, which they no longer needed, and in the educational financial climate we are in it was very gratefully welcomed when there simply isn't spare money for additional chairs, bookcases, and display cases. I know a number of colleagues feel that this is a scenario that would never have been envisaged when it wasn't too long ago a Prime Minister promised "education, education, education". However, there is no luxury of reflection when it comes to being resourceful and doing what we can as school leaders to ensure the quality of the education in our schools doesn't falter. We are the lightning conductors for our school communities always. The offer from Cardiff Met University illustrated for me less a charitable handout to a school but a wonderful example of what can be achieved when we collaborate in education.

I did reflect and realise on Monday that if I did want to work in Suffolk a four-hour tortuous commute from Bristol was probably not a wise idea. I managed to arrive at the impressive new campus of West Suffolk College with plenty of time to spare, to speak at the International Festival of Learning (IFL). Over 1000 teachers and educators attended this great event in the spring sunshine and I managed to catch the first panel discussion with Amanda Spielman, chief inspector of Ofsted, and Geoff Barton, general secretary of the school leaders union, ASCL. Amanda Spielman certainly comes across as a much more compassionate chief inspector of Ofsted, and her comments last year about the focus being on the curriculum echo very much with the strategy and ethos of Wyedean School's approach. She made the point in the room on Monday that the curriculum in many schools has just "fizzled out". I wish she was wrong but I have lost count of the number of school leaders I have spoken to who make the astonished look of surprise when I tell them about Wyedean's rich and deep curriculum and educational experience that sees the arts, sport, music, languages, design, etc., at the heart of our school alongside other subjects. Geoff Barton lamented how many schools are now essentially reducing the curriculum and becoming qualification focussed from Year 8 onwards. He said Key Stage 3 is a learning stage in its own right and no research shows options after less than two years in secondary school does anything but reduce curriculum exposure to a broad range of subjects and learning experiences. Linking this to well-being, how much pressure is on young people at the ages of 12-13 to make such decisions when we want them to be engaged, challenged and enjoying school?

One of the highlights about Monday's IFL is the sheer number of schools, educators, and related organisations and agencies that were able to get together in the same place and discuss education. I drove back home after I had given my talk to the conference and I thought about a quote I had read recently from a superintendent of schools in Washington State, Judith Billings:

"Children are the priority. Change is the reality. Collaboration is the strategy".

The key emphasis in my talk to the audience in Bury St Edmunds focussed on the school improvement strategy at Wyedean over the last few years, based on a very simple but determined strategy. Wyedean could not exist in an introverted isolation at the southern end of the Forest of Dean, pushed up against a hard Welsh education border where collaboration or even willingness to collaborate is non-existent. The game-changer for Wyedean, looking out to the confluence of the Wye and Severn, "blessed is the eye between the Severn and the Wye", and the wider sea; along the M4 corridor to Bristol, the south west, and towards London, was to engage with networks, partnerships, and anyone who could offer an external perspective and challenge to Wyedean School. If we hadn't engaged on a twin strategy of a positive school culture focused on compelling education and wider collaborative engagement, the last few years that have been so significant in how the school has improved would have been very different. Moreover, it is not just Ofsted who see this significant improvement but Challenge Partners, the British Council, the IB, local universities, the CLF, the RSC, local primary schools and a whole host of parents and children who want to come to Wyedean for their education.

To return to the crux of Superintendent Billing's quote, one school and one school leader does not have all the answers especially in the very complex and fluid educational picture we inhabit in 2018. Through collaboration we can be challenged in our approaches and thinking that pulls down the walls of our own self-constructed echo chambers. I always find it fascinating that the central tenet of a student's "education" is not so much about skills and knowledge acquisition, very important to learn but against each other, a false dichotomy... a blog for another day, but being challenged, and open to question, and to be intellectually curious. In all of this to be prepared to change opinion and views held through this process. As the IB learner profile challenges oneself, "How do we know we know?" Collaboration and meaningful partnerships achieves this for a school in education. I have lost count on the times I have been asked if either Wyedean is going to start a MAT or join a MAT. There are a huge number of MATs such as the CLF in Bristol, where that organisation based on collaboration has made a significant difference in school improvement. There are also many examples like the now defunct WCAT in Yorkshire where that model did not work. What has worked for Wyedean School is the ethos of wanting our school to be immersed in World Class education and for our school to exude a positive school culture that allows our education to be a transformative force for good in the lives of our young people and the community we serve. The MAT model of collaboration and partnership for school improvement for Wyedean School is not one that would allow us to have achieved what we have over the last few years. Partnerships like Challenge Partners and now becoming an IB World School candidate are the collaboration networks that align with our school ethos of global learning and C21st World Class education that run through our school values and ethos like a stick of Blackpool rock. A key part of our school ethos is our commitment to work with any school and to collaborate to develop education and meaningful experience that continues to enhance the education at Wyedean and those we have the privilege to work with. We also know that we do not have all the answers as a school community. We often do not even know the questions. However, we know where to find them in our networks, both formal and informal.

In that spirit I am really pleased that the director of Teaching and Learning, my colleague Julie Smith, has been invited to speak at a major global learning conference in Europe in early May, about our innovative approach to learning in a positive school culture that empowers the teacher and therefore the learning rather than unnecessarily overburdening colleagues with fads and a punitive workload. I am looking forward to speaking at my former school, Royal Wootton Bassett Academy, at their "Empowering Young People" conference next week and meeting up again with my former colleague, the brilliant Dr Nicola Wetherall who has done so much important work in schools around Holocaust and Genocide awareness education. Nic has done so much to bring together leading academics, schools and public figures to develop further intellectual curiosity and understanding of key historical events, historic like the Armenian Genocide of

1915 and the Nazi Holocaust to more recent times in Rwanda and Bosnia. The impact of such educational experience as we develop wider understanding and link it to the climate and events of our own World in places such as Syria is immeasurable, but we know as educators that introverted isolation for our schools, our communities, our colleagues, and our students is not the way forward when we think about meaningful education in 2018. The meeting of Commonwealth leaders in London this week is representative of 53 nations, a third of the global population, looking to work further together and the education aspect of the global Commonwealth community is a powerful force of good around the globe. To participate in education and belong to a formal and informal school community is in itself an act of sharing and collaboration and can only be a force of positive good as we go forward.

2 May 2018

In education we are always influencing the next generation of leaders.

"Plus est en vous" (More is in you/There is more in you than you think) Gordonstoun school motto

"Education must enable young people to effect what they have recognised to be right, despite hardships, despite dangers, despite inner scepticism, despite boredom and despite mockery from the World." Kurt Hahn

It is not very often I start a critical thinking lesson asking students for their thoughts about the ongoing events in Republic Square, Yerevan, as I did this week with my sixth formers. The "Velvet Revolution" being played out carefully in Armenia currently illustrates well the thoughts I have been rolling over about whether or not our education system and curriculum really allows the development of young people to take up the reins from the previous generation. The huge crowds of protesters in the streets of Yerevan that peacefully called for the removal of the former president, Serzh Sargsyan from becoming PM and effectively continuing his rule, largely came from the young people of Armenia in a spring like, almost carnival atmosphere as they decided they wanted their future to be determined differently. I know the well-known quote attributed to the Girondist, Vergniaud that "revolutions devour their children", but the educator optimist in me is seeing more and more signs that the next generation are showing more and more signs that the mistakes and mess of the previous generation across a range of global issues from power, climate change, sustainability, refugees, technology, war, human rights, etc. are going to be led differently, more ethically. What is happening in Armenia right now speaks volumes about the people of Armenia, especially its young people.

Education should not be in some abstract bubble as we teach our students not only skills and knowledge in their formal and informal curriculum, but also through our values and ethos that underpin the collective spirit and purpose of our education and schools. I witnessed so many examples last weekend at my former school, Royal Wootton Bassett Academy. I had the pleasure of attending their innovative "Empowering young people" conference with the added privilege of being the keynote speaker that closed the conference on Saturday afternoon. There really cannot be many schools that have taken Human Rights and Holocaust education and put them at the centre of a curriculum that brings together every age group and subject in the school in a meaningful, educational, and empowering strategy. The work of its lead and founder, Dr Nicola Wetherall, is awe-inspiring and is a powerful example of grassroots leadership influencing the school organisation and community in a positive way. The ripples from this work has linked Holocaust and genocide survivors, academics, other schools, organisations, and most importantly young people. The leadership of young people evidenced in this conference and through the awards evening on the Friday evening filled the well of educational optimism about the next generation of leaders and the values they want to see underpinning the world. The young people in the streets of Armenia are also the descendants of one of the very worst and first horrors of modern societies systematically killing a whole race of people through hate and that was the 1915-16 Armenian Genocide committed by the Ottoman Empire in WWI. History and the link to building a better World with human rights and human values is not lost on this country.

I would recommend looking at this US article and study on the work of RWBA:

http://blogs.edweek.org/edweek/global_learning/2018/04/exemplary_holocaust_education_learning_from_the_united_kingdom.html?cmp=soc-twitter-shr

The drive back along the M4 to Bristol on Saturday teatime made me think about one of my education heroes, Kurt Hahn, and the importance and relevance he placed on the development of the next generation of young people in all the schools he established from Salem, to Gordonstoun, and Atlantic College, and movements like the DoE, Round Square International, and of course UWC. Hahn's concept of "experiential learning" meant children should not just sit and do things to "receive" education; they should be "doing" things in school. The concept of "project" education is an everyday part of education but when Hahn introduced it at Gordonstoun in the 1940s/50s it was very innovative education that would enable young people to develop independent learning skills, self-esteem, and build their leadership capacity. Linked to this is Hahn's belief in the power of failure in education, and how as educators we develop a lens of common humanity through creating compassion in our school experiences.

I have spent this week so far thinking about how we put this into practice as educators. I took my last assembly with Year 11 on Monday just before they go on study leave for the summer examinations. They are a great year with brilliant tutors and led with complete compassion and an educator's heart and year head in my brilliant colleague Claire Rush. I chose not to do the traditional Headmaster "Work hard for your exams; don't fail; you get out what you put in..." etc. but instead talked about self-esteem and status as they are about to leave this significant stage of their lives by leaving school. I even managed to get will. i. am singing, *"What I am"* on Sesame Street into the end, I think they appreciated it. I know the next generation of leaders at Wyedean are already leading; the sixth form group that have worked tirelessly with local charities collecting clothes for Syrian refugees is another great example of the compassion and the values we want to see our young people develop and own. The British Council and the NAHT delivered a very strong case to the government this week concerning the issues around schools visits and opportunities for global learning by visiting our own continent of Europe post Brexit. I made the case again at Royal Wootton Bassett for the importance of international education and global learning for "Global Britain" post 2019. I hope we do not have to fight for this powerful intrinsic education model of curriculum enrichment, lost in the narrowness of bloody-minded politicians. With this in mind, we have welcomed two French partner schools in the last week to Wyedean to work, visit, and share with our school community. On Monday, I had the pleasure of working with the Moldovan English Teachers Association as I delivered a webinar on the importance of global learning for our young people. It struck me how important it is for this post-Soviet country to engage in the wider world and create a society and opportunities for young Moldovans to thrive. I am honoured to be delivering a seminar on global learning for COBIS 18 in London in May. The same theme in a recent TES article I contributed for the British Council:

https://www.tes.com/news/why-global-citizenship-more-important-ever

In more than twenty years as a teacher and a school leader, I have found myself returning constantly in times of doubt to the direction of education to Kurt Hahn's ideas as a global educator and about the direction and development of young people in our duty of care and who will take the torch from this generation and carry it forward to the next. Hahn felt education should be to develop young people who were ready to be citizens of a new kind of world and as we approach the 2020s, we see these young people more prepared to lead with integrity, spirit, foresight and humanity in the World. There is so much more in them than you and I could dare to imagine and that is why the well of optimism for the future is full.

25 May 2018

Do schools kill creativity?

"Art washes away from the soul the dust of everyday life." Picasso

"Creativity takes courage." Matisse

I had the honour of meeting and shaking hands with the man who shook the hands of the Beatles, Sean Connery, Jane Fonda and many other famous icons over the post war decades, as he photographed them in their heyday promoting their art. World-renowned photographer and local Wye Valley Tintern resident David Hurn is self-taught and because of his dyslexia at school he joined the school camera club. David has astonishingly agreed to work with my colleagues and students in the Creative Learning Area on a number of projects and our Creativity Coordinator, Jane Collins, has led the project to bring David's talent into school. David has also agreed with Jane to support our annual Creativity Festival which is being held on Friday 6th July. Jane is one of those extraordinary colleagues who epitomises the love of their subject and conveys that to every student. Jane's role as Creativity Coordinator in the school also means creativity is at the heart of the curriculum and not on the periphery, marginalised or relegated to an after school club in pursuit of a narrow skills focus, based on the job market alone. A principle of education that so many school curriculum models seem to have been designed on now. The government's own press release from November 2017 celebrates the fact that the creative industries alone are worth £92 billion to the UK economy and are growing at twice the rate of the economy making a record contribution:

https://www.gov.uk/government/news/creative-industries-record-contribution-to-uk-economy.

The question for many in education and in business is "Why is creativity being killed in schools?", as Sir Ken Robinson debated in 2006 in the most viewed TED Talk ever. In a near identical experience to David Hurn, Sir Ken battled hurdles in his Liverpool school as he overcame childhood polio and used the transformative power of education, learning, and knowledge to progress through school and to university. He is now one of the most powerful advocates for creativity being central in the curriculum. What we call nowadays "social mobility", Sir Ken famously described as being his enlightened teachers seeing *something in me I didn't see in myself*. I would recommend his interview on BBC Radio 4's "The Educators" as well as his TED Talk; always good to listen to, particularly when the Gradgrind (the late Ted Wragg's infamous fictional academy) gets you really down:

https://www.bbc.co.uk/programmes/b04d4nvv

https://www.ted.com/talks/ken_robinson_says_schools_kill_creativity

Artists like David Hurn wanting to support the next generation of young people to access the arts, and realise the potential of creativity, educators like my colleague Jane Collins who sees potential in students when they don't, and powerful and articulate advocates like Ken Robinson make the forceful case for the curriculum to be broad, rich and definitely full of creativity, so that students have a choice in their futures in a globalised economy and world. "Social Mobility" again.

We had the privilege on Monday of working with a long time old colleague from the IB, Dr Peter Fidczuk, who spent the morning at Wyedean looking at the possible subject models for our IB Careers Programme when we launch it. I caught the eye of my Director of Sixth Form, Johnathan Lane, at one point as we marvelled at the subjects on offer that we could have in our IBCP. The routes, pathways, career plans, study programme; whatever we choose to call them, could potentially engage and open up experiences and potential that our students from the Forest of Dean and the Welsh borders often don't see in themselves. They have had such a heavy, narrow diet of necessary information which is not always a worldly education in itself. I remember in the policy dialogue I was asked to contribute to in London back in November upsetting the CEO of a MAT somewhere in the north. I pointed out the damage that the relentless pursuit of Ebacc in England by some schools and the DfE has done to wipe out the curriculum of so many creative subjects leaving only a narrow core. I want to say it again here: the Ebacc is not a "Baccalaureate" in any sense of the educational concept. Read the IB's mission statements and look at their "joined-up" curriculum models and programmes, starting with an aspirational learner profile, to see how narrow and short-sighted the Ebacc actually is. The problem in England for the last 10-15 years is exactly what Geoff Barton, the general secretary of ASCL, emphasised in his blog and on the Today Programme this week: School leaders and educators have given up "leadership" of their profession and need to grab it back. Doctors and Lawyers haven't allowed civil servants and politicians to take over their professional judgements and teachers should be no different. An interesting development to support Barton's rallying cry is the way school leaders are increasingly challenging the long held shibboleths of English education like the Ofsted inspection judgements, league tables, validity and fairness of attainment and progress measurements, school structure models, school improvement models, and teaching and learning effectiveness practices. It is refreshing to see this tackled, finally, and a real dialogue taking hold in the profession about the purpose and meaning of education as we approach the 2020s in less than two years. My fear is the number of brilliant art, language, music, and DT teachers we have lost. As a result of this we are now in a permanent recruitment crisis because working in education is no longer seen as an attractive vocation, precisely because of the misguided approach to raising standards by all shades of the political spectrum over the last 20 years. I will leave cruel and punitive quality assurance systems destroying great teachers for another blog.

Last week I was invited to take part in a BBC Radio Gloucestershire debate on the new two year linear A Levels. Essentially a "false binary" dichotomy was set up by the BBC producer with another Head arguing against my viewpoint. We both came to the same conclusion that some coursework was still good and we will need to wait to see how these A Levels work out. I also made the point that we need to prepare our young people for a global jobs market and we do need to expose them to testing, but that bit is about how much we put pressure on our young people with factors like the sheer number and hours of exams.

I have been trying to work out, in this context, what I think of Lucy Crehan's book *"Cleverlands"* as she looks at the five perceived global educational success stories of Finland, Japan, Singapore, Shanghai, and Canada. Having worked with these countries a lot in global education, I have found myself at odds with some of her conclusions, in particular from what I know of my collaboration with colleagues in Finland for example. The Finns believe their greatest challenge is to avoid the temptation to rest on their laurels of PISA and their structural reforms in education of decades ago. As a consequence, they are going to take a risk and design a more fluid curriculum, less based on traditional subjects, but rather based on the skills associated with creative, digital and global learning, and critical thinking. I worked extensively with schools in Singapore about 10 years ago. The drive for these schools and educators was finding ways to bring more arts into their curriculum, and I remember standing in Tintern Abbey one Saturday with a whole group of Singaporean teachers reading Wordsworth's famous poem and discussing methods to include more creative poetry and drama in their curriculum, rather than just literacy skills.

It is funny how life can come around in full circle, as I sat in Tintern Abbey in the glorious sunshine a couple of weeks ago thinking of those Singaporean colleagues from St Nicholas school. I was transfixed by the astonishing surrealism of the *"Museum of the Moon"* a piece of glorious public art by Luke Jerram and the music composed by Dan Jones. A Bristolian and a Welshman: always a good combination! A replica detailed model of the Moon hung down in the middle of the ruined nave of the abbey and it was so beautiful, bold, challenging, and thought provoking. Art should challenge and move us. Art should be integral in our lives always and to paraphrase Ken Robinson, Creativity should be just as important as Maths.

The Wye "Festival of the River" brought so many people together and made them think about where they live, where they are in their lives, as well as the beauty and appreciation of what they have right now in that moment of time. I thought about the collaborative power of music this week as I watched and listened to the people of Manchester sing Oasis' "Don't look back in anger" as they reflected, one year on, from the senseless terror attack on young people in the Manchester Arena. I thought of the images from Sante Fe, as another senseless US school shooting took place, killing 10 people so soon after Parkland was supposed to be the turning point where this murder of teachers and students stopped. I thought of this as I sat in the Sixth Form café today where Year 13 were in full fancy dress, despite the rain, celebrating their milestone of leaving school singing collectively Jason's Mraz's "I'm Yours". It was just wonderful. Young, joyous faces ready to move onto university, careers, jobs and lives, but right at that moment they were singing and expressing their inner selves. Young people should have the world at their feet and the ability to dream the impossible without fear of the future. I did like the fact the smart phones provided the "lighter" effect of the concert though. It is 2018 after all.

I met, by chance, in London at the O2 Conference Centre one of my education school leader heroes this month, Brian Christian, principal of the British School Tokyo. Brian was in the audience when I spoke at the COBIS conference about global learning and leadership for the British Council. Brian's approach and philosophy for his school is one we should all aspire to as school leaders. It is inclusive, it is global, it is about sustainability, it is digital, it is about character and well-being, it is about achievement and preparation for life. It is about loving learning and wanting to be curious about the world. I greatly appreciated the long conversation I had with him in London, demonstrating again the power of collaboration, sharing, and partnership across education systems and countries. That part of Lucy Crehan's book, I agree with entirely, she was the keynote speaker at the end of the day. Brian tweeted this week a picture of the beautiful English cottage garden on his school campus in Tokyo. One of the most enjoyable enrichment activities we have at Wyedean is the Sixth Form gardening club run by Johnathan Lane. Students who are studying maths and physics also enjoy Wednesday afternoon enrichment, growing peonies and squashes. I do think two-year linear Post 16 courses allow Year 12 to actually do something different in the summer of Year 12 instead of countless exams. We have made that a key part of Wyedean's ethos and culture.

I was going to avoid mentioning the wedding of Harry and Meghan in this blog, but in the context of creativity in schools and the wider curriculum it is almost impossible to leave out. Meghan's dresses were astonishing creations by the very best of British talent in Clare Waight Keller and Stella McCartney. Kanneh Mason's beautiful cello solo in St George's chapel must have made the whole of Nottingham, and not just his old school of Trinity, burst with pride as this confident, supremely talented young musician played to the great and good invited from British royalty to Hollywood A Listers. Bishop Michael Curry reminded the whole world of the power of beautiful oratory as he quoted MLK, talked about child poverty around the World, the legacy of slavery and all, with the running theme of the redemptive power of love. When a gospel choir serenaded with Ben E King's "Stand by Me" the sheer beauty of the voices was awe inspiring to anyone hearing it.

It is up to all of us what we want to see in our schools and in the curriculum for young people to learn. What do we value? What values do we want for the future generations? What are we preparing them for in schools? COBIS schools don't offer their students a diet of a few narrow skills. Like the IB, they offer a broad, challenging, coherent, compelling learning, and life preparing education. The same goes for schools where the values that underpin the culture and ethos are not shaped by short-term politics, or sacrificed on the tight budgets we all face. Why did a school I once worked with in West Java offer the most comprehensive enrichment programme that I had ever seen, when it was operating on a total budget equivalent to one subject dept. in a UK school, let alone an entire school? The answer lies in what the school, school leaders and community wanted for those young Indonesians in their curriculum and their education. We have to lead in education again as educators and be brave enough to lead education knowing that creativity allows us to find the things in our young people they didn't know existed. Far from killing creativity, we should be looking to grow it, encourage it and develop it as the teachers of Kanneh Mason did, Bishop Curry's did, Ken Robinson's did, and my colleague Jane Collins' once did. What schools should kill is ignorance and apathy in our young people. You don't achieve this by killing creativity and the opportunities that go with such a curriculum and approach to education.

"It is the supreme art of the teacher to awaken joy in creative expression and knowledge." Albert Einstein

12 June 2018

How do we decide in schools a strategy for a "preferred future" and avoid "cutting edge futurism"?

"Class of 2018, it's not the technology you build that will define you. It's the teams you build and what people do with the technology you build." Sheryl Sandberg

"The secret of change is to focus all of your energy, not on fighting the old, but on the building the new." Socrates

In my principal's study in school, amongst the paintings, I have a copy of a print by the artist Tom Freeman depicting the night of August 24th, 1814, when a force of British soldiers led by Major General Robert Ross burnt down the White House and the Capitol buildings in the War of 1812. Most students remember this event from the 1812 War, especially Dolley Madison, saving the portrait of George Washington from the White House just before the redcoats got there, and of course the story of the British arriving to find no President Madison only fine presidential wines and a delicious meal laid out which they promptly devoured before their arson act of revenge and cultural vandalism. Students of this war also remember "Old Hickory" and the future 7th President, Andrew Jackson, defeating the British at the Battle of New Orleans just after the war had ended because news of the Treaty of Ghent hadn't made it across the Atlantic in time. I looked at this painting this morning at my desk and normally it reminds me of when my colleagues in Virginia gave it to me as a gift; as an ironic present to take with me back home to the mother country. Today, I thought about the weekend's furore of the G7 summit in Canada, where the richest nations were supposed to be planning the global future but instead President Trump, in a summit eve conversation with Prime Minister Trudeau, accused the Canadians of burning Washington DC in the War of 1812. Not one to let facts get in the way of a good tweet, many commentators made the same point about Trump's poor grasp of historical facts and knowledge especially in someone who has made it as president and a president who cites historically "old Hickory", another outsider to the White House, as his hero. The point was also made that Trump graduated from an Ivy League school, Pennsylvania, and should know that Canada was still part of the British Empire in 1812 and it was the British who burnt Washington DC, in revenge for the burning of York (Toronto) in Lower Canada at the start of the war. Then there were a few commentators who talked about "Google knowledge" and how we don't need to know facts, events, dates or just knowledge anymore, and Trump was no different.

This set off a chain of thoughts in my thinking, especially as a former Head of History, who loves and values dearly historical knowledge, about how this type of comment around the purpose of education is taking more and more hold of the debate concerning what we will be and what we should be delivering in schools for now and the future, especially viewed through the digital learning lens. Even in the late 1990s I remember a school bursar arguing with me over my request for a set of text books because "in the future there would be no more paper". Like all things around predicting the future, the flying cars and cities on the Moon etc., they haven't quite come to fruition yet. Unfortunately, in education capricious fads come thick and fast and I have been struck over the weekend on #Edu-Twitter by one commentator referring jokingly to "cutting edge futurism" with reference to those who use the term "C21st learning". As someone who references this a fair bit, it did make me go back and question how I was using it in explaining the educational approaches of Wyedean School and the point of global learning in general. It's made me think even more introspectively because Wyedean is about to embark on a widescale consultation with all parts of its community (sorry, cannot say "stakeholders") looking at the "preferred futures" and the vision of the school going into the 2020s.

What I do know is this: the "knowledge v skills" debate is about as useful as the "Man v Food" programme on Dave. Certainly not as entertaining as the TV version of another false binary dichotomy in a zero-sum game. There are so many snake oil salespeople still in education. I've sat in "cutting edge futurism" conferences in the UK and overseas and listened to very well paid "gurus" with about 5 mins total teaching experience in front of adolescents on a cold wet dark Wednesday afternoon in November, to tell stressed and hard-working educators capricious statements such as 1) there will be no curriculum content in the future; 2) Coding will replace MFL or 3) the "3Rs will be replaced by the 3Cs". And of course, no one will have textbooks and all teachers will be robots. The way the profession has been treated poorly on a range of issues from pay awards to performance management and punitive QA systems has almost turned hardworking teachers that are still left in the profession into robots. But as the Welsh sing "Yma o Hyd" – "we are still here". The 3Rs are fundamental and have underpinned education in the past and will continue to be important but so will creativity, communication, and collaboration in learning. Coding is a vitally important area of computer science and digital learning which we need to invest in with more funding. Wyedean has recently begun working with the National Cyber Security Centre to develop this key area of the curriculum. This is one of the most exciting initiatives I have seen in over 20 years of education. My brilliant colleague and faculty leader, Emma Williams, is now simply "Agent Williams" and it is engaging so many learners and using outside agencies like the NCSC to positively influence education.

We are also aware of the fundamental importance of learning more than one language and there are a number of recent British Council studies emphasising the damage being done as the UK moves to a "linguaphobic" situation:

https://www.theguardian.com/books/2018/may/28/british-linguaphobia-has-deepened-since-brexit-vote-say-experts

I refuse to believe that tools like Google Translator, useful at a facilitating level, will replace learning languages and all that knowledge acquiring means to a learner when they use it to engage people and culture in a wider global society that isn't monoglot English. What has been illuminating in the initial discussions I have had with colleagues, governors and teachers about the future of education in Wyedean is that no one is falling into the "curriculum reductivism" model in the discussions or suggesting learning is all about "skills". The noises coming out of Ofsted and the new framework in 2019 is focusing all around the curriculum and for schools to have a much more strategic approach to why they are delivering the model to their students. This is actually to be welcomed and there are very few systems in the World where there is a coherent strategy around the skills, knowledge, and understanding students will acquire in their experiences of the informal and formal curriculum that will form their education model through their schooling. More importantly, aiming for a purpose beyond school and linked to the values and positive contributions individuals make to their local, national, and global societies.

It was well received news last week that in Wales the recommendations were to allow the inspection service, Estyn, a break from inspecting schools to actually allow them time to implement the very interesting curriculum reforms of Graham Donaldson on the Welsh system. More strategic thinking like this on the English side of the border would be more welcome. I am speaking at a British Council event for Welsh senior school leaders on school improvement strategy in Cardiff next week and I will certainly be praising them for this refreshing approach to actually allow something to be developed and established, especially something as important as a nation's approach to curriculum and its future through the education of young people.

The American author, William Doyle, stresses the following six things we all need to consider in education when we speculate what the future of education will be:

1) Students' well-being;

2) Teachers' well-being;

3) Social and cultural well-being;

4) Nature-Play;

5) Collaboration, professionalisation and research;

6) Post digital schools & non-digital oasis – effective but limited use of screens.

Doyle's points echo the very things we miss when we fall into simple, easy, lazy, and fractious arguments, often based on the personal becoming the general in debates about the purpose and direction of education for the 2020s and beyond. The strategy I had when I first became principal of Wyedean in 2015, which had underpinned my approach as an educator and school leader since I started teaching in the mid-1990s, (staffrooms not stinking of cigarette smoke as they did back then is clear progress) is the curriculum needed strands to join it up and in particular the strands of global, digital, creative, and sustainable learning. There are more, but these are the four I focused on. When we look at social mobility issues in the C21st or BAME or gender equality or LGBTQ+, the socio-economic and equity elements of education should be considered more in the curriculum and the education experience in our schools. This is something I feel I could be doing more to lead on as a school leader going forward, as this has not been raised nearly enough in broader education debates especially at the supra-national level. When I first became involved in the IB at the start of the millennium, it was the IB Learner Profile and the type of student that would emerge from the whole IB experience which impressed me and still blows my mind as an educator, and just makes sense whenever I catch a progressive /conservative /neoliberal /liberal education debate on what we teach in schools and how we teach it:

Currently, my good friend and colleague from Gar-Field High School, Virginia, and presenter of the White House burning painting to me, Brian Bassett, is with his IB students and colleagues in Ghana working with partner schools and communities to build libraries full of those old fashioned educational quirky things Guttenberg called "books" all those centuries ago. Everything about an educational philosophy, approach, and lasting legacy you would want for the C21st and for that matter the C22nd, which some of these students may just make it into to pass on a baton to the next generation. On a similar note it is very welcome that the European Commission is offering young people age 18 a free travel pass this summer to see Europe through their Discover EU scheme and a number of my sixth formers at Wyedean are applying for this horizon widening opportunity. Brexit means we are leaving the structures of the EU, not the continental geography of our allies and neighbours of Europe.

I have been very fortunate to begin working with one of the most inspirational global educators around, and a 2018 Varkey Global Teacher prize finalist, the Norwegian teacher, Barbara A Zielonka. Barbara is a passionate advocate of the Sustainable Development Goals (SDGs). From this September her #bethechangetakethechallenge1819 initiative is being launched in over 100 schools worldwide to raise awareness of the SDG by using digital learning to link global classrooms, subjects, and develop skills such as the American academic

Patrick Kyllonen defined as C21st century learning in 2012 as cognitive, inter-personal, and intra-personal competencies. I am very honoured to be the UK ambassador for this initiative and to work and share ideas with incredible educators across the globe. Barbara is also behind initiatives such as "How can technology empower the class of 2030?". More of that cutting-edge futurism but only this time it is! It is in Wales where the teaching of the SDGs is compulsory in the curriculum, something else we could learn from over the border of the River Wye. I feel I can look Barbara in the eye especially now the school's solar panels covering the entire roof space have been installed and switched on. Chepstow announced it is "plastic free" on the weekend and the BBC announced "plastic" was the children's word of the year. I am in awe of the schools that are committed to be plastic free by 2020, and this is something I will look at in Wyedean. The power of "The Blue Planet" changing attitudes and approaches as we are truly all in the process of being educated. This theme of the SDG is always linked to our annual Wyedean Creativity festival and this is being held on the 6th July.

My colleague, vice principal academic and best timetabler on the planet I have ever seen, Gwennan Jeremiah, is attending a SW RSC conference this week on curriculum approaches. I am hoping it is not just about how we squeeze the curriculum into the politicised EBacc. Believing in the future is also to be an optimist by default I keep telling myself. My colleague and Wyedean's director of teaching and learning, Julie Smith, wrote an article in last week's TES on the school's approach to "stretch and challenge" learning and we are speaking to Eastern European colleagues online at the MTEA annual summer conference next week about this inclusive approach at Wyedean to creating compelling learning opportunities through challenge:

https://www.tes.com/news/gt-we-must-stretch-all-students-not-privileged-few

Often the "preferred future" is the one that is already happening and the one that has always been underpinning the very essence of what we do in education always. Not a panacea, silver bullet or any guru's snake oil to miraculously solve overnight all society's ills through education and our schools. To return to Socrates, who I quoted at the start of this blog, 2500 years ago I am sure his "Socratic method" of teaching was being sneered at because it was seen in Ancient Athens as "cutting edge futurism" by his peers. Well, it has stood the test of time and tomorrow I will deliver an assembly to Year 10 and a critical thinking lesson to Year 12 using near enough the same methods of teaching and learning from the Classical Greeks. It still seems to be working well in 2018 and when you work with young people in education, you are always building the new. The "preferred future" is a decent one for the next generation avoiding the mistakes so often made by others in the past.

21 June 2018

Real Digital Learning is not Digital Distraction. Why we need to move past seeing technology as the "enemy of the age" and educate, beyond our schools, the crucial integrated facilitating role it already plays across global society in the C21st.

"Can you imagine teaching, or indeed day-to-day life, without technology? Although many people view the future of our world as digital - they are wrong. Our world is already digital - as any teacher or schoolchild will readily attest. This environment moves fast..." Julia Adamson, Director of Education at BCS, The Chartered Institute for IT

"The technology itself is not transformative. It's the school, the pedagogy, which is transformative." Tanya Byron

"The place of mobile phones in the classroom seems to me dubious at best." Amanda Spielman, Chief Inspector of Ofsted speaking at the Wellington Festival of Education, June 2018

I sat in a meeting of school leaders this week and what I noticed is something that is now such an everyday part of human interactions that we take it for granted. No one appeared to be listening and everyone appeared to be distracted by their technology. We have greater connectivity and facilitating technology than ever before, but we are becoming more disconnected it would seem. Let me go back to the beginning of my sentence; this wasn't a classroom full of children or even a packed commuter train where you would expect people to be glued to their devices for music, books, newspapers, email, social media, videos etc. This was a room full of school leaders. School leaders lamenting about the decline in standards of behaviour and about students not engaged with school.

I wanted to write a blog piece about the phenomenal impact digital learning has had on Wyedean School as a key strand of learning but this week there were a number of comments and reports that should not be unchallenged. The thing that happens in education too many times is a new agenda will be announced, and then already overburdened school leaders and teachers will get to the end of a long academic year feeling they can't quite rest because someone very important and influential has made an announcement, and no one is quite sure if it is a policy, in the Ofsted framework or just advisory. This week first the Culture Secretary, not the Education Secretary, Mike Hancock, announced that mobile phones, but not devices, should be banned in school because they disrupt and cause low-level poor behaviour. No study cited. At the Wellington Festival of Education, the Chief Inspector of Ofsted, almost word for word, has made the same call. As a school principal of 1100 students aged 11-19, I think this is a very worthwhile debate to explore and to have in education right now even alongside the chronic underfunding, the recruitment crisis of teachers, the narrowing of the curriculum, and the dysfunctionality of local-national accountability and responsibility of academies, MATs and the local authorities. The reason why we need this debate, informed by randomised control trials across schools and age groups, is because it is a debate that needs to be moved on conclusively. I read the annual Roehampton University TRACER report this week and I have referenced the opening quote in the foreword by Julie Adamson at the start of this blog. Anyone with an opinion on technology and young people should not only think about their own relationship and interactions with technology, but also think carefully and deeply about the place of technology in our digital world. For me, this quote should be at the start of any informed debate.

For many schools, poor low level disruptive behaviour is the main barrier to progress and school improvement success and I have no doubt the use of mobile devices not only distracts but causes untold issues when used in a negative, undermining way, but won't solve chronic underfunding, poor aspirations or unpreparedness for a global and digital society. What these schools need is a greater panacea than Ofsted "helpfully" suggesting that mobile phones are banned. Greater funding and deeper understanding of the issues around social mobility and aspiration may be a place to start. Not driving out hard-working teachers and school leaders labelled as "failures" by Ofsted from the very schools and communities that need them most would be another. No doubt we will also hear that an imitation loud grammar school blazer with a good crest and silent corridors will solve all the ills of these schools. The recent report from Stephen Tierney, of the think-tank, Heads' Roundtable, report in this week's TES about Ofsted not being fit to "judge" a school in a deprived area because it is more than five times likely to be failing than one from an affluent area is powerful evidence. We need to move beyond blaming a phone, a community, a student or an educator, and beyond looking for simple short-term solutions that may have initial impact but are not sustainable and ultimately the old problems with deep root causes soon reappear. The link to the TES here:

https://www.tes.com/news/Ofsted-fit-judge-deprived-schools

Anecdotally, mobile phones were banned in a rural school I worked in, after many hours poring over a draft policy. Here is the thing, the policy said only phones. The "knowledgeable" adults could not think past their own digital experiences and knowledge; and students just brought in other digital devices; and the perceived issues remained. The rural locality with the long bus journeys, winter nights, and dark lanes meant parents had no way of being in communication when their child left to and from school. There were very real and serious safeguarding issues caused by the fact students could not contact home not just after school but also for school clubs, trips, and revision sessions after school. The student council fed back and said the hour or so commute was valuable reading time, music time to relax for good well-being and time to revise, all using their phones and or devices.

On the longest day of the year and summer solstice, with the wonderful sound outside my window of the Year 6s here for transition week and the anticipation of this next cohort joining us in September, I met with my brilliant group of Year 9 Critical Thinkers this morning. I was all set for Refugee Week debate and ready on throwing into the critical forum Trump and the disgraceful practice he has ordered of separating young refugee children from their families on the Mexico-US border along with the new Italian government's "tribute" to the 1930s and their approaches to the Italian Roma communities. We went for a discussion on technology, digital learning and young people, and mobile devices. I will repeat again a point made in many blogs; I talk to the students of Wyedean and I am filled with so much hope at the wisdom and decision making abilities of this generation for the future compared to the present one. So in no particular order of discussion from critical thinking Year 9s:

1) Safety and safeguarding: the majority of students here catch buses, often living in rural areas especially in the Forest of Dean. Having a phone is vital for communication alone. A bus broke down on the A48 yesterday on the way home and students were able to call individual parents/carers in advance. School texted home as well as a post on Facebook and an alert on our Wyedean App.

2) Policing: Would we have scary and intimidating security and body scans/airport scans at the school gates with a huge queue of students entering the building each morning? Personally, I prefer the current school culture of standing out at the front of the drop off and just wishing students a great day with a smile. Liability of storage of 1100 phones in school?

3) Effective use in learning: Online tools and apps are used extensively in innovative and engaging learning and access through mobile devices is now an everyday part of learning culture. For example, use of the app Kahoot and interactive class knowledge quizzes, Show My Home Work is now invaluable to us in not only for the setting of work but also allowing independent learning and home involvement. Students also use this in their free periods, at break, and lunch around the campus extensively.

4) School has a robust behaviour policy and misuse of devices already as our core commitment to a positive learning

environment for everyone: Good schools set these boundaries and enforce them.

5) The social media World continues after school: There is no "cut off" for our duty of care or partnership with parents at 3:30.

6) Adults are often worse than young people for digital distraction and inappropriate use of phones: What have people such as Trump demonstrated about aggressive trolling and unacceptable behaviour to women, minorities, children without consequence?

7) Digital society preparedness: how would removing technology help anyone prepare for a globalised society functioning with so much technology? Pay apps are very popular on phones with young people so they do not carry hard cash for example.

8) Global Learning: How many countries and schools are we able to connect with using Skype, Zoom, and Google Hangouts etc. On Monday, I presented to Eastern European colleagues in their conference in Chisinau an hour-long presentation on "Stretch and Challenge Learning for all". We need global connectedness for a post Brexit "Global Britain" even more.

9) Wider access to learn through World Universities through MOOCs and already alternative additional curriculums exist for individual learners in school using edx, FutureLearn and others. Many use their devices in the library and common rooms to study on these.

10) Like everything, social media has a negative side but we use it in a very positive and celebratory way in school: Students who aren't sporty can see the sports team doing well like the Softball, Rounders and Athletics teams this week. The Year 7 "First Give" presentations in the JK Rowling library used digital learning and shared with home and the wider world this way. Huge thanks to the Mayor of Gloucester for being a judge! She tweeted it too!

I want to add here a very thoughtful piece by the American EdTech expert, Ethan Miller, on the ever-brilliant "TeacherToolkit" this week looking at the question of "too much technology being bad for students". I would extend that to adults as well. The link is below and there are four very real points policy makers, educators, parents and young people should consider what Miller posits:

https://www.teachertoolkit.co.uk/2018/06/19/too-much-technology/

• Social media addiction and cyber bullying

• Rise in physical and mental health problems

• Disconnect from the real World

• Too much Edtech can be overwhelming for students

I am aware this is a long blog but sometimes these things cannot be dealt with in "280" characters even if the president of the USA thinks it is possible to solve most complex issues this way. I will leave this with the discussion from Year 9s: *"We still love reading books, taking a walk, having a coffee with friends, playing real sports/games, and seeing live events. Schools have had money cut dramatically from well-being and counselling services to a record low. Go figure. Minecraft or Fortnite are crazes for young people in the same way that crazes for young people have always existed. Adults need to stop "worrying".*

https://www.newyorker.com/magazine/2018/05/21/how-fortnite-captured-teens-hearts-and-minds

We need to build into schools more outdoor learning like the DofE weekend my students and colleagues had in the Wye Valley last weekend. Sports, well-being, enrichment need more status in the curriculum – gardening club is very popular here. Technology and digital learning are as fundamental to young people as literacy and numeracy. Global learning is wonderful online but seeing visitors like our Japanese partner school this July cannot be replaced as a "real experience". Final word, adults need to model the values, priorities, and behaviours they want to see in young people. This "technology/behaviour" issue is as much a young person issue as much as a wider society issue where "poor behaviour" in every form is now the norm for adults all over the online world. See Guardian article link:

https://www.theguardian.com/books/2018/may/30/ten-arguments-deleting-your-social-media-accounts-right-now-jaron-lanier

So to the positive. Digital Learning is a key learning strand of the curriculum at Wyedean School, connecting subjects, and facilitates innovative learning, as it should in all schools. It is not about gimmicks, expensive white elephants or looking for "cutting edge futurism". The worry highlighted in the Roehampton report this week is the smaller number of girls taking Computer Science and the overall take up for the subject with the removal of the more general ICT qualification. In a digital World that already exists and is getting more sophisticated, we should be prioritising Computer Science and digital learning even more. I would like influential educators and government ministers shouting this from the rooftops rather than talking about banning all mobile phones in schools. The French have passed a law to do this in schools from September. Yet it was President Macron this week who recorded his face-to-face put down of a school student then trolled it on social media for the more powerful moral figure in French society to make his cheap political point at the expense of a French teenager online for the World to see.

My innovative and tireless colleague, Emma Williams, has been truly transformative in her leadership and vision of digital learning at Wyedean. This is nowhere better illustrated than the partnership she has developed working with Newent School and with the National Cyber Security Centre (NCSC) as a "Cyber School". The partnership with the NCSC has just been a remarkable development.

I recommend https://twitter.com/WyedeanComputes if you want to see compelling, innovative, and digital learning across the curriculum and some of the recent digital learning events like the Dragons Den, the Coding Club, AI, outside speakers or just using the Raspberry Pi that have all added to incredible transformative digital learning at Wyedean. I think to when Bill Gates said, *"Technology is just a tool, in terms of getting the kids working together and motivating them, the teacher is the most important."* Educators like Emma are such teachers who motivate students and enabling them access to technology and digital learning to engage them and prepare them for their future lives and their world.

I want to finish with a lovely comment made by two Wyedean parents on Twitter today about their son being able to take part in the Coding Club. This is why digital learning needs to continually be placed at the heart of the curriculum and we move away from the "digital distraction" debates.

"Thanks for putting on this club. My son is loving it and learning so much. Really appreciate the efforts you go to at Wyedean to give our kids such brilliant opportunities."

Working in education is the best job in the World! Digital, Global, Creative, Caring, and a Sustainable World.

2 July 2018

We must harness the power of agency in education to improve social mobility.

"Geography is destiny." Abraham Verghese, physician-author

"The need for political leadership in this area has never been more pressing. Social mobility is one of the biggest challenges facing our country today. It is not just the poorest in society who are losing out. Whole communities and parts of Britain are being left behind economically and hollowed out socially. The growing sense that we have become an "us and them" society is deeply corrosive of our cohesion as a nation." Rt Hon Alan Milburn, former Chair of the Social Mobility Commission

"Education is the civil rights issue of our generation." Arne Duncan, former US Secretary of Education

My former teacher and mentor, Les Jones, was born just outside Wrexham in North Wales around the time of the dreadful Gresford Colliery disaster of 1934 that took 266 lives of that close-knit mining community, including members of his family. A coal miner's son and the youngest of four he would go on to take his place at the local grammar school, Grove Park, and later to win a scholarship and place at Magdalen College, Oxford. I once asked him what had been the significant factors that had enabled what the experts would now call "intragenerational social mobility", an individual's upwardly mobile socio-economic class strata shift hard to achieve even in 2018 but especially in a Depression/World War era, class ridden British society in the mid Twentieth Century. His reply was twofold: Firstly, his family and the strong community stability of his colliery town that provided him with so much support, aspiration, and love. It really does take a village! Secondly, the access to education and learning he had growing up. In Wrexham, the great nineteenth century Scottish-American steel magnate, Andrew Carnegie, had built one of his many public libraries across Britain and USA in one of the most significant philanthropic gestures of that era. Akin to the work of the Gates Foundation today. My old teacher benefited completely from this foresight in allowing the masses access to learning and, similar to the approach to education of self-taught revolutionary leader Mao Zedong, who Les often said he took the lesson from, as he read every book available in Carnegie's generous gift of that library to the inhabitants of industrial Wrexham. It worked and after university he never looked back, and continued to learn and put back into society through his career as an educator, community leader, artist, and a wise holistic teacher to so many students in the UK and around the World over the decades. He is still doing it now in retirement from his rural home in the hills of mid Wales.

The Indo-American sociologist, Anindya Kunda, asked the crucial question of our time in his 2017 TED Talk, "*How can disadvantaged students succeed?*" and he used his own background growing up in America with an Indian heritage and other stories from his career as an example of how that is possible. He categorically rejects the easy notion that these students from very disadvantaged backgrounds simply had "grit and resilience" and "pulled themselves up by the bootstraps" which often seems the opinion of the privileged and the elites when viewing such cases. Kunda as a sociologist focusses on other factors that influenced their agency, built their capacity, and allowed them to navigate the system. A system in America where aspiration and doing better than the previous generation is so ingrained it goes as far back as colonial times and is enshrined in the constitution. Andrew Carnegie was a poor Scottish immigrant arriving in that country hoping for social mobility as much as another later Scottish immigrant in Mary Anne Trump, nee MacLeod or the

Slovakian immigrant Melania Knavs arriving in New York in 1996. Kunda in his talk looked at the pathways, support, programmes, and social scaffolding that allowed very disadvantaged individuals to become socially mobile. Learning simple skills that most socially mobile people have, like having networks, relevant skills and cultural capital through education for example. Kunda puts the important caveat in all of this success and said we should think of people who obtain social mobility as being "exceptional" not the "exception". By thinking of them as exceptions, we take away society's responsibility to help people, students, and families in similar circumstances. I am also hoping that the use of and the sneering around "Vicki Pollard" type working class characters has long gone from the stereotypes some sections of the media and professional classes have when they view the working class.

https://www.ted.com/talks/anindya_kundu_the_boost_students_need_to_overcome_obstacles

When former President Obama's Secretary for Education, Arne Duncan, made his call to arms in 2010 by declaring that "education was the civil rights issue of our time" using the very powerful analogy of a fundamental societal problem to solve with the first black President sitting in the Oval Office, that clarion call echoed across similar Western societies including a post-industrial Britain. Looking at the issue of increasing greater social mobility opportunities for disadvantaged children, families, and communities ranging from coastal towns, former coal mining towns, and areas of rural deprivation has occupied governments for a long time and certainly has become a priority in the 21st Century to try to tackle poverty, poor attainment, and perceived poor aspirational attitudes. Education is more than the silver bullet here. Education is critical to the success of offering a lasting solution and having a wider resonating legacy throughout these communities. All governments recognise this and it was the cross-party commission on social mobility led by former Labour minister, Alan Milburn, and former Conservative minister, Gillian Shephard, which spent most of this decade looking at solutions to tackle deprivation and how to increase social mobility for some of the poorest communities of the UK. The last two years of British politics has seen a political agenda dominated by one item since the 2016 referendum vote and that is Brexit. As a consequence of this, Alan Milburn resigned from chairing the social mobility commission frustrated by his perceived lack of progress and support from the government. The Commission's November 2017 report is still relevant and remains one of the most detailed, comprehensive, and analytical reports into deprivation, lack of opportunity, and poor social mobility in the UK. The report highlighted the "cold spots" in the UK, where there are poor social mobility opportunities and that included the Forest of Dean. For example, many young people in low and low/middle income families will do worse economically than their parents. In some of the "cold spots" less than 10% of young people will go onto Higher Education. It is vitally important for the Forest of Dean that Post 16 centres thrive like the one we have at Wyedean, offering academic and vocational routes and aspirations to our young people, and Wyedean is supporting the proposal for a Sixth Form for Dene Magna School in the central/north part of the Forest of Dean. The 2017 report also found UK levels of social mobility for young people were far lower than many other countries. Those from high income and professional backgrounds who have all the structural and cultural capital that social mobility requires still predominantly dominate the top professions and universities.

Connectivity is also a key factor and to echo the writer Verghese, it really is about where we are from. Wrexham or the Forest of Dean or even Appalachia. The 2017 Commission spent a long time highlighting the urban/rural split in term of social mobility and education. Connectivity is the key not only addressing poor transport for remote areas but also in terms of connectivity and digital literacy. I had the pleasure of talking at length earlier this week with Dame Sue John, the Executive Director of Challenge Partners, formerly, known as the London Challenge. London does stand out from the rest of the UK and the next 20 UK cities for being a "hot spot" for social mobility. The London Challenge, and subsequent Challenge Partners of now over 400 English schools, also stands out as one of the most remarkable peer to peer school improvement networks and this has had a knock-on effect on the quality of education being delivered in London and so many other schools like Wyedean. London schools are achieving higher than the Kent grammar schools. I spoke to colleagues in Wales this week in Cardiff about school improvement through global learning and lamented the waste of money thrown at an ill thought out imitation of Challenge Partners for Welsh education a few years ago, Challenge Cymru. It took huge amounts of money from already struggling schools in the Valleys, wasted it on educational "gurus" and was eventually brought to an end with no clear impact at all. Another costly failure on trying to improve schools, education, and social mobility.

At Wellington College's annual Festival of Education in June, the Chief Inspector of Ofsted, Amanda Spielman, contributed to the social mobility and education debate with this missive: *"Many local working-class communities have felt the full brunt of economic dislocation in recent years, and, perhaps as a result, can lack the aspiration and drive seen in many migrant communities"*. What was encouraging to see across the educational chattering classes on social media and subsequent media responses was a robust debate around social mobility, lack of opportunity, the white working class, deprivation in the UK, aspiration, and the perceived higher "drive and aspiration" of migrant communities. Including the purpose of Ofsted being debated in its current form and the negative contribution it has sometimes played in damning so many of these schools. In these very areas Ofsted focusses only on outcomes to make its overall judgement with little regard to socio-economic context as these schools continue to struggle with poor funding, disengagement, deep societal issues, and the damning instability of frequent staff turnover of around 70%. Her predecessor, Sir Michael Wilshaw, also waded in. A man many would hold responsible for the aggressive and narrow focus of OFSTED that is linked to harsh punitive accountability climates and a poor imitation of private school cultures being adopted to "raise standards" like the garish blazers, Ebacc drive, mis-understood house systems, and binary behaviour systems. All so loved by the short term "hero Heads" finally falling out of fashion when school improvement has always been a collective endeavour. And, of course, the now shrill call for mobiles to be banned in schools. A notion so counterintuitive to the very idea of digital learning and preparing working class kids for their already existing digital world. In these schools this approach fostered by the likes of Wilshaw's leadership has led to so many good irreplaceable teachers simply leaving the profession because of unrealistic workloads especially in the very areas they are most needed. To be fair to the current chief inspector she did also state; *"Schools in white working-class communities have a harder job to do than others"*. But since this speech, the new professionalism and desire to claim back leadership of education by so many educators and school leaders has seen the power of their agency taking to task these comments and OFSTED's entire approach to schools in deprived areas already struggling in difficult circumstances. This Tuesday an important piece of research by Toby Greaney and Rob Higham of UCL for Nuffield into the structural impact of changes in England will further add to the power of agency of educators to take on the "perceived wisdom" that presides:

https://amp.theguardian.com/education/2018/jun/30/market-led-education-system-puts-finances-before-pupils?__twitter_impression=true

Wilshaw's description of England's state education system as "mediocre" speaks more about his past leadership of HM Schools inspectorate for his years in charge of standards in education, rather than on hard working colleagues and communities battling a rapidly changing globalised society affecting and demanding on their corner of the World.

Dr Zubaida Haque wrote a 10-point response back to Amanda Spielman in the TES and this is not the first time Dr Haque has taken issue before with Spielman, especially over her comments about banning the hijab in schools last year. People seem to want to ban so much in schools. What I found worthy in Dr Haque's points is the first point: Career aspirations don't just come from home. Also point 2 – social capital matters.

It led me to have a look at the book review of Robert Verkaik's "Posh Boys" which looks at the place of independent schools in the UK in the 21st Century. The Guardian described it as *"A trenchant j'accuse against the old-boy chumocracy and the "apartheid education system" that perpetuates social inequality"*. As the principal of the very school Hogwarts probably originated from and the school least likely to look like Hogwarts even with the odd rickety staircase and ex caretaker who is more than a passing resemblance to Hagrid, I think this kind of argument doesn't actually help or add anything in the social mobility debate. If private school aspirations are about a "Hogwarts" model as school leaders told me at the COBIS conference in London in May, then their students are going to be suffering poor social mobility in the globalised and digital society of the 2020s and beyond as much as their white working-class counterparts in the coastal towns of England. And parents will be paying a lot of money for their child's privilege of fanciful 19th century idealised educational fiction and not being able to be socially mobile outside of a narrow English confine which no one knows what will even look like post Brexit-Global Britain. I have worked in and work with a range of schools, and whatever label we give them, what I have always found is all parents and carers want the best for the children. Working class parents want the very best for their children as much as any socio-economic class of parents. It was ill-judged for the chief inspector to say they had no drive or aspiration. I have also seen some of the worst and best lessons, school leadership, curriculum design, and safeguarding in independent schools and to say the private school system existing prevents social mobility is too crude and lets so many other factors off the hook in this fundamental debate.

Two things these last few weeks at Wyedean have given me very clear signs of hope, which is again about the drive and aspirations of our young people to want to use education to make something of themselves and navigate successfully a complex globalised society.

Firstly, seeing the future cohorts coming to Wyedean from our local primary schools as well as being able to take time in the very warm weather to talk to our existing students as we come to the end of a long academic year with the summer holidays ahead. The Year 11 Prom last week, a wonderful American idea that allows our young people to mark the end of school formally and make a rite of passage in their young lives. It made me so proud of how these students have grown in confidence especially with the stress of so many hours of exams this summer term.

The second is reading a captivating and hopeful article on the recommendation of my great colleague and inspirational global educator, Barbara Zielonka in HundrEd by Josephine Lister. The article is below and what it illustrated for me is the continued narrowness of the national confines of debates in the UK around issues like social mobility and the need to look for international comparisons and examples to inform our debates and search for solutions in a much wider way. I was blown away at the notion put forward by global strategist, Parag Khanna, that far from the revival of nationalism and aggressive populism that we see in Europe and America right now, the actual global trend is the continued rise of the urban megacity having much less in common with their nation's rural hinterland and more connectivity to other world cities. London already illustrates this in the UK along with cities like Paris and New York. One of my main aims for Wyedean and our part of the Forest of Dean and borders is to be proud of our area but make sure we are outward facing. This mentality alone is a key factor in the power of agency in developing social mobility for our students. Lister also references the work of the NGO BRAC in Bangladesh, a country suffering the impact of climate change with the constant flooding from the Bengal Delta. The solution for the young people, especially girls, is to get an education and to have special boats which could connect rural areas and act as schools if needed. Education is critical to social mobility as I have seen only too often in so many countries where it is not taken for granted. We can ban mobile phones all we want, but the key to education in the 21st Century can now exist on just two things – a device and a connection. The research of Professor Sugata Mitra and founder of SOLE has proved that with a more technologically literate generation than ever when school is not an option, young people in India and other places struggling to climb the social strata for a better life can do so because they can now access education through a device and a connection. "I *understand democracy as something that gives the weak the same chances of the strong.*" Gandhi

https://hundred.org/en/articles/there-s-a-growing-educational-gap-between-rural-and-urban-areas-connectivity-could-help-solve-it

I know the power of agency in education to improve social mobility, as a young secondary school student in the mid-1980s living in a former mining town, coming from a council estate and a large family where my father had been digging coal underground since the age of 15. I knew even then that I would need the drive to harness the power of agency to fulfil my aspirations through education. I was very fortunate that my brilliantly caring, funny, engaging, creative, and challenging woodwork teacher shared a similar background and somehow was in my school despite having a PPE from Oxford University and could name-drop his famous contemporaries impressing most people. I had teachers who took us to West Berlin, the Wall came down by chance, whilst we were there, a real moment of history. Teachers who made us so proud of our town and county's history and local identity that I still get a thrill driving past the barn when Charles II hid in 1651 after the Battle of Worcester and thinking "What if...?". A school where languages, Art, Drama, IT, Food Tech, Music, Creativity, Sports were as equal in the curriculum as other subjects. Teachers who gave us a love of learning, of books, and ideas. Who taught us how to debate and to critically think. Who brought the outside World to our corner of it, so we could talk to people in different professions and walks of life raising our experiences and life chances. Who didn't sneer at our popular culture because they saw it in the context of interacting with visiting museums, galleries, libraries, allowing us our heroes of the day akin to Gareth Bale, Harry Kane, Ariana Grande.

I have had more conversations from my own students about the World Cup and Russia this last week, and they looked shocked when I shared with them my own stories of visiting and working with schools and agencies in Moscow and Siberia. How did my own trajectory from the "neck-end of Madeley" get me to delivering lectures on History at Tomsk State University 10 years ago? My own daughters have enjoyed the film "*The Greatest Showman*", and PT Barnum is almost the classic example and advocate of social mobility in 19th century America as well as widening popular culture to the people. My daughters looked very surprised when I said to them at the end of the film, at the scene where Barnum is watching "*Swan Lake*" with his two daughters performing, that I had seen the actual lake outside Moscow where Tchaikovsky composed the ballet score. I have experienced this, all thanks to my teachers, who made going to university sound so natural despite the fact that we were the first in our families to do so. Families worked with the school and wanted such high aspirations for their children. I am not sure as a teenager in 2018 that I would be able to have the same path as I did in the 1980s and 1990s through education in the climate of today.

My late father in law, Peter Whittle, is another example of a white working-class boy who accessed education from the poverty of Royston Street, Edge Hill, L6 in a post war Liverpool and went onto study History at the University of Bristol, despite his mother refusing to sign his admissions and grant forms. When we scattered his ashes on the cliffs above his beloved Brehac plage on the Côtes d'Armor two years ago, we looked back at a life of social mobility of a solid cricketer, writer on the Liverpool Echo, teacher, yachtsman, brilliant chef and restaurateur as well as a man who learned languages and epitomised everything that was good about being a cosmopolitan European and being English. Although passing on his love of Everton FC to my three daughters has been raised a few times.

Education is critical to social mobility through high aspirations. The Observer article from the weekend starkly illustrated the deep challenges facing English education going into the next decade:

https://www.theguardian.com/education/commentisfree /2018/jun/30/observer-view-on-role-of-schools-generating-inequality-admissions

For education to mean something by playing a determining role in allowing social mobility for all, we do need to level the playing field but in the sense of greater opportunity, investment, and wider society by having high aspirations for all our young people and not just a few. We need it for the sake of cohesiveness and mutual prosperity. We are committed to it for the young people of our communities in the Forest of Dean and Wye Valley at Wyedean as all educators are in their communities as well.

"Aspire Together, Achieve Together: Wyedean is an academic and nurturing global school committed to World Class C21st learning for all. We aim to turn dreams into Futures." Wyedean School mission statement on the school website.

12 July 2018

In praise of the place of lazy summers in education.

"Rest is not idleness, and to lie sometimes on the grass under the trees on a summer's day, listening to the murmur of water, or watching the clouds float across the sky is by no means a waste of time." John Lubbock

"I love how summer wraps its arms around you like a warm blanket." Kellie Elmore

"A life without love is like a year without the summer." Swedish proverb

It was a bit of shock to answer the Skype call in my study on Monday morning at 9am to see the awesome students of Pinnacle College, Kyalami, Johannesburg, sitting in their coats and scarves. Especially after the weekly meeting of the staff to thank them for last week's work, briefing them of the events for the new week ahead, and mentioning the approach we have to coping with the unprecedented heatwave of the last few weeks in the UK. There are some real memorable moments of this job and getting to talk to the students and colleagues on Monday morning for over an hour about education in South Africa and Britain, diversity in our societies, the World Cup and England's chances, Welsh v SA rugby, J.K. Rowling and Wyedean, and even to have a lovely rendition of their school song is such a moment in education. I took them on a tour of the campus here at Wyedean courtesy of my mobile in the warm sunshine and asked students and staff here to say hello and answer questions, especially the new Year 12s from other schools for the Sixth Form transition week. The power of this global learning never diminishes and it is an important part of my role as a British Council ambassador and a Skype Classroom /Microsoft educator to ensure these connecting classrooms and schools around the World happen frequently. However, the coats and scarves in Johannesburg? Seemed so odd but the geographers here were at least able to talk about the Southern Hemisphere winter and how South Africa can also get cold. Dedicated colleagues like

Rose Lean and Principal Naidoo in South Africa are doing tremendous work in bringing the World into their school for the benefit of their community.

In between the end of term events, finishing off the key things for the academic year like the Principal and Leadership report to full governors, school evaluation of the year, and the summer newsletter to parents, I am trying to get through my 4 week online administrator/Principal's IBCP course. I never thought that I was a great student and to misquote Winston Churchill, I prefer to learn rather than be taught. How true for many of the students I have met as well as the glee when they found out Churchill had never been to university but still became Prime Minister and won the Nobel Prize for literature.

On Monday afternoon I took part in a conference call with the group of educators who are also working on the course. I listened to my colleague from an IB school in Texas talk about the racial tensions and gun safety issues they faced in their school in comparison to the UK and as I did, I did take a moment to savour and fully appreciate what an "outward facing global school" really looks like. This was and is it! It was also seen in a different and lighter way in the amazing energy from the phenomenal students from Kosei Girls' School Tokyo who spent the week with Wyedean students teaching them origami, calligraphy, traditional dances, songs, and just interacted together as global teenagers. In the IBCP conference Skype another colleague from South Korea, originally from Canada, raised some of the well-being issues she faces as Dean of Students at her campus because of the stresses and pressures teenagers, parents, and society places on them to succeed in Asian cultures like Japan, South Korea, China, and Singapore. In Lucy Crehan's book, "Cleverlands" there are many interesting points made, but what never is really addressed for me is the intense mental health pressure and issues around young people and their well-being in Asia. More importantly, what is being done to address well-being and mental health for young people? My colleague from South Korea said it was a real concern for her to actually get her students into some down time and not to be constantly studying late at night at home and early in the morning at school.

The heatwave currently in Britain makes my daily drive across the old Severn Bridge from Bristol and the view to the Forest of Dean and South Wales more akin to southern Spain right now, with the parched brown and yellow landscape desperate for rain. I "enjoy" the emails, texts and WhatsApp messages from friends and colleagues telling me their school/country broke up for summer "vacation" back at the end of May or June and why are we still in school? To be perfectly honest there is still so much to do and one of the best things we have done to cope with the heatwave in school is to anticipate it and be pragmatic about it. Students have been allowed to wear their PE Kit and shorts from the very start. If they are too hot and uncomfortable with the heat, still wearing a blazer and tie without access to water how on earth will they learn? I have taken the same sensible approach with staff who are expected to run the school and teach the students.

There are so many summer term events going on in Wyedean that it is hard to take stock of everything. For the last few months, I am conscious that the weekly Monday briefing is still half way through when the bell goes for registration as we are still thanking colleagues for their hard work and reading out the week's events. This week alone we have a Duke of Edinburgh expedition out, year group reward trips, Year 10 and 12 work experience, Year 11 Sixth Form induction, Year 9 Critical Thinking to the Bosnian Genocide conference at my old school RWBA, Public Speaking finals, Gospel choir events, PE teams are competing in country athletics and Rounders; the list goes on. Moreover, this is what schools should be doing in this summer term. The outward facing global school is also a school that believes passionately in the wider and enriching curriculum developing all students holistically and not paying lip service to it with a couple of outdated brochure pictures and references at new parents evening. Look at our school Twitter to see how rich the education is at Wyedean. In all of this activity, I know when I speak daily to students in the corridor and yard how much they are enjoying the variety and pace of the term. This is hopefully looking less like a treadmill of grinding education as possible.

Today, my colleague and director of teaching and learning, Julie Smith, presented to the weekly Teaching and Learning briefing on metacognition and self-regulation approaches to help students think and reflect about their learning and to follow more a study by the EEF this year. Julie gave colleagues time to think about these questions:

• Which explicit strategies can you teach your students to help them plan, monitor, and evaluate specific aspects of their learning?

• How can you give them opportunities to use these strategies with support, and then independently?

• How can you ensure you set an appropriate level of challenge to develop students' self-regulation and metacognition in relation to specific learning tasks?

• In the classroom, how can you promote and develop metacognitive talk related to your lesson objectives?

What occurred to me listening to colleagues discuss these questions is just how important the summer term and the summer holidays are for students especially, to have the time to reflect on their academic year and to take time to relax, read something or engage in something on a much deeper level without distraction. For students to become metacognitive and self-regulate, they need the balance and time to do exactly this and not an education system some of my global colleagues seem to be describing in the societies they work. The answer? The summer holiday/vacation! I have a whole heap of articles from various newspapers and journals that stretch back a few years over the same theme about the summer holidays. That they are, in no particular order: too long, Victorian summer farm work culture no longer needed in 2018, students forget what they have been taught, and the priceless classic, people who work in education have "all those holidays" – notice it is never accompanied by "and all that pay" and "all those additional hours on a weekend, week nights, half term breaks, etc.", that are put in just to get ready to teach during term time and deal with the complex issues around young people and education in 2018. However, to digress dealing with these viewpoints is not the aim of this blog.

I have given an assembly around the theme of the summer break and what makes us happy to the different year groups in the last couple of weeks, as I see them formally for the last time before the break. I even managed to retell the "happiness" anecdote to Year 10 around a dinner with President de Gaulle, Prime Minister MacMillan, and "Tante"

Yvonne in the early 1960s back when Britain was desperate to join the EEC. The assemblies I gave to students amounts to the same advice and that is to use the summer as a rest, to reflect, and take time to do something. At Wyedean, we believe strongly in "stretch and challenge learning for all" and on our website, there is a link to reading lists and activities to ensure that as well as taking time out to be lazy, getting up late, spending the day not doing much, there is at least something to look at as an alternative. It is not about young people being addictive to their devices and screen time either for the next 6 weeks.

http://www.wyedean.gloucs.sch.uk/Stretch-and-Challenge-2017-18/

Like all things, there is a cost and what society is willing to pay through taxation to build a progressive society for all, but I have always been impressed with the American, Canadian, and Nordic approach to summer camps/summer schools during the break to structure activities and opportunities for young people and actually to get them outside and a change of scenery. In a week in amongst the "turmoil" where those 12 young lads and their coach were finally rescued from the caves in Thailand; a week that Harolds' MacMillan & Wilson would have definitely described as "events, dear boy" and "a long time in politics"; there were two things that I read with interest in the context of the investment we place in our future through education and young people. The Public Accounts Committee released their parliamentary report into the cost of academies and MATS in England since 2011 and highlighted some of the worst cases of poor oversight of trusts, wasteful spending and profligacy with little impact on young people and their communities. A very dear colleague and the eminent professor of education at the University of Gdansk and visiting professor of education at John Hopkins University, Maria Mendel, released her book "Pedagogy of Common Places" which is a long study into an alternative to neo-liberalism and economics in the development of education in countries like the USA and UK, to try and get policy makers to focus on a humanising alternative based on sustainable community schools. Maria looks at the impact of the Charter School model in the USA and I was very fortunate to be asked to contribute on education in England and Wales. In the current binary education system of either/or, Maria's research looks at

196

communities where schools have improved through a systemic approach linked to learning, raising standards, and creating World Class opportunities but it is in the context of developing people and capacity focussed on young people as the main priority being prepared for a globalised society. Connected to that approach is a move away from the relentless testing for its own sake, and a culture ensuring schools are then anchored in the very communities which they serve. I saw this in evidence at the Wyedean annual Creativity Festival last Friday as a great learning, holistic, whole school, celebratory, community event in the July Friday evening sun. Listening to the Year 9 group at the festival singing the Red Hot Chili Peppers "By the Way" as my five year old daughter danced along was one of the most relaxing and best moments of the term. These students are so talented! We need to encourage and see this side of them more through these opportunities.

Dr Isabelle Moreau, of UCL believes we should contextualise "laziness" in space and time instead of contrasting it with "hard work". She believes just as we go for slow food, quality over quantity movements, in the summer we should go for slow work and that should extend to our students and colleagues at the end of the academic year to recharge and reflect, ready for when the autumn brings a different pace and priority as we start a new academic year. There are those like Dr Sandi Mann of the University of Central Lancashire who actually believe boredom now and again is actually good for us and plays a vital role in society: *"When we are bored we look for neutral stimulation. One way to achieve this is to go inwards and let our minds wander and daydream. When we are freed from the shackles of conscious restraints, we may see things differently and look at ways of doing things...it can be a catalyst for change and help us cope with information overload."* In Tanith Carey's book "Taming the Tiger Parent", she writes as a mother of two about the concept of a child's spark and this is something every child has and can get lost in as they are allowed the less formal structured time. They can only do this, she argues, if they have the opportunity to be left to their own devices – that does not mean mobiles or tablets! Tanith believes that some of the best learning is through being left alone to reflect and enjoy the freedoms to watch a film, go on a bike ride, read a book, meet with friends, listen to music,

197

visit the park or even sit under a tree and watch the world go by. This is why we will always need the periods of down time in the education calendar, to allow good memoires to form and to have less fear about the future. It is ok to be "lazy" in the summer.

I am looking forward to my own summer break, not necessarily the four days at Euro Disney my wife has booked, which my three daughters, aged 5, 7 and 9 are looking forward to, but seeing Paris and the two weeks in France visiting places we know well seeing family and friends. I am hoping to finish a biography on Charles de Gaulle *"The Last Great Frenchman"*, Mbappé may have something to say on this, by Charles William. I keep putting this down though and I need to stay away definitely from any leadership theory books for 6 weeks only picking up fiction, history or biography. I've got Madeline Albright's Fascism: *"A Warning"* lined up next. Light reading for the beaches of southern Brittany I know. After Sunday, we will also know if Football is coming home finally to England or will it be a case of "Allez Les Bleus" again. Bastille Day this weekend could be a spectacular one for France potentially. For so many, the 2018 World Cup in Russia has been a wonderful global event to be involved with whoever lifts the trophy as World Champions and to echo the wise words and leadership of England coach Gareth Southgate:

"Our country's been through some difficult moments recently in terms of its unity. And I think sport has the power to do that. And football in particular has the power to do that. So for us we can feel the energy and we can feel the support from home and that's a very special feeling. It's a privilege for us".

#GarethSouthgate would definitely want a well-earned rest, relaxation and reflection for any team or school community or even country that has worked so hard all year and need time out ready for it to all start up again during the autumn.

Have a great and lazy summer.

3 September 2018

Navigating a new academic year in a dysfunctional educational landscape through leadership.

"That one is never ready for the next step in life's journey, we learn what we need to know on the road itself." Quaker Faith & Practice 22-33, Elsie Boulding

"The pupils from this school, will leave with a lifelong sense of hope, a feeling for community, a passion for social change." Parker J. Palmer, *"Let your life speak"*

There was a Monday in August where I woke early even though it was the holidays due to the sound of the sea crashing against the granite rose coast shoreline. It was so compelling to listen to, especially combined with a spectacular sunrise due to the bay in this part of Brittany where my father in law lived facing east. Like anyone connected with education, the summer break and the changing of routines was very welcome particularly after another full-on academic year at Wyedean including the January Ofsted inspection. Lunch at a French family friend's house turned into a Gallic feast lasting four hours on one day. I think the average educator in a school is lucky to grab four minutes to wolf a sandwich down. But this is what the summer break is for in many respects, to break the routines, reflect, repair, and take stock ready for the new academic year in the autumn. It is hard to completely switch the mind off school and I am not sure I have ever gone away at the end of July to not even think about the year just gone and the year to come. I have found as a school principal, like the police, one is never really "off duty" and although the day to day changes for a few weeks, social media, and the two sets of exam results for Year 11s and 13s mean it is never a six-week absence without so much as a glance over the shoulder. There are three phases of the summer holiday for an educator; the beginning is where most brave the traffic jams on the motorways and the queues at ports and airports because in a few hours there will be a completely different environment and humanity slowly returns. My children commented how much more relaxed my face looked by the second week in France. Then there is the middle section of August with results and then at the end the preparation for the new academic year ahead. I enjoy all sections of the school break. The very precious time with family and recuperating; the sharing and celebrating success and being a support for students and parents on results days and now this final section of reflection and looking ahead.

My colleagues from the Music department gave up the first few days of their break to take the school orchestra and choir to Tuscany as they were performing in a number of concerts and events. At a time when this summer the status of creative subjects in the curriculum in most schools is looking critical as the arts are squeezed more out of schools in pursuit of a narrowing of the curriculum, music and the arts are flourishing at Wyedean. This was demonstrated in the very strong exam results obtained this summer and the numbers taking these subjects. The same goes for languages at Wyedean where the results and numbers opting for KS4 and KS5 are successful. They are a key part of the broad holistic curriculum we believe passionately in at Wyedean. The quote from Parker J. Palmer is in my cabin study at home and I aspire to this belief when I look at the priorities for Wyedean School. There were two brilliant examples of the school culture and ethos living up to Palmer's belief about the purpose of education and the mission of schools. Two sixth formers, Laura Willingham and Beth Garland, are members of the Gloucestershire National Citizen Service and this summer raised over £1k to help towards funding of the Opportunity Centre in Coleford. I am so proud of these two for what they are doing for children in their Forest of Dean community. The other example this summer is Lotte now going into Year 10. Lotte raised money in school at the end of last term for the Newport charity supporting people living on the streets, The Wallich, in aid of homeless people. I cannot wait for this generation to be leading their communities and country. In

200

this last week three sixth formers, Matt, Stuart, and Haydn were given a unique opportunity to further their digital learning and cyber skills with a work experience with Cyber Security Associates Ltd as part of the school's links to the National Cyber Security Centre. These lads had an informative summer placement and the company praised how proud they were of them. In between pushing out the "Stretch and Challenge" reading lists for potentially bored students who need something to occupy them that could be useful, it has been a busy summer. I even read and "enjoyed" a number of anticipated books including Madeline Albright's book "Fascism" and Julian Jackson's biography on de Gaulle. Mental note not to talk about de Gaulle and Macron in the same breadth in certain circles in northern Brittany and Paris again.

Preparing for the new year ahead is one of the key tasks for all school leaders, it comes with the territory of leading, and I know how colleagues must feel as they want to welcome back the school community and get the new year launched and underway. Even finding feet and easing back into routines is hard enough for staff, parents, and students. Definitely no four-hour lunches and especially no Sancerre to go with it. I have sat in the audience of the first day back in September and watched a few "state of the union" addresses from varying degrees of school leaders. The best ones don't try to solve the minutiae of the summer results with the uncomfortable "blame game" and certainly don't bombard with too much detail of every line of the school improvement plan. The best ones celebrate the success, reflect, and allow the new year to unfold with the key messages succinct for everyone. It's also the time when you look around the room at colleagues you haven't seen for six weeks, see new faces, and make sure they feel welcomed as we all started somewhere new once and as a community you miss those colleagues who left or retired in July. The strategic launch and ambition in school soon gives way to the operational day to day and the glorious stretch of the new autumn term, hopefully with an Indian summer, moves without warning to less daylight and the cold weather. Students are joining us for the first time in Year 7 and I always think how they must feel coming up from primary school. Most seem very confident and a good school community ensures they are part of it from day one. But not all settle straight away and therefore the nonsense around "not smiling before Christmas" has hopefully gone the way of "brain gym" and other "gems" of education. I believe passionately in the power of the school community at Wyedean and why having a positive school culture that believes in all people is key to the school's success. The autumn Open Evenings for the Year 6s and Year 11s wanting to join us next year is where we begin the fundamentals of this relationship between home, school and the student.

I start my 24th year in education since I first began at Bootham School York all those years ago as a teacher. I would like to say it has got easier especially with experience and the advances in pedagogy and technology. I have tried to avoid looking at national educational headlines this summer, but it is hard not to when education has two central days in a slow news month like August with the results focus. Bootham School was only a year in my career but knowing the brilliant Head and educator there at the time, Ian Small, and the school community he led based on a positive school culture, achievement, respect, and aspiration for all, has stayed with me. I hope some of his leadership is something I try to emulate as a principal now. In particular, his focus on what was best for the school community of Bootham linked to preparing the students for global citizenship as individuals with a decent set of shared common humanistic values and qualifications and skills to lead and live happy fulfilling lives. That challenge has never changed for any educator or school leader, but it is a challenge that seems to become increasingly difficult in an increasingly dysfunctional educational climate. As I prepared my talk for my colleagues at Wyedean over the weekend, I noticed I was reaching deeper into my leadership well of optimism as I read more and more about the educational climate we now operate in. I stopped reading, took a long walk with the dog, had a cup of tea, and then a quote from Stephen R. Covey caught my eye:

"I am not a product of my circumstances. I am a product of my decision."

Despite my disgust at the reduced funding situation for schools, the deliberate narrowing of the curriculum, the cut in SEND budgets, the false link to grammar schools aiding social mobility recently made, the sheer hours of exams and stress young people face as guinea pigs only to be sneeringly referred to by some as "millennial snowflakes", as well as a whole host of looking into the abyss situations such as the dire recruitment crisis of teachers and the growth of inequity and corruption stories around certain schools and MATs, I can choose to be a product of the decisions I make for Wyedean School. That is my role and duty as a school leader. I am the lightning conductor that can soak up most external pressures and create the culture for my colleagues to ensure the students of the communities we are proud to serve as their local school can experience compelling learning and unique opportunities that launch leaders like Lotte, Laura & Beth on their way to find their path in life with the skills and experiences we expose them to and embed so they *"...will leave with a lifelong sense of hope, a feeling for community, a passion for social change"*

This is how we learn to navigate the dysfunctional educational landscape of 2018-19 by repeating frequently our belief in the power of transformative education, supporting one another in a positive culture and using leadership to make sure success happens for all our young people. That is what I will be telling my colleagues when I stand before them for the first time this week and we launch another academic year together. As ever, I will be smiling from day one in September because I am privileged to lead a remarkable group of educators and support staff with our brilliant young people's futures in our sacred care as we work with the families and communities we are so proud to be a part of, day in and day out. We continue to work tirelessly for what is best for Wyedean.

9 October 2018

What does a 'good school' actually look like and mean in practice?

"There are schools that put mission before politics." David Barrs, Headteacher Anglo European School

"The education system the World over is still teaching for the 20th century." Sir Anthony Seldon, Chancellor of the University of Buckingham

The American educator from Colorado on the other end of the Skype conference call asked me a very simple but at the same time complex question last week when we met: "How would you sum up your school?" As a principal, I spend a great deal of time "summing up my school" and it means I have to think about the purpose and mission of Wyedean School constantly. My governors, colleagues, and parents would argue I should, I am the principal after all. It does not mean I am complacent about it or do not reflect upon it as a leader. The International Baccalaureate consultant asked me the very same thing on Friday when she came for two days to work with my colleagues, as we get ready to implement the IBCP in our curriculum and become an IB World School. I drove home over the Severn Bridge wondering if my answers were exactly the same or had I left anything out. We have the label "Good" from Ofsted following our formal HMI inspection in 2014 and 2018 but what does it actually mean? A couple of weeks earlier I had spoken to prospective Year 7 students and their parents and carers for the Year 6 Open Evening about not necessarily why they should choose Wyedean for their secondary school but what Wyedean School's education, ethos, and values meant for the holistic development of our young people in our care in our community. I spoke about three key aspects of the Wyedean mission: 1) Positive School Culture; 2) The outward facing school and 3) 21st century education.

I read something on Twitter on the weekend that summed up the role of the principal with regard to the importance of positive school culture and the influence on the school community climate. *"The school takes on the personality of the principal. If the principal is mean, the staff will be mean to one another and the kids will be mean to one another. If the principal is full of energy, excitement, and enthusiasm, the teachers will be energised to teach and the students will be excited about learning. The principal can either be a flame of positivity or ignite a flame of hope. The principal is responsible for the culture and mood of their school"*. I think this is true of any school, Head, or Principal even in a system where they are less autonomous say in a MAT, or in more centrally controlled education systems as in Wales. The first aim in Wyedean school's priorities is to believe in people. If we do not, then we have a negative school culture characterised by high staff turnover, fear, overzealous rules, and effectively compliance rather than true-shared learning and belief in the transformative power of education. I often feel so fortunate to have worked for and with so many inspirational colleagues, leaders, parents, and students that to not believe in people just feels so wrong. Every "good" school believes in its staff, its community and, most of all, its students.

The "competitiveness" between schools is one of the worst aspects of our modern day education system and it is not what we should be doing as places of learning. However, it exists. It was interesting to see this week that Singapore, an education system Lucy Crehan used in "Cleverlands", is abolishing school ranking: "Learning is not competition". A mission statement for any department of education. To listen to David Barrs speak at the RSA seminar in London to celebrate the 50th anniversary of the IB and hear him remind the audience that there were still good schools who focussed on their mission and not politics was a refreshing reminder that education doesn't have to be this way. The most powerful models that drive school improvement are when organisations and educators network, partner, and collaborate. That is why Wyedean is working to be an IB World School in a global network of 5000 schools. It is why we are in Challenge Partners working with over 400 schools in England. It is why we are a British Council Ambassador school working with phenomenal schools and teachers in the UK and around the World, and it is why we work with schools closer to home locally in the Forest of Dean and Gloucestershire formally. The border between England and Wales, as far as education is concerned, has become an unnecessary hard border and the only alignment now between two very diverse national education systems is that we only share the same names for qualifications. I fear the hardening of more borders going into the 2020s around the globe. I pray that I am wrong. It is a real shame when schools are forced to compete instead of collaborate. Students lose out.

Good schools share good practices. Gloucestershire is a selective county with grammar schools and when Gloucestershire Heads meet, this divide is often apparent especially around funding and resources. It was therefore encouraging a couple of weeks ago at a meeting of county secondary Heads to see unanimity against the further detrimental cuts in educational funding to school budgets.

This is where working together matters as schools face the gravest challenges with the funding forecast getting even worse. This is why normally apolitical school leaders marched on Downing Street in September. It is why the UK Statistics Authority taking to task the DfE's repeatedly misleading stats on school funding is a step in the right direction on the biggest challenge and crisis facing England's schools. It was the former Secretary of State, Justine Greening, who recently pointed out the inward mind-set of policy makers when she said: *"The Treasury sees education as a cost not an investment"*. Even the most forward looking, high performing, high achieving schools are struggling facing a future where funding has been reduced, according to the respected IFS think tank, of around 8%, and more costs like underfunded national pay awards and pension contributions are being pushed onto schools about to or now running at a deficit. Education is not a burden; it is an investment in the country's future.

The outward facing school is a good school for lots of reasons not least because it means bringing the community and World into the classroom. My first assemblies across all year groups this half term have been around "Languages" and I have focused them on the three aspects of learning more than one language, the vocabulary and communication we individually have as well as the importance of non-verbal communication. I always liked the quote *"Everyone smiles in the same language"*. Another sign of a "Good" school when everyone walks around the campus smiling and greeting one another. The "happiest" and the most smiles in schools I have ever seen was working in Indonesia, tragically now dealing with the aftermath of last week's tsunami that hit Sulawesi.

I am following the developments of the new Ofsted framework due next year not because I slavishly watch everything Ofsted does and base Wyedean's direction on an external inspection system, but because the curriculum is going to feature heavily in the new framework. A good school does not narrow the curriculum and approaches the curriculum from the point of view of holistic learning using a broad and rich curriculum. Someone said recently in most schools now the curriculum is just simply the syllabus studied in order to take an exam at the end. Maybe this is the case in some schools.

One of the main attractions for Wyedean looking at the IB is because their approach to the curriculum and developing the learner is the opposite of an exams factory educational approach. Hearing Sir Anthony Seldon speak at the same RSA-IB event as David Barrs, stating the majority of education systems are still teaching for the 20th century, reminded me why even in 2018 we have to talk about the 21st century as if educators and policy makers were unaware we are in this present century.

Last week when I had the pleasure of talking to Mary Murphy of Douglas County school board Colorado to plan collaborative work between our schools around global citizenship, the United Nations SDGs, all using a Microsoft learning platform, it made me think again about the potential we have in our schools every day for transformative learning. When I worked with the positive and energetic students of Heritage International School in Chisinau, Moldova, and their brilliant global educator, Tatiana Popa, for European Day of Languages through Skype last week, it brought home the compelling international learning we have in our schools. Every day my colleague Emma Williams is pushing the boundaries of learning with the work she does with Cyber and Digital learning in Wyedean. The author, Sarah Franklin, author of the WWII book, "Shelter", set here in the Forest of Dean, came into school to work with Year 11 students for National Poetry Day. The English department and our JK Rowling library work tirelessly to develop literacy and a love of reading in students. They are always holding an extra opportunity for further involvement in reading and their daily lessons are just superb to see walking around. I see the caring and nurturing work of the Wyedean pastoral teams daily to ensure that in a World where mental health problems for young people are on the increase with resources scaled back, my dedicated colleagues stay late, work early, and do all they can to support students to cope and deal with complex issues. My assembly this week to the Sixth Form is on Mental Health Awareness and I will make it very clear that not all adults over 30 castigate young people as "Millennial snowflakes".

A "good" school is not an Ofsted label. A good school is a school where the people who work there would gladly put their own children on that school's roll to be educated. A good school is a school where the climate and culture is completely based around learning and young people. Maybe this is the time of the year where the "open evening" and the marketing of a school does bring into focus the question of "how would you sum up your school?" and allows school leaders to reflect on exactly what the school stands for, and equally important, what it doesn't stand for. A good school should also stand for certainty in uncertain times so that we are sure that the complex global problems we face in our common humanity have future leaders who know how to work towards solving them, when reports appear in newspapers like the respected Washington Post stating we have around ten years to solve climate change through a collective drive on sustainability and give the planet and the generations to come a good future. We also cannot afford to lose sight of our mission in good schools for the sake of short-term narrow politics in the education of our young people.

8 November 2018

Why our education system always rests on Hope and Optimism even in the most challenging of times.

"Our ability to change a child's life is beyond imagination." Sir Anthony Seldon

"Optimism is the faith that leads to achievement. Nothing can be done without hope and confidence." Helen Keller

In Manchester last week, the British Council asked me to give the keynote talk at the start of their two-day Connecting Classrooms conference to a variety of organisations involved in global education ahead of the launch of the new version of this programme to schools in the UK. I was not feeling particularly optimistic though after a long day in school to deliver in the words of the organisers *"an inspiring talk about Wyedean and global learning"*. This was the first week after the half term break, all thoughts of autumn and Halloween with family in mid Wales diminishing fast, the clocks going back and the convoluted long train journey from Bristol, across to Newport, up through the Marches to arrive in Manchester late at night in the rain. As I stumbled tired around Sainsbury's at Piccadilly station to get a bottle of water, it was the very patient shop assistant, with the broadest and friendliest Coronation Street accent that put me back on track ready for the talk the following day. It really is the smallest acts of human kindness and decency sometimes that makes all the difference.

What the British Council continues to do in supporting schools and global education gives anyone in education working with them hope and optimism. The same case can be made easily for the remarkable work of DfID and the government's aid spending commitments around the globe, as well as the incredible range of organisations in the conference last week who are working with schools to support and inspire them as they develop international education. I had asked my Year 10 and Sixth Form Critical Thinking groups at the start of the week if they could provide a short-film discussion for me to share with the delegates. I used this in my talk at the start to ensure there was not a disconnect with the aims of the Connecting Classrooms programme and the very young people here in the UK and around the World who we want to fill with hope, optimism, and empowerment. The film link is here on YouTube:

https://www.youtube.com/watch?v=qd6c6iKCIok&feature=youtu.be&safe=true

It is funny sometimes the connection you can have with a place without realising it and Manchester for me is one of those places. As a young undergraduate in the early 1990s, I remember going to see the now late Labour leader, John Smith, in Whitworth Hall at the University of Manchester, give one of the most compelling cases of hope for Europe and cooperation in the post-Soviet World; this seems a very long time ago now in all respects. In my talk last week, I used the example of how teachers inspired me as a young person especially, instilling a love of learning and desire to find out more about the World. I was very fortunate to be on an A Level History school trip to Berlin when the Berlin Wall came down, and I was able to clamber up the Wall in front of the Brandenburg Gate to get a photo in the newspapers just before the DDR border guards kindly eased back us all down onto the Western side of the Iron Curtain. I used this illustration in the conference as an example of hope and optimism in education,

and the power of committed and inspiring educators. This
hope and optimism was still there when John Smith spoke in
1992 to me in the audience, only this time as a university
student, about the collapse of the USSR and the new post-
Soviet Europe and World we needed to build for the fast
approaching Millennium. The connection with Manchester has
led to a number of talks and opportunities to speak in that great
historic industrial northern city about global learning to all sorts of
audiences over the years. In 2017, I was asked to speak for the
British Council's Ambassador Conference on the Saturday
afternoon as the post lunch "pick up" – no pressure. I
remember quoting a line from Virgil I had read in the Classics
lesson in Wyedean the week before, as it just seemed to be so
apt at a time when hope and optimism were fading fast;
*"Durate et vosmet rebus servate secundis." – "Carry on and
preserve yourselves for better times."*

I thought of this quote when I watched the new BBC2
documentary "Schools" on the funding impact which was
filmed literally just across the eastern side of the Severn from
Wyedean. Knowing what we have had to do here over the last
few years to ensure that we removed a significant budget
deficit, which meant tough efficiency decisions grew the
school in a falling roll and kept true to our mission about our
educational principles with the students centre stage as
always. My heart went out to colleagues going through the
same process in South Gloucestershire as they reduced their
capacity to meet reduced funding:

https://www.bristolpost.co.uk/news/bristol-
news/worried-children-future-bbc-series-2192446

The "competition" culture in the English state system
makes me really miss the collaborative one I left behind in
Wales, but at least the hope from the broadcasting of "School"
and the raw honesty and despair in that MAT produce more of
the empathy and support seen on social media during and
following from the education community. It may even speak
some "truth to power" to help us all. The uncertainty around
funding and the general dysfunctional educational landscape
that requires skilful, resilient, and resourceful leadership is
something I spoke about at length in Manchester. I walk into
Wyedean every day and give thanks for the colleagues, teams,
governors, parents, and community we are so fortunate to
have this side of the Severn supporting Wyedean students. I

do not know even where to begin when a Chancellor of the Exchequer tells the House of Commons in a budget speech that he is making a one off payment to struggling schools after years of austerity for the "little extras". More money for filling in potholes than financing schools adequately. Words fail especially when the brilliant vice principal for Business and Finance Jodie Howells and her financial team get the school on a balanced budget that still keeps a broad curriculum at Wyedean true to compelling learning and enriching opportunities. This is before we are hit unexpectedly for pension contributions and an underfunded pay award that knocks out a delicately balanced budget.

Sir Anthony Seldon is however absolutely right. Our ability in education to change young people's lives through transformative education keeps us optimistic and gives us hope even in the most difficult of circumstances, and this is what keeps people working in education going. This extraordinary commitment and dedication is what most schools are now barely running on, as there seems no end in sight to the better times we are preserving ourselves for, according to Virgil. I cannot think of any time when I have been an advocate of what my great American friend and colleague from the Old Dominion calls "Macho BS leadership". Unfortunately it does exist in too many organisations, but it achieves very unstainable short-term gains and is always toxic. My talks this year ranging from working with colleagues in Heritage International School Moldova, META, Eastern European Foundation, COBIS, HET, and the British Council have been loosely around the mission and culture of Wyedean as an outward facing global school. The questions I use with audiences are what I regularly ask of my school community and myself as we keep away from a certain type of toxic leadership but keep our leadership always hopeful, optimistic, and focussed on the mission as a positive school culture:

• How narrow and inward are we as educators?

• Are we more about the mission or more about politics in schools?

• Are we preparing our young people for a global society and the challenges for the 2020s?

• Where does our leadership fit into all of this to challenge a "negative narrative" that seems to be gaining ground?

• How vital is a culture of professional collaboration in supporting schools?

So what does this look like at Wyedean? Not in any particular order, the following is a flavour of why walking through the doors here first thing every morning over the last few weeks continues to fill us all with hope and optimism in our positive school culture at Wyedean:

We welcomed our latest batch of around ten new teacher trainees from our partner universities for this term's placement with us. This gives me hope that teaching is still attracting good people into our ranks.

We have just been through the annual appraisal cycle with all staff, setting objectives to continue to develop careers and contribute to the school. This is such an important part of making sure people are valued and treated as professionals in the organisation.

We are currently preparing for our annual Challenge Partners Review and the team are here as critical peers from the 19th-21st November. This is a key part of our school improvement, quality assurance and ensuring we are involved with over 400 of the best schools in the UK in this outward looking dynamic network and partnership.

We are preparing in school to commemorate at the end of this week for the 11th November the 100th anniversary of the Armistice and Remembrance Day with our community.

Thanks to the extraordinary generosity and faith in Wyedean School by a member of our local community, we have been able to use their donation to commence building the Study Garden that will provide a designated outdoor learning space and an area for quiet well-being. This gives me so much hope to see this work underway although I do feel for the builders in the cold wet rain right now.

Before the half term break, the entire school community celebrated the life of former student Tirion Ray and raised money for the Lily Foundation to honour our late student.

We have been working with several community organisations including collecting for the Chepstow Foodbank and Year 7 students have produced amazing artwork as part of the 70th celebrations of the NHS to brighten up the X-Ray dept. in Lydney Hospital.

The community has also given back to us so much and we have promises of donations of several Christmas trees ready to be decorated at the start of December to make sure Wyedean looks festive. Also in time to welcome Year 11s from Gloucestershire and Monmouthshire to see the incredible success of our Post 16 education for Sixth Form Open Evening on the 29th November.

The strong relationship with the University of Bristol and the school has led to a number of opportunities over the last few weeks including a widening access scheme aimed at securing places for students supporting social mobility and lectures at the university for students especially for science and geography.

We are currently working with the University of Oxford to get Year 10s from Wyedean and other local Forest schools to visit and raise future aspirations for these students who may not see this particular path at this point of their lives. The University of Gloucestershire has been brilliant in their support of Wyedean especially assisting Sixth Form students write university applications. Cardiff Met University have also been in school last week working with students interested in careers in Law.

The phenomenal work of my colleague Emma Williams continues in the development of digital and cyber education at Wyedean through the partnership as a cyber-school linked to the NCSC. I would recommend anyone to view this on the "@WyedeanICTComputing" twitter feed. We do not fear the role, power, and technology in the lives of our young people now and for their future and a key part of our job is preparing them well for all of this, especially getting more girls into STEM subjects. It is also why banning mobile phones is not the answer for us in our school. It is so counter-intuitive to digital learning.

It has been wonderful to continue World Class global education over the last few weeks with Mary Murphy and her colleagues in Colorado and the brilliant Narattama Shama and her students at BSP Pilani, Rajasthan. Happy Diwali to all of our Indian colleagues and partner schools.

As I stood last week in Manchester watching my own students on the screen in the conference hall speaking to the delegates about their World, their aspirations, and their hopes I felt so much pride as their school principal and I am fully aware of the privilege we hold in education to potentially change lives beyond imaginations.

The reason so many people and organisations were brought together for two days by the British Council is to ensure by "connecting classrooms" in the UK and around the World, we ensure these global learning opportunities continue and transform communities through hope and optimism. From the Forest of Dean and Welsh borders to the mountains of Colorado or the suburbs of Chisinau. We are starting to see narratives being challenged everywhere again, and this is where our hope and optimism for the 2020s and the longer term future need to make sure we are preserved as we carry ourselves forward. From the hundreds of thousands of people marching in the London sunshine recently to the lines of queues standing patiently to vote in the US mid-terms, there is hope and optimism that our young people are not apathetic or indifferent to what is going on in their society. They will challenge and call out hate and they will replace it with hope.

I read recently not to shout louder in an argument but to make the argument more effective. We need debate and dialogue to get back to being able to disagree without being disagreeable. The young student who stood on the Berlin Wall stunned because he thought it would never come down, and the one who listened to the hope John Smith spoke about for the 21st century all those years ago knows as a now older educator and student of history that nothing remains the same forever. If this time has a purpose maybe it is to have taught us to value more what we have always had. Whatever colour the poppy, the symbolism of the poppy being worn and displayed in November for me is as much about remembrance as it is about looking to the future with hope and optimism that things will improve and get better. Hope is knowing there are better times; optimism is how we get back to achieving them through the transformative change power of education. Even in the most challenging of times, we cannot lose both in our schools and in society.

13 December 2018

School leadership for the 2020s, what should it look like?

"The greatest danger in times of turbulence; it is to act with yesterday's logic." Peter Drucker

"If you want to make God laugh, tell him your plans." Woody Allen

I recently had the pleasure of meeting and having dinner with a group of international school founders and IB school principals. The conversations were wide ranging especially around the issues of what international mindedness and a holistic curriculum looked like in practice in their schools. What has been left more in my mind, as I reflected later on, is the discussion we had around school leadership and the development of future school leaders, especially looking ahead to the challenges and changing landscape of education in the coming 2020s. A school founder who was new to investing in education made the point in the discussion that in her mind a school leader, whatever the national context and culture, needed to have the following approach for now and the next new decade: a commercial CEO's mind, an intellectually curious soul, and an educator's heart. A stimulating discussion and a delicious meal aside, I have been pondering this last point for a few days since the meeting, and not only wondering at the difference in a school leader in a more commercial independent school setting rather than a state/public school setting, but also questioning whether this is the case or not at all for all school leaders regardless. Finally, will school leadership be markedly different in the 2020s?

School leadership here in the UK, and in similar education systems around the World, has been transformed on all levels since before the start of the Millennium. The strong emphasis on more autonomy in the role coupled with a significant increase in accountability and responsibility means the job description and role I have today as Wyedean principal is a lot different from the very first Wyedean principal, and probable role model for JK Rowling's "Dumbledore", my predecessor,

Ken Smith. I have often looked around my room and wondered what all four of my predecessors must have thought at various times as they faced the challenges of their stewardship leading Wyedean School. The managerial and operational heavy role of my predecessors is more obvious when I look at documents like the old school log book, and they certainly didn't have the senior and middle leaders to support them as I am very fortunate to have now in 2018. There are many aspects of the role of leading a school community that have remained timeless, including the very crucial task of being the person who leads and guides the whole school community. When I first took up the role as principal it was this very fact that seemed the most daunting. My good friend and colleague in the US, Dr Cherif Sadki, a very wise and experienced school leader, likened being principal to being mayor of a small town. Cherif went on to say: *"Everyone wants a piece of you and there is never a moment to yourself."*

One of the reasons I wanted to write a blog on school leadership looking ahead to the 2020s is partially down to the fact there is a real concern that there are not enough school leaders emerging through the system, but also the calibre of school leaders who can deal with the challenges in leading a school is also an issue. I will state quite clearly here, being a school leader and principal of Wyedean School is an absolute privilege and it is my honour to be able to have the trust of my school community and the wider community to lead their school and serve in this role. But it is also fair to say that it is not without its challenges, not least adapting and preparing for a more challenging, changing, dysfunctional, fluid, and unpredictable educational landscape. When I think back to my very first job interviews as a young history teacher and inevitably, there was the final question along the lines of "Where do you see yourself in say four/five years?" I certainly didn't answer "Headteacher".

My ambition was always to be a good teacher and enjoy what I did as a teacher of history and politics having an impact on the students I taught. I was very fortunate to have worked for and with so many inspirational school leaders that, as my career become more established and I began the route into middle and senior leadership as a head of history, IB coordinator, director of 6th Form, I found I enjoyed the ability to lead and have a positive influence over a wider range of educational areas from curriculum to pedagogy. One of the crucial lessons that has stayed with me all of my career is that in education we have to have a love of learning and a continuing interest in learning.

The best schools are those that have these remarkable professional learning communities in operation, characterised by the absence of formal titles as individuals lead and instruct developing the learning community. This is one of the strongest features of Wyedean School and the director of Teaching and Learning, Julie Smith, herself studying for a PhD, has been instrumental in the drive behind this, especially using the Lesson Study programme for staff professional development. Both Ofsted in January and Challenge Partners in November strongly recognised the "re-professionalisation" of teachers at Wyedean and the autonomy and trust they have been given. The notion of a positive school culture is something I am responsible for, and I get to establish what that will look like and directly influence day to day culture as principal. I can influence the curriculum, learning in the classroom, and the pastoral care but the organisation, systems, and individuals in school all operating in a climate of professional trust and responsibility emanating from me as the principal is something that is timeless for effective school leadership. It was a feature in the best schools of the 1970s and it will be a feature of the 2020s.

I am very conscious that I demonstrate that I am constantly involved in learning as the principal. I undertook my Masters in educational leadership as I moved to senior leadership and before becoming a Head I passed the very administrative heavy NPQH here in the UK, a very practical course but an important part of my training; and I have continued to be a student of global learning, history, and politics with various online courses through a range of universities worldwide. There is an interesting debate always about the integrity of the principal in a school in terms of "walking the walk" by being an accomplished teacher and demonstrating that constantly. To be able to "look colleagues in the eye in a Monday morning briefing". My personal belief is that a school leader to be effective in education has to have a background in teaching but I am no way the "best teacher" in my school. I see so many colleagues teach and I am in awe of just how good they are in the classroom. I think it is very difficult to understand what you are leading in schools though by not having this direct classroom experience. Conversely, it is a very "British" idea for the Headteacher/Principal to be in the classroom more, whereas in the US, senior leaders are not in the classroom. The most important role for me is to be able to allow the teachers to teach in a well-run organisation with a strong educational vision and climate. The students are their number one priority but in order for that to be the sole focus, a school leader for me has to make sure the organisation is effective, efficient, and has a plan to where it is going. When I have spoken to aspiring Heads/Principals, I have illustrated the importance of being highly visible and energetic, but in terms of walking the walk there are so many ways that can be achieved through scheduled assemblies, some classroom teaching, intervention groups and mentoring, covering colleagues, taking on some specialist classes/clubs outside the formal curriculum. Just knowing the kids and not the ones who get sent to you for contravening the behaviour code. It is up to the individual school leader but to undertake this role outside of the daily joy of working with young people, sharing their trials and tribulations, sharing their success and failures, and just being there for them to ensure they have certainty and guidance is part and parcel of the fundamentals of why being involved is the only way.

One of the more frequent debates I read is about "moral or ethical leadership" in schools. I find it astonishing that this has to be explicitly made because for me it is obvious that if you work in education and you are fortunate to be entrusted with the progress and development of young people then your leadership couldn't be anything else but moral and ethical. Working in education is not for the faint hearted nor is it a career that you go into lightly. It is a vocation and from Day 1 it is apparent that this is like no other job. The rewards are incredible and the lows can leave you reflecting a long time after the event. Well-being, the perceived isolation, and our sheer resilience as the roles grow more complex as much more support is needed for school leaders is something I hope the 2020s continues to develop more in depth as this is much needed from the current position. School leaders are not machines, we have families and we do occasionally get things wrong. Shock horror! Back in the 1970s I am fairly sure my predecessor Ken Smith didn't contend with social media and the proliferation of daily life being played out online in the way we have to think about now both in our individual lives and in public. This will only increase in the 2020s but so will our ability to use it in a positive way and close down the abuse and negative way it is used. And we are very much human when all said and done.

Which brings me back to my posh dinner with the school founders/owners and IB principals. One of the facets of being a school leader, I came to realise very early on in my career, is that a good commercial mind was key to understanding and leading a complex organisation. I was fortunate to see and experience this in the US with American counterparts running their schools this way, and in the independent school system in the UK. The school leader of the 2020s has been reading articles in publications such as Forbes and the Harvard Business Review for a number of years. In the US and UK a school leader is much more responsible for a whole range of areas outside of just leading teaching and learning, ranging from Health & Safety, marketing, public liability, safeguarding, legal, financial management and accounts, and the list goes on. As budgets in the public purse shrink further, astute commercial skills are needed to look at how additional income is generated to support the core business of the school – students and their learning. This is also why it is crucial to be an outward facing school and use a range of partnerships and networks that bring benefit and value to the organisation.

The "educators heart" is something that is timeless and the best school leaders never lose sight of why they came into teaching and that thrill of the classroom introducing a new topic or idea and watching fires being lit, rather than the pails filled or the shape of the spoon being taught. The best times of the day and week are these moments, especially if I am grappling with a complex issue around educational law or the budget. My Year 13 Critical Thinkers did exactly this for me on Tuesday as we held our weekly class and there was no better place to discuss the extraordinary developments happening in Westminster this week than with my A Level Politics classes. I think the point in the discussion about the skills of the modern school leader going forward in the 2020s became more heated when we talked about a school leader having an "intellectually curious soul". For the school founders and owners this seemed to be almost a luxury add on at best and at worst an irrelevant quirk more suitable in the time of Mr Chips or even Dumbledore. Naturally, anyone immersed in the IB philosophy would disagree and to love learning and ideas is the very essence of education. The point was well made that we were all arguing that three aspects were needed in a "holy trinity" for the school leader, and each on their own would not have the same level of success and effectiveness. One colleague summed this up best when they said this was about always wanting to learn and not dismissive of new ideas or even being satiated with what we already know. I have to say, it has been a long time since I have heard any colleague disparagingly say to a struggling class or student, "well, I have my GCSES and A Levels". I am never sure how apocryphal this story is but I have always liked the idea that the future famous Welsh poet, Dylan Thomas, was skipping school in his hometown of Swansea and got caught by his Headteacher. "Where are you going Dylan?" the Head asked, to which Dylan replied "I am going home to write poetry". To which the Head replied, "hurry up then before you get caught". Dylan Thomas's father of course was the Head of English at the school. My other similar story but converse is of the New York high school principal who told a very young John McEnroe not to miss school to play tennis because it would never amount to anything. What do educators know anyhow?

What also connects this "holy trinity" together is the ego of the leader, or rather the lack of one. It's been a while since headlines have shouted about "Super Heads" or "Hero Heads" and what is more and more apparent in modern times is that, whilst there is no denying that the principal does play a decisive role in the leadership and culture of the school, to ignore or not allow other leaders to also flourish and operate is very detrimental to the organisation. Lots of people can bring so much more to the table and the worst organisations, be it schools or private companies, flounder if they build their leadership model on the skills and the talents of one individual's ego, no matter how good they have proven themselves. It is not sustainable and it goes when they leave. Without a constant flow of leadership talent and a systemic approach towards not only enabling actual real leadership, with real decision making ability and trust, but also developing the leadership capacity and succession planning, the organisation is only as good as the ego it is built on. School leadership in the 2020s will reflect increasingly this model of leadership rather than a thin veil of paying lip service to ideas like distributed leadership when the reality means control and power is in the arbitrary hands of one person. Leadership in the 2020s will reflect the times we are in and what may have worked in the 1970s or even the early part of the Millennium certainly won't be the approach in the 2020s. In the UK we can already see this in the once sacred shibboleths of graded lesson observations, punitive quality assurance models, performance management linked to conduct and capability, and a whole host of dumb practices that have led to so many good educators leaving the profession in droves. To go back to Dr Sadki's idea of the school principal being akin to a mayor of a small town, this implies that the mayor is an elected servant of the people, listening and acting for the people with a wide range of stakeholders and communities to serve. Not an authoritarian ruler leading in a capricious way.

In "The Pepper Effect", US principal Sean Gaillard, makes the compelling case for creativity, collaboration, and innovation being at the centre of education going forward as well as communication and critical thinking making up his "4 x Cs". Gaillard places great emphasis on his role as principal not only setting the right culture and vision people can aspire to in the school but how central developing leaders and the notion of the professional group working together collaboratively towards the common and shared vision is the core idea in this model. Wyedean School had its annual visit from the Challenge Partners Review team at the end of November and the report is available from this link:

http://www.wyedean.gloucs.sch.uk/docs/Wyedean_School_and_Sixth_Form_Centre_Challenge_Partner_Report_November_2018.pdf

Our membership of Challenge Partners is about being in a dynamic network of schools that is outward facing but also central to drive up standards in education and allow the development of leadership to thrive in the school. The educationalist, Tim Brighouse, famously wrote about the stages of leading a school and he said the 3-7 period is where a leader is established and really flourishes. It is downhill after

7 years though. Well, I thought about Brighouse a lot when I read the third annual report from Challenge Partners this week. I hope this doesn't read as my vanity, but I was so proud to see what the review team had picked up and had observed in the school culture and strategy here at Wyedean. Reading it I felt that the strategy and hard work we had all spent throwing out a previously toxic culture and replacing it with professionalism, trust, a positive school culture, a learning community, a rich curriculum, a caring environment, and leadership everywhere had been established and embedded in Wyedean. This is what leaders should be achieving now and for the 2020s through the mind-set, right approaches, and skills:

"The strong ethos for learning and the collective and collaborative culture that supports students and staff "the Wyedean Way" is palpable. Leaders are determined to make sure that each individual achieves highly and benefits fully from the many opportunities offered. Wyedean is a very strong community where expectations are high, learning is for all, and engagement is the norm. Students and staff feel strongly supported and are rightly extremely proud to be members of the Wyedean family."

"Leadership is distributed widely and opportunities to develop leaders are seized upon."

"Leaders have a very good understanding of the school's strengths and areas for improvement. They are highly reflective and use the individual and collective strengths of the team well to address priorities swiftly but thoughtfully."

"The leadership of teaching and learning is high quality".

"Middle leaders are strong, enthusiastic, and confident leaders. They feel empowered to develop their own ideas and innovate and value highly the unstinting support and collaborative approach of the senior team."

Extracts from the Challenge Partners Review report on Wyedean School, Nov 2018.

Finally, school leaders in the 2020s will need to keep at the front of their minds the need for balance, family, rest, retaining a sense of humour, a break from routines, perspective and a hinterland, especially when the inevitable pressure points bite in the academic year. As the old lags will tell you in the staffroom, this is a marathon not a sprint. Modelling this to aspiring colleagues who will take over one day soon in leadership roles is crucial. It is why I enjoyed seeing my own daughters in their nativity play this week and why other colleagues are doing the same as we get to the end of this very busy but rewarding term. I am hoping for holiday time in my cabin to read the new book on school leadership "Nuance" from my great hero, Michael Fullan, fingers crossed there for Christmas (hint hint family) alongside the great historian Doris Kearns Goodwin's new book "What it takes to lead in turbulent times". I wish everyone a Merry Christmas and best wishes for 2019. The 2020s will only be 12 months away when we return in the New Year and after this decade I think we are more than ready for the promise of the new one.

10 January 2019

Why Global Britain, Education & Europe will continue to connect Young People in the 2020s.

"The Freedom to travel, study, work, live and retire will remain an inalienable Human Right for the 21st Century.
One of the most powerful things...having an education in a different country opens your eyes, not only to the World and the country you study in it gives you a perspective on your own country as well."
Sir Ciaran Devane, CEO of the British Council speaking recently to a House of Lords inquiry.

I have been quietly grateful for the burst of winter sunshine that has greeted the Wyedean School community this morning back after the Christmas break ready for 2019 and the new academic term ahead. It's always a good sign, and one of the best moments of the job, when students return after any break smiling, saying hello, and looking eager to start a new term. The contrast in weather here in the UK with my colleagues in Siberia was made clear to me when I looked at photos sent over the break showing temperatures in Tomsk down to minus 34C, and the River Ob completely frozen over with thick ice. I was cheekily asked a few times by returning students though "any chance of a snow day this term Sir?" I seemed to recall that students were only sent home in Tomsk when the temperatures fell below minus 30C. I think the last time the Forest of Dean and Wye Valley experienced those temperatures were back in the Ice Age.

My mind went back to Siberia over the break, and the first time I took A Level and IB students from my then school in Bristol to work with schools in Russia back in the early part of the Millennium, as part of an Anglo-Russian British Council Connecting Classrooms project. It was during July/August though and I couldn't get over how hot Moscow was and how stifling the heat was in landlocked Siberia at the height of summer. Those then A Level and IB students organised activities such as English language summer schools for local children as well as working with summer camps where the cricket was a surprise hit with Siberian school children. But then so was the Russian bat and ball game lapta with our students. First known in the C14th predating the MCC a little. When we returned via Heathrow airport the HSBC bank had launched an advertising poster campaign aimed at promoting the idea that it was the "World's local bank". What worked particularly well was the use of contrasting the same image/value and how that could be interpreted very differently around the globe, depending on the culture and the country. For example, one poster showed three images of a cow and on each one it either said "leather", "deity" or "dinner". Another poster showed three images of a very shaven male head with either the word "style", "soldier" or "survivor". One of my favourites was two sets of photos showing a man with a suit and tie and one wearing jeans. Both had the words "leader" and "follower" across the images. It was a very thought provoking idea and HSBC were very kind to donate a set of these posters to support global learning education when I established the South Gloucestershire International Education Centre. At the start of this year HSBC launched a new ad campaign "Together we Thrive", with what some, according to which comments thread you read on social media, believe is either a clever social awareness message or a very overt political one adding to a very divisive climate already:

"We are not an island. We are a Colombian coffee drinking, American movie watching, Swedish flat pack assembling, Korean tablet tapping, Belgian striker

supporting, Dutch cheers-ing, Tikka Masala eating, wonderful little lump of land in the middle of the sea. We are part of something far, far bigger."

Probably useful at this point of the blog to make a couple of things clear. This is not a pro or anti Brexit piece. This is also not a political blog. I am a public servant, tax payer funded educator. The motivation to comment about what we are potentially losing in education and from the experience of young people as the UK moves forward to whatever future it has in the 2020s is far more important than any of these things. I have made the point over the last three years in my blog that too often debates are presented in a false binary zero sum way, and from an educational and critical thinking point of view, this is not how dialogue develops; we live in a World where people seem far too concerned about being disagreeable than actually just disagreeing. It is actually dreadful to witness so many of the "debates" around key issues that will impact their lives conducted often in such narrow, nasty, and violent terms. Hardly a shining example for young people.

What I found encouraging in the sentiment of the HSBC ad as well as every time the Prime Minister, or anyone, or any organisation similar talks about "Global Britain" is that it reminds me that we are not, and have never been, insular islands cut off from the World. In a globalised 21st century where the very imminent and real World issues ranging from climate change, to refugees, to poverty impact on 1all countries and citizens *"we are all very much part of something bigger"*. It is this sense of global perspective that we have to recapture and re-enforce in our educational ethos and culture as we approach the 2020s whatever the confines of the current political debate. The UK will need Europe and the wider World and vice versa. There is an almost inexhaustible list of positive contributions this wonderful lump of land in the sea has made to science, music, art, literature, technology, the international order framework, and so on. Now is not the time to allow a small minority to control the debate of the outward facing country and education debate, confining it to a false binary choice between two extremist points. Back in May as I stood in the main foyer of the hotel adjoining the O2 arena in London waiting to speak to a COBIS international audience about Wyedean's approach to education as an "outward facing school", I noticed the old West India dock hidden amongst the skyscrapers of Canary Wharf. The history student in me thought about the global links, people, trade, and influences that have been coming in and out of the British Isles and old docks like this one for so many centuries. Ironic that modern global capitalism is now juxtaposed against Victorian mercantile trade on this stretch of the Thames in East London as a natural progression.

I believe we are at a crucial moment in 2019 where we are in real danger of losing the freedoms of movement to our continent that previous generations have enjoyed and seen as a normal part of their globalised World. It makes me feel very uncomfortable and saddened at the potential driving aspirations and opportunities lost as a global educator, and someone who has seen daily and regularly for nearly 25 years of being a teacher the transformative power on young people of international education. Whatever is decided now will not last forever and is at best a pyrrhic victory. The case for allowing people the reciprocal freedoms to travel, study, work, live, and retire is an overwhelming one and for the younger generations this is not something they want to lose. When they hold the reins of power, as we are seeing the shifts now in other democracies like the new House of Representatives in the USA, these rights and freedoms will come back to the fore as the overwhelming moral, political, and social case is allowed to stand in its own truth. In our schools and education daily the positive global influence in learning is ever prevalent and is transforming the aspirations and realising the hopes of young people. Technology itself has transformed our ability to connect deeper and celebrate and reaffirm what we are proud of in our own local identity as well as learn and gain new ideas from the rest of the World. Our nearest neighbours and friends in Europe are central in this experience, and putting the political aspect of the EU aside, we need the media and politicians to move on from the demonising language and toxic debate that has blighted the last few years, so we can continue to forge our close partnerships through innovative and incredible schemes like Erasmus and networks like ETwinning. This is not in a binary polarised position to being engaged with say the Commonwealth or the rest of the World. They complement and enhance one another. Globalisation has brought many problems which we need to solve, but it has also brought many benefits not least to education, peace, and

226

prosperity. As I told American colleagues before Christmas, I am very proud to be a "globalist" educator. Young people don't fear the future. The future is where they will realise their dreams.

I want to conclude with two examples which illustrate the power of our connected continent and World coupled with the freedom to move around it, to experience it, to learn from it, and to have the wisdom to know it. From my own adopted city of Bristol, the city that sent Cabot on a voyage of discovery to Newfoundland in 1497, where the name Colston still reminds the inhabitants of the less than glorious chapter of its history through the central role of the slave trade, the city of Edmund Burke, the Frys, and Airbus and Rolls Royce where an Anglo-French collaboration designed one of the greatest planes of all time. An example below of how a diverse modern Bristol is moving forward.

Here is the link to the article:

https://www.gazette-news.co.uk/news/17303440.essex-uni-lecturer-swim-channel-help-syrian-refugees/

"People come, start their life and they make a contribution - both to the economy and to the civic life of the city ... Having an international population in a city gives you phenomenal connectivity." - Mayor Marvin Rees of Bristol, UK

On a much more personal level is the example of one of my former IB students who took advantage of the ability to move around Europe and came to Bristol to study an international qualification from the Czech Republic. At Christmas, Sasha asked me to help verify her residence in the UK like millions of our students, colleagues, friends, family, and neighbours who are facing uncertainty in the last few months before the 29th March. Sasha went to university in the UK, pays her taxes, worked for local charities and has made a very successful career in a blue chip financial services company. Sasha embodies the aspirations and opportunities we should be continuing to give to all of our young people. All of our people. I forwarded on to Sasha the link to the original BBC online article about the movement of young people coming to Bristol to study the IB, and it makes me proud to read but at the same time sad at what we are potentially losing:

http://news.bbc.co.uk/1/hi/education/6745503.stm

I will be telling colleagues and students of Moldova, who I am very fortunate to be visiting in Chisinau and Heritage International School later on in January, the very essence of why it is important for them to be proud of Moldova but also to be outward facing embracing the deeper connectivity of their education to a global World. Similarly to the senior school leaders I will be working with in Tunisia in February for the British Council as we look to work together on common issues and share experiences in our education systems. There is far too much at stake, and we have got used to the fact by now that nowhere in our shared World and common humanity is just a lump of rock in the middle of nowhere.

"We're going to win not by fighting what we hate, but saving what we love!" Rose Tico, *Star Wars VIII*

12 February 2019

Whatever happened to the self-improving school led system?

"...even the best teachers can be rendered ineffective in a dysfunctional school, or that a great principal can turn into a good teacher into an extraordinary educator. But even today, reformers rarely take the impact of the principals into account." Rahm Emanuel, Mayor of Chicago

"I dwell in possibility." Emily Dickinson, poet and writer

"It's not the structures but the outcomes" Sir David Carter, former National Schools Commissioner.

"So, education is generally dysfunctional and chaotic in England?" the nodding heads of teachers and school leaders in Chisinau, all agreeing with the question their Eastern European colleague had just put to me once I had finished speaking to them. My reply was "not exactly" and I certainly hadn't set out to convey that impression when I spoke a few weeks ago about the systems, changes, and reforms in England over the last decade. I had in fact set out to illustrate

228

the dynamism, innovation, energy, and leadership that the English education system has in abundance and in many, many inspirational examples as an education system to be admired globally, especially compared to post-Soviet societies where the pull away from authoritarianism, especially in the public services, still has a long way to go. I had felt very confident in fact when comparing the approaches taken in countries like the UK to Eastern European countries in areas of leadership, school improvement, teaching and learning, safeguarding, curriculum, diversity, well-being, to name but a few. My mind quickly did a reflective spin on its rolodex-like recall over the last 30 or so minutes as I blustered a very poor Hugh Grantesque Englishman abroad impression. I was sure that what I had said wasn't how the questioner had described back to me, but I soon realised that to my audience, the system, processes, practices, culture, direction, and vision of education in England must seem very alien to an audience of educators where a centralised ministry of education still has so much sway. A system where leadership is often summed up by one word "Soviet", where public workers are more akin to civil servants, and public buildings and infrastructure are in urgent need of capital investment.

On the plane home I reflected on making sense of what has been happening to education in England for so many years, in almost a permanent revolution of constant new ideas and innovation all against the very real backdrop of severe under funding and a chronic lack of investment across the board. One of the reasons I am a passionate global educator advocate is because there are so many ideas and innovations to be gained through cooperation and collaboration between systems around the World. The students I had spent some time with in Chisinau talking about the state of the World in lessons were articulate, fluent in a second language, and had an extraordinarily focussed ambition to study and learn. I would like to export that back to the UK alone. The dedication and professionalism of teachers is also something that is always inspirational to have the privilege to see if I am invited into a classroom in the UK or abroad. I was bowled over by the dedicated and hard-working school leaders and teachers I met in Chisinau.

I want to return to the idea of "Soviet" leadership (management) which seemed to crop up in so many discussions. There is a legacy of the Soviet Bloc that still lingers understandably in this part of the World, and I remember having a similar conversation with the eminent academic Professor Maria Mendel, in Jagiellonian University in Krakow in the autumn of 2017. Professor Mendel, both a fellow of the University of Gdansk and John Hopkins University, is well placed to comment on this model still pervading in education in Eastern Europe. Where her research has been particularly prominent recently in offering a different lens to view with, is how the model of education in the UK and the USA was supposed to release greater freedoms and leadership based on schools and their communities 10-15 years ago, but the reality is that has not always happened. When I speak about Wyedean I speak about the place it has serving the people of its community here in the Wye Valley and Forest of Dean borders. Anchoring the school in its community and educating the children of the community is one of the central tenets of state education in the UK for me as a school leader. When I spoke with Maria and when we have corresponded, I highlighted as one of the strengths of the English system how self-improvement has been given back to schools and school communities to lead in the system. I read with interest an article in The Atlantic by President Obama's former chief of staff and now mayor of Chicago, Rahm Emanuel, on how he reformed the Chicago school system.

https://www.theatlantic.com/ideas/archive/2019/02/policymakers-need-new-path-education-reform/581995/

He realised and believed in the power of school leadership to be one of the main drivers of reform in the schools. He highlighted the need for principals to be autonomous, have flexibility, and how this would establish the right culture and teams in a school. I have quoted the lines that stood out and resonated for me from Mayor Emanuel at the start of this blog because they illustrate a self-evident truth about where the transformative power of positive change and educational gains in our local community schools comes from.

The need for this type of leadership that is genuinely leading self-improving schools is also advocated by the Canadian Education writer and leadership guru to many, Michael Fullan, in his latest book "Nuance". Fullan acknowledges, as we enter the 2020s, society is worsening and education is becoming less effective in its central role of producing the better citizens we need and want, especially when schooling seems no longer up to the challenges learners face in the 21st century. This call for new leaders, he calls them "nuanced leaders", will be characterised by leaders who can get beneath the surface and what he describes as "leverage deep change for the better". These leaders can motivate, mobilise, and have the best knowledge for solving complex problems. The following lines from Fullan are central in the debate to why we need a self-improving school led system:

"We are bombarded with massive connections to others that ironically are superficial".

"We need leaders who are expert at humanity and expert at networks".

"In threatening times, surfacers (the opposite of nuanced leaders) provide false clarity that allows perverse hidden forces to fester".

"The World is becoming more demanding at the very time that regular schooling is standing still – actually going backwards as fewer and fewer students and teachers buy into what they are required to do".

I believe strongly as a school principal that a self-improving school led system allows the development of leadership that writers like Fullan call for, and the system of education is developing which tackles the problems and purpose of education in the 21st century. It shouldn't be for a minister of education to grab the headlines over a weekend blindly proclaiming that all mobile phones should be banned in schools. It should be up to that school community to decide how they will approach mobile phones in their schools. It was interesting that the minister didn't talk about smart watches or other devices. The disengagement of young people from the curriculum and schools can be reversed if they were listened to more; and some of the issues that are at the forefront of their minds, like the uncertainty of their World from Climate Change to university places to job insecurity to better mental health support should be prioritised. If the relentless focus of schools stopped being competitive against one another and fearful obsession on narrow data targets and instead a more holistic collaborative approach was allowed, a self-improving school could then lead on this for wider benefit. Teachers would want to stay in the system instead of leaving in droves if they felt they were respected, listened to, and allowed to practice teaching for the very reasons they came into the profession: to make a transformative learning and life difference in the lives of young people; not to be soul destroyed and made to feel worthless by an illogical punitive quality assurance system often led by remote bureaucratic managers obsessed with targets and not human beings as a priority. And before someone cries "standards", the best examples of self-improving school systems led by nuanced leaders prove that accountability is much stronger because of personal integrity, professionalism, trust, respect, and a common sense of shared purpose in the school and school community. Too many "surface leaders" provide short-term false clarity and allow the problems to keep manifesting. But they have moved on and up at that point. They would have fitted in well with the Soviet management system back in the heyday of the USSR.

The Nuffield Foundation's UCL Institute of Education (IOE) four year study evaluation of the government's self-improving school led system released in the summer of 2018 made interesting reading for anyone watching education's progress in England. One of the reports main findings was this:

"...despite the government's claims to be 'moving control to the frontline' and giving schools more autonomy, the reality is very different. Schools are more tightly regulated than ever, facing pressure to get good exam results and Ofsted grades or face being taken over by a MAT. Many schools have felt the need to narrow their curriculum and focus relentlessly on test outcomes in response. The government has encouraged schools to collaborate with each other to share their expertise and to support schools that are struggling. But competitive pressures in the system have made this challenging, with schools also incentivised to prioritise their own interests to attract pupils and funding."

I believe that this paragraph is a fair summary of what the vast majority of school leaders and teachers in the system would agree with, as a picture of our system right now, but it is a damning indictment and should be a call to arms to spur

232

on the tribune voices to get us back to the opposite of what the IOE found in their case study. What isn't really mentioned here is the severe financial climate and real terms reduction of funding and services in schools over 10 years that is having a detrimental impact on education in England. Professor Toby Greany, one of the co-authors from IOE went on to add: *"The idea of a "self-improving" system in which schools collaborate on behalf of all children is appealing, but we cannot simply rely on the goodwill and moral purpose of school leaders to make it work. The problem is that the system is hard-wired to encourage selfish behaviour."*

https://www.ucl.ac.uk/ioe/news/2018/jul/chaotic-government-reforms-are-failing-tackle-education-inequality

So, whatever happened to the self-improving school led system? At least self-improving schools could continue developing what they see as a curriculum model for their school community given the autonomy they have in this area and a key reason I personally came back over the border from Wales as that education system embarked on a very centralised top-down approach with its curriculum reform. We have been developing at Wyedean School for the last years a broad and balanced curriculum, both informal and formal, with an holistic learning approach that allows a focus on strands linking subjects like STEM, creativity, sustainability, cyber and of course global learning. Our culture and vision has been developed for Wyedean as an outward facing school engaged in networks and partnerships that are genuinely collaborative, equitable, and serve best the interest of our school community. It is one of the things we are most proud of here and to have Latin and Classics stand alongside Mandarin, DofE, gardening, Coding, and to be invited to become a pilot school for the IB shows what we are doing is right for our community. We have attracted an additional 200 students in the last 3 years who want to be educated here because of our curriculum approach.

Ofsted's new framework was recently put out for consultation and it wasn't the best kept secret that the focus will come onto the curriculum and a new measurement of "education" will replace outcomes for students and quality of teaching and learning. The debate on #EduTwitter and other places has rightly pushed Ofsted on its repeated line that it has *"no preferred pedagogy and no preferred curriculum"*. The EBacc fits the Ofsted belief, in their words, of *"a strong academic core"* at Key Stage 4. Stephen Tierney's recent blog brilliantly shouted no clothes at the Ofsted Emperor on this very issue: https://leadinglearner.me/2019/02/03/ofsteds-great-colon-problem-plus-other-curriculum-issues/

Stephen went onto warn; *"The profession is effectively sleep walking into the new framework; many schools will be ill-prepared for the curriculum debate. Equally, I can see inspectors repeatedly asking schools for their curriculum 'intent, implementation and impact' with nothing more than a few training slides and a wing and a prayer of understanding of what they are asking and the response being given."*

I am flying out on Sunday to Tunisia for half term as I am delivering training and a number of talks to colleagues from North Africa and the Middle East for the British Council. As I have been collating materials I have thought about the conversations in Chisinau in January with Eastern European educators and school leaders. Here's what I think. The best defence of the self-improving school led system comes from one of the prime architects of the MAT model, former National Schools Commissioner, Sir David Carter. Sir David is an extraordinarily inspirational figure in the English education system and I have been fortunate enough to hear him speak a few times, work with him in his "Race to Outstanding" group, and I know well his legacy in Bristol with his brilliant schools in the Cabot Learning Federation. Sir David believes everyone in an organisation is a leader and for me, what I take most heart from, is that he believes it is the outcomes and not the structures we should get focussed on for school improvement. Sir David advocates leadership in the system, not "Soviet" managers.

The self-improving school led model has been very successful at Wyedean in all sorts of ways. It has anchored a school back in its community stewarded by dedicated local governors and trustees who epitomise the very notion of critical friendship as they challenge and support the school. It is the development of leadership to create the very nuanced leaders that Michael Fullans describes. Leaders at middle and senior level who have integrity, are dedicated, professional, caring, and serve fully the school community and its students.

234

Wyedean has a wider community it engages closely with, and our parents and carers have shown remarkable generosity and support at all levels for their school. Our non-silent corridors are full of incredible young people who smile and say hello as they engage their teachers. The support staff of Wyedean are the bedrock of the organisation and ensure the school can undertake its primary purpose of educating young people. We are professional, commercial, supportive, and above all else, a human organisation with well-being at its centre that believes in young people and the transformative power of education. We are not ego driven or beholden to one "charismatic hero". We are a team who all work together daily for the students. I have colleagues giving up valuable family time next week to take the ski trip to Italy or the Year 12 MFL work experience to Spain on an Erasmus programme. I have had staff and students in all weekend working on the final arrangements for the performance of "Sister Act" this week. I have PE colleagues who give up their time to ensure students get to fixtures. I have colleagues who inspire engaging learning every day and raise the status and pride of those students who never get the loud shouts, such as the amazing work last week of my colleagues Jodie Coggins and Marie Groucott, ably supported by Sue Johnson, as GCSE Food Tech students cooked and presented their incredible menus for feedback to staff. One of the best moments all year for me is seeing those students full of pride as people tasted their food and were amazed at the high standards. It's also the daily diligent pastoral work for example, of Head of Year 11, Laura Crum, getting students ready for their exams in 3 months and the meticulous and calm leadership of Sam Bishop and the Sixth Form team as they complete UCAS, interview Year 11s, and work on supporting 12 and 13 through the daily trials and tribulations of young adulthood.

Rahm Emanuel concluded his piece for The Atlantic by stating: "*It's high time we stop fighting about brands, because the only thing that really matters is whether any school is providing a top-notch education*". I couldn't agree more and we need as an education system to look at what happened to the self-improving school led system and attempt to get back to it to allow schools their autonomy and freedoms to innovate and do what is right for the community they serve. We all want "top-notch" education for our children; it doesn't and shouldn't matter about the label or the structure. I am looking forward to seeing what I can learn and bring back from the Tunisian schools I am visiting next week as part of our outward facing ambition for Wyedean School.

13 March 2019

What is "typical" in any school?

"Not everything that counts can be counted, and not everything that can be counted counts." Albert Einstein

"I wanted to thank you so much for taking the time to give me such a wonderful tour of Wyedean School. It really gave me a great idea of what it is like to attend your school. The whole day was thought provoking, inspiring and a joy. As a principal and global educator, you should be proud of the culture you have developed at Wyedean". Barbara Anne Zielonka, Global Educator/Global Teacher Finalist

The Danish school leaders from Herning, seated in the British Council boardroom that overlooks the whole of Whitehall, asked a very simple question to me over skype as I concluded my presentation to them about Wyedean: "so, what is a typical day, week, month like at Wyedean?" Not so simple a question. I told them no day or week or month are the same in school as I reflected over just the last few days. Last week I was sitting in the very same building, a non-descript office block just off Trafalgar Square at the bottom of The Mall. I was there with one of my Year 13s to take part in a guest panel being broadcast live around the globe as part of the British Council's "Schools Now!" online conference talking about how we have developed resilience in schools for our young people. The other school on the panel was Kingsford Community School from East London. Two very diverse and almost polar opposite schools but both invited to talk about the challenges and programmes we have developed around resilience. It is always a deep honour to talk about the education at Wyedean School to any audience but especially to a worldwide one. The remarkable Headteacher of Kingsford is Joan Deslandes. Joan, like every other Headteacher in the country, works tirelessly for the school community she leads, combining those key virtues of compassion, vision, and tough love as she finds a path through the increasingly dysfunctional education landscape and chronic underfunding in schools. Listening to her remarkable Year 10 student Belinda speak about her student leadership to support other students was humbling enough, but when Joan spoke about members of her school community stabbed, senselessly murdered for no reason other than the attacker wanting to prove his ability to be accepted into a gang then the thought of "typical" pales into insignificance. Joan spoke about how she has to continue to bring her community together in the most adverse circumstances and keep a sense of hope, optimism, and belief in the transformative power of education on young lives. Those armchair commentators and politicians who blame underfunded schools for every ill that tragically blights too many young lives need to know there are so many astonishing educators working hard daily for their students in this country to ensure there is no such thing as a typical day in learning.

A "typical" day, week or month does exist in terms of the cycle of the academic year. Right now as we leave the winter behind, although the very warm week experienced in February was a stark reminder why so many young people around Europe and the World are protesting for Climate Change Action, and Storm Gareth batters the UK, students are preparing for summer exams, curriculum leaders are working on staffing and timetable with our World's best timetabler, Senior Vice Principal Gwennan Jeremiah, for the new academic year, parents are meeting teachers, Year 6s have received their school places for September, Year 11s have interviews for Post 16 courses, School Improvement Plans get reviewed, and on it goes. Schools are places of certainty for our communities and need the positive learning and nurturing environment to support our young people progress through their education. When I talk to educators from Canada to India to Indonesia, these things remain the same, unaffected by rapid changes in technology or new fleeting trends in fashion, music or scary characters popping up on Peppa Pig.

Wyedean School has had more than its fair share of visitors over the last few weeks, including a film crew to showcase the school and a British Council team with Wyedean's great supporter and brilliant champion of the British Council's work with schools in the UK and across the World, John Rolfe. John came in on a "typical day" at the end of February and met again with the Year 13 Critical Thinking group, still Brexit and Trump popping up frequently, they are hoping less so in the 2020s as undergraduates. John saw Year 11 English students take part in a video conference with their ETwinning partners in Heritage International School in Chisinau as they spoke about the Moldovan and Romanian traditions of celebrating spring with martisors. My Welsh students spoke to their counterparts 3000kms away about St David's Day and the tradition of Eisteddfods. Both sets of students on opposite ends of Europe are proud of their identity, using technology and sharing their global citizenship. Later on John witnessed another group of Year 8 students talk about SDGs with colleagues and students in the snowy Rocky Mountains at Mesa Middle School in Douglas County. This is a typical day for Wyedean. This is innovative and compelling education allowing young people to engage with their counterparts around the World to discuss the issues that they are concerned about and want to find solutions to.

John spoke to year 12 and 13 Spanish students later in the day who had just returned from working with younger students in Coleg Lestonnac in Vallodolid as part of an EU funded Erasmus programme connecting young people in Europe. The experiences they have gained are astonishing and that clearly came out in the interviews with the film crew. My colleagues, Head of MFL Beky Simpson and Molly Stephens, gave up their break at half term with their families to ensure this opportunity took place in Spain for their students. The annual ski trip had a very successful visit to Italy, successful apart from colleague Mark Brooks breaking his leg and coming back a bit later. Again, these hard-working colleagues, led ably by the assistant principal, Dai Thomas, missed time with their families so students could experience this great opportunity. It isn't typical for teachers to find the energy and time to ensure all this enrichment and wider learning is taking place, and I made this clear to the panel in London, recalling the wise words of my American mentor, Bill Bixby, when I became a principal: *"Positive school culture is everything"*. When government figures show 90% of graduates who started in 2010 have left teaching, the "typical" days, weeks and months in school are in serious jeopardy along with the

238

compelling and challenging education we need to give to our young people. MFL and languages for example, in schools, is an absolute crisis and still no clear strategy emerges.

What seems typical in many state schools is an arts/creative dimension that doesn't sit in the centre of the curriculum as it should, but is relegated to enrichment, after school clubs or privately funded lessons. It is a privilege to see the incredible work of the Arts/Creative faculty at Wyedean and a few weeks ago their whole school production of the musical "Sister Act" was likened by a fair few to being of "West End" standard. The lead performance of Mili Robinson as Delores was just truly astonishing. One of our best students in a school of 1100 best students. Thanks to the hard work of my colleagues Simon Jones, Pat Allard, Sara Greener and Brian Ellam, students from across the school participated in this amazing run of performances. Yours truly even made a cameo as the Pope on the last night bridging a gap to my last performance in upper sixth in New College, Wellington in Moliere's "Tartuffe". Although one would say, every day is a performance on a stage as an educator...I know, move on. One of the strongest aspects of the "typical" day at Wyedean is what the science dept. achieve to encourage students into science, and the annual STEM Fame lab competition leading to the final at the Cheltenham Science festival has done so much for KS3 wider learning enrichment and confidence to speak to an audience about a STEM idea. This year Maya Hall won and there are some great photos on our Twitter feed:

Wyedean Science - Twitter

I was asked by the TES to write an article, which was published last month, about not letting ego get in the way as a leader.

https://www.tes.com/magazine/article/get-over-your-ego-if-you-want-all-pupils-thrive

I used the example of my leadership of the IB and global learning when I set up the South Glos' International Education centre a few years ago in Bristol. I thought about how my colleague Emma Williams has developed cyber learning with the NCSC across this school and working with other schools for all learners, but in particular the success she has had with STEM and girls getting into coding. Emma's tireless leadership, engaging with outside organisations and companies, enabled her to get the very best opportunities for all students and schools involved. It is less typical to see brilliant selfless leaders like Emma developing this incredible facet of learning. I am really looking forward to speaking at the NCSC awards in Gloucester this week where a number of our students will be honoured for their work. Emma's creativity and cross curricula work has extended to the incredible cyber learning she has established in the school's JK Rowling library, including Hagrid's reading hut. I hope our famous alumnus approves especially as we are using it to promote girls into STEM.

Our World Book Day on the 7th March certainly had a great arena and cathedral of learning to celebrate, literature and poetry from around the World. My English Learning Area colleagues and our wonderful librarian, Angela Friel, have done so much to support literacy and love of reading for our students. I went very much for World literature dressing up as "Dan, capitan de Plai" from Vasile Alecsandri's famous Romanian poem. Thank you to the great Moldovan global educator, Tatiana Popa for the beautiful shirt and her mum for the hat!

So, to begin at the beginning, as the Welsh poet and man my dog is named in honour of, Dylan Thomas once said. Wyedean experienced last week an extraordinary visitor who wanted to see us on a typical day, the global educator and Varkey Global Teacher finalist, Barbara Anne Zielonka. Barbara's words, posted online after her visit and quoted at the start of this blog, mean more to this community than your typical official external verifier looking at standards in education every few years. Barbara was recently named by the World Economic Forum, the forum that hosts Davos, as the most influential educator in the World. Barbara has advocated sustainable and digital learning across the World in 1000s of schools in her remarkable career. Barbara is an astonishing advocate of SDGs in the curriculum. She is one of the most powerful voices in education and we need more like Barbara in our national educational debate and shaping typical learning as we enter the 2020s. We did manage to surprise her at least twice. The first surprise was when I picked her up from Chepstow station dressed now, with a quick change, as Leo Tolstoy, still in shock at how few Year 7s had heard of "War and Peace" over say "The Dork Diaries" – I blame the English department or Gove. The second time, Barbara met our very own Moss the Wyedean dog. This very powerful but simple idea advocated by my colleague Angharad Churches, has been a significant game changer in our student support centre and Moss helps to put at ease some of our most vulnerable and hard to reach students who need the certainty and comfort of their school the most. This should definitely be typical in all schools as our first duty of care to ensure our students are safe, looked after, and nurtured. Working with global educators like Barbara and being part of networks that go beyond a few local schools or even your country should be typical for all schools.

There is no typical day in any school. That's why people are drawn to education and want to work with, improve, support, and shape the life chances and opportunities of our young people through transformative learning. There is definitely no typical day at Wyedean but when we reflect and the school is over, I do think of the famous line from the philosopher Hegel;

"The owl of Minerva flies only at dusk." Hegel

Spring is definitely coming, warmer weather and lighter days to come.

19 May 2019

"Dear Rob,

Bravo. Belated but very warm congratulations on your appointment. This is wonderful news for you, your family and the school in Moldova. You are a fantastic head teacher and you have expanded the horizons of Wyedean and all of your pupils in a wonderful way. You will be sorely missed. As you know, I share your passion for international, innovative and transformational education and I know that you will do great things in your new school, and in your role as a British Council ambassador. If there is anything that I can do to assist you with your future tasks, I would be delighted to. With regards to Wyedean, please assure your successor and your colleagues that I strongly support the school and look forward to the continued success of the school and pupils. I very much hope to welcome at least one of them to Somerville

in the not too distant future. I would be so proud. Warm regards, Jan."
Email (4th April 2019) from Baroness Janet Royall, Principal of Somerville College, University of Oxford and former Leader of the House of Lords

"This school is amazing on so many levels." Tweet sent to Wyedean (2nd April, 2019) from Penny Rabiger, Educational Consultant and Advisor: Lyfta

At the third attempt, my Year 10 critical thinkers still couldn't master goodbye in Albanian, as we sent the students at Shaban Jashari school in Kosovo into shrieks of laughter over Skype on Wednesday morning. This was the first time we had ever worked with a school in Kosovo and, thanks to the hard work of our colleagues there, Leonora Gucati and Shkendije Gucati, we were spending a wonderful global learning morning connecting two classrooms either side of Europe. The confidence and fluency in English of the Shaban Jashari school students was very impressive. We had to pull it back somehow, for the honour of Wyedean. I turned to the Year 10s, we nodded in unison, and played our best card. "Do you know what famous children's author was a student here?" You can only play with the cards you are dealt and JK Rowling's association with Wyedean has never failed to impress schools and students, from Kosovo to Japan, from Canada to India, over the four years we have been connecting to classrooms from our corner of the Forest of Dean. This partnership will be another new and exciting link to develop for this outward facing school at the confluence of the Wye and Severn flowing to the sea and the Atlantic.

A few weeks ago we linked up again with my future students and colleagues at Heritage International School to celebrate English Language and Global Learning Day. We covered a huge range of topics with the students in Chisinau and my Year 10s in Wyedean made the point that next time we Skype, I will be on the other side of the screen in Moldova. One of the most hopeful, reflective thoughts I have from this Heart Shaped Land, after four years, is this: the brilliant, engaged, eager, and curious 21st century students in classrooms as far apart as Kosovo, Moldova, Indonesia or Canada, will have brilliant global teachers like Tatiana Popa or Leonora Gucati or Beky Simpson, who will continue bringing the World into classrooms and making real our global society on a daily basis using technology and pedagogy. The thrill of working together across countries and continents, finding out about the differences and similarities in our individual and global societies never gets to be a routine. That Wyedean has placed this in the centre of the curriculum and the school ethos, linking it to global issues such as cyber security, STEM, sustainability, and climate change, has meant learning has never been abstract, but transformative and engaging. We don't have a "jump on the next best thing" approach in the school and we reject the false binary "either/or" approach of a lot of national curricula. We are very proud that our students can learn about both Coding and Classics as subjects. The educational climate of Wyedean that we have created around this continues to be proudly showcased both nationally and internationally.

My colleague Emma Williams, in partnership with the NCSC, continues to develop some of the most exciting and innovative learning for Wyedean students in cyber education. Emma is in demand to share her work and ideas with audiences around the country for the NCSC and her integrity rests completely on the fact she is working daily with her students in the classroom. Another reflective thought that gives me complete hope as a school leader is the way in which the strategic development of individuals has been such a success and has released the talents of so many of the phenomenal educators that it has been a privilege to serve and work with at Wyedean. Emma is a perfect example of this approach. This belief in people, a positive school culture, proactive and meaningful wellbeing is a legacy I am very proud to be leaving, particularly in contrast with the toxic cultures, climates, and fake gimmicks masking the "control freakery" that so many organisations in education still seem to be mired in.Teaching should have the very best, they should be beating the door down to join the profession. We should not be in the dire retention and recruitment crisis we are suffering in the UK.

One of the best moments of the week for me is the Wednesday teaching & Learning briefing. The incredible

Director of Teaching & Learning, Julie Smith, has crafted a culture of teaching & Learning that underpins the educational success of Wyedean. She reflects the old idea that attitudes are "caught, not taught" and every teacher at Wyedean has been released from toxic & punitive cultures of old, and re-professionalised – acknowledged as the experts in their field, and actively encouraged & allowed to do what they came into this profession for: to teach and to inspire. The education of our young people by brilliant educators should be a national mission of any government. I have had the pleasure of meeting so many great candidates over the last few months wanting to come to teach a range of subjects from music to science at Wyedean, because we have created a positive school culture and an outward facing school.

One of my favourite historians is the American, David McCullough. I picked up again his outstanding biography on the second US president, John Adams, the other weekend, whilst me and my dog Dylan were taking a break from the hot weather in my cabin. John Adams didn't see being President as the pinnacle of his life. His influence on everything in public life in that period is astonishing: from the appointment of Washington as the army commander, to Jefferson writing the Declaration of Independence, to John Marshall being made chief justice. Adams is also the author of the oldest continual written constitution in the World, the Commonwealth of Massachusetts. As we look at our current crop of politicians, the stagnation in public policy, and the continual chronic underfunding of schools destroying our very educational framework, it is worth politicians noting this from an 18th century Founding Father: Adams deliberately specified not only the importance of education being a public good and right, but also the importance to be able to study subjects such as literature and the sciences. Adams stressed the vital importance of education to a functioning democracy and an educated citizenry for the protection of our rights and liberties. A message never more needed in the times we live in right now. As educators, our mission is to provide this for our communities.

If I have taken anything from the past four years here at Wyedean, it is the absolute importance of the trust and partnership with parents and families. Education is always about the future and it is always about hope. Watching Year 8 science students talk over Skype to Dr Karl Kruszelnicki from Sydney University last week in my room, thanks to the constant dedication and efforts of my colleague, Chris Jones, epitomised exactly this. My colleague in science, Stuart Motson, has also been relentless in getting students into STEM, and providing wider learning opportunities.

Never one to exist in the intellectual abstract, I had the honour of being invited, a couple of weeks ago, to contribute to an All Party Parliamentary Group roundtable discussion in the Palace of Westminster with MPs and Lords as the only UK secondary principal involved. The discussion was part of an eventual report on global learning, languages, and Europe for Britain post Brexit. My great friend, colleague, and primary school principal, Jo Speak, was also there and once John Baron MP opened the discussions we had a very fruitful exchange of views over the course of the next couple of hours. What is clear, and what we made clear in Parliament, is that "Global Britain" is just Orwellian doublespeak if, in a spate of nationalist petulance and short-sightedness, we "close the Channel" to our closest friends and neighbours in Europe. The power of global learning is self-evident from student engagement, careers, identity, and understanding of a globalised World. The demise of languages in this country is frankly, a disgrace. Britain needs to do more to engage with the World and not less. I am not sure four English clubs competing in the finals of Europe's highest club football tournaments for the first time should be taken too much out of context, but the remarkable and moving scenes at Anfield where Catalans and Scousers joined in unison to sing Gerry and the Pacemakers' Liverpool anthem after a thrilling match with footballers from around Europe and Africa, show what a globalised society looks like approaching the 2020s. I am fairly sure Catalans and Scousers are more than proud of their local identities: Jurgen Klopp is just a German Bill Shankly after all, who was also Scottish.

Wyedean's global learning and commitment to languages continues and these two new British Council films promoting global learning and the BC's programmes are testament to the school's development of this integral part of 21st century education in any school in any country. My mission in Moldova and Eastern Europe after 31st May is to continue to develop concepts such as international mindedness and global learning in the remarkable young people of my new school.

"Our school's international journey":

https://vimeo.com/332186583/29c6844a01

"How we brought the world into our classroom":

https://vimeo.com/332187785/f4435ebe4f

It has been bandied around a lot by certain self-styled educational gurus on EduTwitter recently, to coincide with the release of Ofsted's new framework with a sharper focus on curriculum, that the English state system needs to be able to provide more "confidence and polish" for young people. I am sure the Headmaster of Stowe had this in mind when he gave his interview to The Times last week about the "threat" and the inequity of the state system on the independent system. Having worked in both I think it falls under the category of false binary, polarised viewpoints again. One of the hopeful thoughts I keep coming back to is the incredible work of my colleagues Tom Rugg, Jodie Coggins, and Rachel Barbato in their work on putting sustainability and changing our entire school approach towards this key SDG focus in education. Tom has also created a hugely successful Duke of Edinburgh outdoor learning programme in school that benefits so many students. My thanks to all the staff who supported the Bronze practice walk in the beautiful Wye Valley in the sunshine last Sunday.

As Mental Health Awareness Week draws to a close, it is gratifying to see the school's new study garden is already being used by all sorts of groups, especially in the exam season, where a quiet reflective area of the school is essential for good well-being. The pressure on young people, the lack of a clear finishing line, mental health anxieties, are all things that, unfortunately, will only increase going into the 2020s in schools. There are many good examples we can use and share in the educational community to mitigate and lead by example. I watched the Year 11 and 13s leave last week to start study leave and the work dedicated heads of year like Laura Crum, and Sixth Form leaders like Sam Bishop and John Lane do with their teams, day in and day out, preparing and supporting our young people, makes me proud of our approach to the pastoral welfare system. We stand on the shoulders of giants here at Wyedean, with the past examples of Martin Jenkins and Claire Rush as just two great pastoral senior leaders who cared for and supported so many cohorts through their school years. I see the legacy in the Year Heads bringing their groups through now, especially Marie Groucott and Anna Jones as the respective Heads of 9 and 10 and the daily issues they are constantly facing and supporting our young people and families with. We don't always get this right, it is always a work in progress, particularly as societal demands change rapidly, but I am very proud of the model we have at Wyedean for looking after our young people so they can achieve academically and develop as individuals.

I sat for the last time in my now empty room with my Year 13 critical thinkers for our final session together before they left that day for study leave and to hit the books that afternoon... It occurred to me that this group has been with me from Day 1 for four years every Tuesday, more or less, as we have discussed ideas, politics, society's ill, hopes, the future, as well occasionally Trump and Brexit. We looked at the idea of "What makes us an adult?" which started off well but went onto the very deep, intellectual, and erudite topics of chest hair and males carrying handkerchiefs. These are remarkable young people and they have kept my sanity and feet anchored as an educator for the whole of my time at Wyedean. I am very proud of all my students and it reminds me daily why we are in this wonderful profession.

My greatest friend and mentor, Les Jones, has given me many lessons over our 35 years of knowing one another, and still continues to do so, but when I was 14 he inscribed a book for me with the words "Carry the flame, defend the weak". These get recalled often as an educator, even more so as a school leader. I looked over my presentation to governors from four years ago and one of the points I had underlined on my cue card was this: "Good leaders see around corners". I think I have been trying to do this throughout my career. My friend and colleague from Virginia, Bill Bixby, gave me this advice as a new principal: "Be highly energetic, be highly visible and always read the tea leaves". All three crucial, all three getting harder. Global educator and friend of Wyedean, Barbara Zielonka, very kindly sent me Andrew Marotta's book "The Principal – Surviving and Thriving". I have found the "survive and thrive" approach has effectively been the school improvement strategy in this constant dysfunctional education system. I have never believed in a leadership theory of the "hero Head". All staff, academic and support, have made the school the success it is, with a governing body who are from the community and provide real, critical friendship to the team and school. I have the privilege to work with an extraordinarily talented group of senior colleagues who I will miss dearly. Wyedean is in very safe hands with this leadership team, supported ably by Mel and Tina, and my friend and colleague Gwennan Jeremiah, proudly to be the school's first female principal. I do hold the honour though, of being the first one not to retire. Gwen epitomises the very best of dedicated school leadership, public service, and skills set second to none. She is supported ably in pastoral by Dai Thomas as Vice Principal, and in finance and business by Vice Principal Jodie Howells. Three people who I would walk through the gates of Hell with and the colleagues you would want by your side in a crisis and to celebrate the incredible education we offer daily here at Wyedean.

I know I am going on to work with a visionary founder in Moldova and great school leaders who I am working with now already but I will miss the Wyedean team and their ethos of being student centred, willing to take risks, and always looking for a way to engage and offer hope for our young people. The ultimate question of interview; "are they Wyedean?"

I want to close my final blog, there will be a new one from Moldova, to say I will reflect and be hopeful always because of the incredible families and communities here in the Forest of Dean and Welsh borders. I hope I always live up to the very warm and generous words of Baroness Royall at the start of this blog post. It hasn't always been easy conversations and we are dealing with 1100 individual young people developing and becoming young adults in our school community. Our community has supported the school and worked in real partnership delivering education for our young people. I am fortunate to have always worked in schools with similarly great communities and families, and I know I go to Heritage International School with exactly the same supportive, involved and collaborative community as Wyedean, as Bootham, as Ridings, as Wootton Bassett, as Crickhowell.

Dennis Potter once famously said of the Forest of Dean/borders:

"A strange and beautiful place, with a people as warm as anywhere else, but they seemed warmer to me."

They do to me too, and always will. It's been a privilege and a pleasure to serve Wyedean.

The End

Glossary

A Level: Advanced Levels. Post 16 individual subjects that are examined after two years and used as a basis for university entrance. Students normally take 3 or 4 A Levels depending on their GCSE results and obtaining at least Maths and English at Level 4/5 (equivalent to an old B/C) and at least another 3 GCSEs depending on the A Levels. An average A Level student has around 8 GCSEs at C/B or 4/5 and above.

BTEC: Key Stage 4 and 5 vocational qualifications.

COBIS: Council of British International Schools

DfE: department for education in England.

Estyn: Welsh agency for standards in education inspectorate service.

ETwinning: EU's schools' formal network for collaboration across Europe of schools on education projects.

GCSE: General Certification of Secondary Education – awarded for individual subjects at the end of two years at Key Stage 4 and used as a national benchmark of progress and attainment of 8 key subjects, including English and Maths, to measure success of English schools in effective league tables (Progress 8 and Attainment 8).

HET: Holocaust Educational Trust

IB: International Baccalaureate - global curriculum and qualifications.

Key Stage: chronological division of ages in the U.K. for teaching - KS1 and KS2 for primary, KS3 for 11-14 year old, KS4 for 14-16 year old, KS5 (also known as 6th Form and Post 16) for 16-19 year old.

MAT: Multi Academy Trusts. Unique to England. They are groups of academies (schools) under one CEO.

META: Moldovan English Teachers Association

NCSC: National Cyber Security Centre.

NCSL: National College of School Leadership. It was set up under the Labour government in the late 1990 and is the awarding authority f the NPQH leadership qualifications.

NPQH: post graduate National Professional Qualification for Headship.

OfSTED: Office for Standards in Education for England; Schools inspectorate service.

PGCE: Post Graduate Certificate of Education.

RSC: Regional Schools Commissioner; 9 in England; they are responsible for Academies and schools not in Local Authority control.

STEM subjects: Science, Technology, Engineering and Mathematics subjects

UCAS : university & college application service.

The author

Rob lives in Bristol and Chisinau, is married to Genevieve and they have three daughters. Rob was born and educated in Shropshire where his father was a coal miner. Rob studied politics and history at the University of York before starting his teaching career at Bootham School in York. He was heavily influenced by the school's Quaker internationalism and went on to get his PGCE at Aberystwyth University. Rob taught and led his history department in Bristol for many years and set up the International Baccalaureate as a lead international education school. Rob obtained his Masters and NPQH and led the Sixth Form at Royal Wootton Bassett School and later as deputy head in Crickhowell in Wales.

Rob is Director of Heritage International School in Chisinau, Moldova, the first international school in Moldova based on global learning principles. Rob was previously Principal of Wyedean School, Gloucestershire, where for four years he led a school nationally and internationally known for its innovative holistic curriculum and developed model of global learning. Rob has been a senior leader in leading schools in Wales and England. He is committed as an educator and school leader to the principles of international education & global learning, the IB as well as the power of transformative digital learning, sustainability & creativity in developing the learner holistically. Rob is a long serving British Council Ambassador and has worked with and advised schools and school boards on global learning, leadership, curriculum, and school improvement education policy around the World. Rob was the founder co-chair of the IB SW region of schools. He has served as a trustee of the Windfall Trust, a children's charity in mid Wales and as a trustee of the education training group Adfecto.

Rob has contributed to several journals and books on global learning including his most recent articles on global learning, curriculum and leadership in the TES, and contributions to the 2018 OECD/Asian Society publication on global education, Professor Maria Mendel's "The City, Community & Education" and the recently published Canadian "The Leader Reader". He has been heavily involved in International Education for over 20 years & was a speaker and contributor with the Microsoft-British Council's ASEAN "Deep Learning" policy seminar series in SE Asia focussing on the impact of global learning in the curriculum and classroom. Over the last year Rob contributed talks to a number of global learning conferences including the Mid Atlantic IB group, the Eastern European education group META, COBIS, the Cabot Learning Federation, British Council & the Holocaust Education Trust.

He can be contacted via his blog "Mail From Moldova": https://mailfrommoldova.home.blog/author/robford73/

Printed in Great Britain
by Amazon